BY THE EDITORS OF

CONSUMER GUIDE®

With technical assistance from
THE AMERICAN DIETETIC ASSOCIATION
and the National Center for Nutrition and Dietetics

FAT REDUCTION

Trim Fat from Your Life

Publications International, Ltd.

ISBN 0-7853-1962-X

NOTICE:
The Editors of CONSUMER GUIDE® and Publications International, Ltd., the contributors, the consultants, and the publisher take no responsibility for any possible consequences from the use of the material in this publication. The publisher advises the reader to check with a physician before beginning any dietary program or therapy, exercise program, or weight-control program. This publication does not take the place of your physician's recommendations for diet or lifestyle modification. It is not intended as a medically therapeutic program nor as a substitute for medically approved diet plans for individuals on fat-, cholesterol-, or sodium-restricted diets. Every effort has been made to ensure that the information in this book is accurate and current at the time of printing.

ACKNOWLEDGMENT:
This publication was reviewed by The American Dietetic Association (ADA). The ADA, with more than 67,000 members, is the largest group of food and nutrition professionals in the world. The ADA's goal is to provide optimal health and nutritional status for Americans. The National Center for Nutrition and Dietetics is the public education initiative of the ADA. Technical review by The American Dietetic Association does not constitute endorsement or recommendation of any brand-name product mentioned in the recipe section of this publication. Although the contents are the responsibility of the authors and editors, appreciation is extended to the following for their review of the manuscript: Karen Donato, M.S., R.D.; Marsha Hudnall, M.S., R.D.; and Alicia Moag-Stahlberg, M.S., R.D.

CONTRIBUTING AUTHORS:
ARLINE MCDONALD, PH.D., is a nutritionist with Scientific Nutrition Consulting in Chicago. She also serves as adjunct assistant professor with both the Department of Preventive Medicine at Northwestern University Medical School in Chicago and the Department of Human Nutrition and Dietetics at the University of Illinois at Chicago.

NEIL J. STONE, M.D., is an associate professor of medicine at Northwestern University Medical School in Chicago. He is a practicing internist, cardiologist, and lipidologist and has contributed to over 60 publications in his field. He serves on the Clinical Affairs subcommittee of the Arteriosclerosis Council and is a past member of the first Adult Treatment Panel of the National Cholesterol Education Program.

Consultant:
PHYLLIS E. BOWEN, PH.D., is an associate professor in the Department of Nutritional and Medical Dietetics at the University of Illinois at Chicago, where she is also the associate head for graduate studies and research and the director of the Nutrition and Metabolism Laboratory. Ms. Bowen consulted on the "Dietary Fat and Cancer" chapter.

RECIPE ACKNOWLEDGMENTS:
The publishers would like to thank the companies and organizations listed below for the use of their recipes in this publication.

Almond Board of California
Armour Swift-Eckrich
Blue Diamond Growers
Borden Kitchens, Borden, Inc.
California Cling Peach Advisory Board
Chef Paul Prudhomme's Magic Seasoning Blends™
The Dole Food Company
Florida Tomato Committee
Heinz U.S.A.
Keebler Company
Kellogg Company
Kraft General Foods, Inc.
McIlhenny Company

Mott's U.S.A., A division of Cadbury Beverages Inc.
Nabisco Foods Company
National Fisheries Institute
National Turkey Federation
Pet Incorporated
The Proctor & Gamble Company, Inc.
The Quaker Oats Company
Sargento Cheese Company, Inc.
StarKist Seafood Company
USA Rice Council
Western New York Apple Growers Association, Inc.
Wisconsin Milk Marketing Board

CONTENTS

Introduction

As you would expect from its title, this book is about reducing fat—from your diet and your waistline. But it is also about a great deal more. This book is about taking control of your lifestyle, so your eating, exercise, and other habits can work for you rather than against you. It is about making wiser choices to help improve your appearance, your health, and the way you feel about yourself. It is about creating a new way of living, a new low-fat lifestyle.

A recent medical article asked "What if Americans ate less fat?" The authors noted that if all Americans restricted the amount of fat they eat daily to no more than 30 percent of calories, the number of deaths from heart attack might be reduced by 5 to 20 percent. The authors further suggested that, proportionally, the reduction in the number of deaths from fat-related cancers could be even greater. If their assumptions are correct, about 42,000 of the 2.3 million deaths that would have occurred could be avoided.

The message, then, is clear. One key to a healthier and perhaps even a longer life is fat reduction. You may be saying, "Easier said than done." But the fact is more and more Americans are reducing their fat intake. Reports from the 1970s showed that Americans got an average of 42 percent or more of their calories from dietary fat. Recent studies have pegged the current average at about 37 percent. Still, there is wide agreement that the desirable daily intake of total fat is less than 30 percent of calories. Clearly, we still have a way to go to reduce fat to a level that may help ward off heart disease, certain cancers, and obesity.

Coronary heart disease, cancer, and obesity develop gradually over time. While you may not feel especially vulnerable to them at this moment, you need to keep in mind that the seeds of these diseases are planted early and the habits of a lifetime can affect their development. Making healthier choices now may help prevent the ravages of these diseases later on.

But you really don't have to look that far in the future to find benefits from adopting a low-fat lifestyle. Incorporating a low-fat diet and regular exercise into your life can help you to start looking and feeling better now. These essential ingredients of a low-fat lifestyle can help you lose body fat and tone your muscles, so you'll look better and your body will work more efficiently. What's more, they can help you control your weight, which in turn can help you decrease your risk of coronary heart disease and obesity in the future. These benefits can be greatly enhanced if you also make a conscious decision to avoid cigarette smoking and excessive alcohol consumption.

So where does *Fat Reduction* come in? This book is designed to give you the information and motivation you need to adopt a low-fat lifestyle today and to start reaping the many benefits it provides in terms of health and fitness.

Part I of this book reveals why reducing fat is important. There is a clear and easy-to-follow discussion of fat in the diet and fat in the body. There is also an explanation of how saturated fat, cholesterol, and excess calories in the diet can increase your blood-cholesterol levels and your risk of coronary heart disease. There is a discussion of blood-cholesterol testing, a tool you and your doctor can use to assess your risk of coronary heart disease and gauge your progress in lowering that risk as you modify your diet and your exercise habits. There is also a discussion on how a diet high in fat can increase the risk of cancers of the breast, prostate, and colon. Part I of this book concludes with a review of the health risks associated with overweight and obesity and the ways in which a high-fat diet coupled with inactivity can encourage the storage of excess body fat.

Part II explains how you can trim the fat from your life through a low-fat diet, exercise, and weight control. These are the basic elements of a low-fat lifestyle. In this section, there is a review of the guidelines and recommendations from a variety of organizations devoted to preventing heart disease and cancer. You may be surprised to find how similar they are and, consequently, how the changes you make to lower your risk of one disease can help lower your risk of the other. There is an explanation of how essential exercise is to reducing body fat, controlling body weight, and improving overall health. And, if you're looking for a more structured approach to losing body fat, there is even an entire chapter to guide you in choosing a weight-loss method that is safe, healthy, and effective.

Finally, in Part III, there is a description of the tools you need to start adopting a healthier diet lower in fat, saturated fat, and cholesterol. We'll help set goals for improving your current diet. There are tips for planning meals, shopping for groceries, and preparing more healthful foods. There are even tips for modifying your favorite recipes so that they're both tasty and low

in fat and cholesterol. Part III also includes recipes, complete with nutritional information, for a variety of flavorful foods that can fit easily into a low-fat diet. There is also a counter that provides total fat, saturated fat, cholesterol, and calorie values for hundreds of brand-name and generic foods.

In other words, you are holding in your hands a map to a healthier, low-fat way of living. It is not a lifestyle of denial. Rather, it's a lifestyle built on choices that are better for your health, better for your appearance, and better for your future. That lifestyle can include a variety of tasty foods, an abundance of invigorating activity, and the health and energy to enjoy them. A low-fat lifestyle can include all this and more. The choice is yours.

Chapter 1: Understanding Fat

Fat is most simply described as one of a group of compounds called lipids that cannot mix readily with water. Chemically, fat can be defined by the arrangement of its molecules. Physically, it can be identified by its form as either a solid mass or a liquid oil. From a sensory standpoint, it can be detected by the flavors, aromas, and textures it imparts to foods. We are most familiar with fats found in foods or used in their preparation, but fat has industrial uses as well, such as in the manufacture of soap. We also recognize fat when it alters the body's shape by adding bulk to the stomach, thighs, hips, and other areas.

The chemical, physical, and sensory properties of fat have made it a vitally important ingredient in our food supply. Consumer preference for fat-rich foods remains high despite mounting evidence that these foods might pose risks to health. Consuming too many fat-rich foods makes weight control more difficult. In addition, a diet that is high in a particular type of fat—namely saturated fat—is now believed to play a major role in the development of heart disease. And a high-fat diet may be involved in the development of some forms of cancer. But before you can understand the links between dietary fat and overweight or disease, you need to understand the properties of fat and how it functions in the human body.

The Nature of Fat

Fat is important to living systems because it is nature's storehouse of energy-yielding fuel. Most fats are made up primarily of triglycerides—three fatty-acid chains attached to a glycerol molecule. To use the energy stored in fat, the body breaks down triglycerides into fatty acids. Individual cells then oxidize, or burn, the fatty acids for energy. Protein and carbohydrates such as sugars and starches also provide energy, but fat, with over two times as much energy available per gram, is a denser and thus far more economical source of energy for the body.

All living organisms, including plants, have the ability to manufacture fatty acids and assemble them into molecules of fat in order to store energy. Different species tend to manufacture different types of fat. As a general rule, animals manufacture a fat composed mainly of saturated and monounsaturated fatty acids, and plants manufacture a fat that is rich in polyunsaturated fatty acids. Some plants also manufacture monounsaturated fatty acids, which are similar to polyunsaturated fatty acids but are much less complex. The terms saturated and unsaturated refer to the number of hydrogen atoms found in the fatty acids that make up dietary fat—saturated fats have the maximum number of hydrogen atoms; polyunsaturated have the fewest. The degree of saturation, along with the number of carbons in the fatty-acid chains, determines which form (solid or liquid) the fat takes at room temperature, how useful it is in cooking and baking, and (as you'll see later) how it affects your blood-cholesterol levels.

Types of Unsaturated Fat

The degree of saturation contributes to the determination of what form a fatty acid will take and how the body will ultimately use it. Because they do not have the full complement of hydrogens that saturated fatty acids do, unsaturated fatty acids have gaps, or empty spots, on their chains where hydrogens are missing. Monounsaturated fatty acids have one such gap; polyunsaturated fats have two or more gaps. The location of these gaps helps the body to identify the fatty acids and determine how they will be used. Polyunsaturated fatty acids fall into either the omega-3 group or the omega-6 group, depending on where the first hydrogen gap appears. Almost all dietary monounsaturated fats belong to the omega-9 group.

Hydrogen gaps can sometimes be moved around on the chain when unsaturated fats are chemically modified by processing. When this happens, two gaps may switch to opposite sides on the chain instead of side by side, as they normally occur. This change makes the fatty acid a *trans* fatty acid. *Trans* fatty acids look more like saturated fatty acids than unsaturated ones because their chains are straight rather than folded like those of naturally occurring unsaturated fatty acids. Because *trans* fatty acids are formed by processing natural fats, they are handled differently by the body than naturally occurring fatty acids. By substituting for these natural fatty acids, *trans* fatty acids may interfere with normal fat metabolism and may adversely affect a number of critical cell functions. Scientists are still trying to understand the role *trans* fatty acids may play in heart disease.

Fat in Food

Fats found in foods are composites of different types of fatty acids. Dietary fats, therefore, are identified by the most common fatty acids present in the mix. For example, fats that consist primarily of saturated fatty acids are called saturated fats. They are typically solid at room temperature. Butter, lard, and the marbling and visible fat in meats are saturated fats. Much of the fat in milk is also saturated and solid at room temperature, but a process called homogenization breaks down the fat into fine particles and scatters it throughout the liquid portion of the milk.

Polyunsaturated fats, on the other hand, are usually liquid at room temperature. These liquid oils are found mostly in the seeds of plants. The oils from safflowers, sunflowers, corn, soybeans, and cotton are polyunsaturated fats made up primarily of polyunsaturated fatty acids. Vegetable oils are made up of mostly omega-6 fatty acids, although soybean oil also contains small amounts of omega-3 fatty acids.

Like polyunsaturated fats, monounsaturated fats are also liquid at room temperature. Examples of fats rich in monounsaturated fatty acids are olive oil and canola, or rapeseed, oil. The fats in avocados, peanuts, and many other nuts are mainly monounsaturated. Almost all of the monounsaturated fatty acids in these foods are from the omega-9 group.

Sometimes vegetable oils are chemically modified to change some of their polyunsaturated fatty acids to saturated ones. This process, called hydrogenation, is useful commercially because it lengthens the shelf life of the oils and allows the less expensive vegetable oils to acquire important baking properties that are normally found in the more costly animal fats. Hydrogenated or partially hydrogenated vegetable oils are more saturated than the original oils from which they're made, although they're generally less saturated than fats such as butter. In addition, the processing may change some of the remaining unsaturated fatty acids in the oils into *trans* fatty acids. The more hydrogenated or "harder" fats will contain more of these *trans* fatty acids. Margarine and vegetable shortening are examples of hydrogenated or partially hydrogenated vegetable oils that are commonly used in commercially prepared baked goods and nondairy creamers.

Although most animal fats are usually saturated and most vegetable fats unsaturated, there are some noteworthy exceptions. Fish and chicken fats have fewer saturated fatty acids and more polyunsaturated fatty acids than do red meats such as beef, veal, lamb, and pork. The fat from fish is actually so rich in polyunsaturated fatty acids, especially in omega-3s, that it takes the form of an oil at room temperature just like fats usually found only in vegetables.

By the same token, a few vegetable fats are so rich in saturated fats that they are solid at room temperature. Palm oil, coconut oil, and palm kernel oil contain between 50 and 80 percent saturated fat. Coconut oil and palm oil were once widely used in the commercial production of nondairy creamers, snacks such as popcorn or chips, baked goods, and candy, but their use has declined under consumer pressure for lower levels of saturated fat in processed foods. Cocoa butter, the fat found in chocolates, is also rich in saturated fatty acids.

Foods rich in fat are usually those prepared by frying; basting; or marinating in butter, margarine, oil, or drippings from meats and poultry. Fat-rich foods can also be detected by their greasy textures. Sometimes fat can be seen as a solid, whitish substance around the edges of a cut of meat or running through it. Much of the fat in poultry is concentrated in and just below the skin. Dairy products such as whole milk, ice cream, and most cheeses are also rich sources of saturated fat. Sometimes, however, it's hard to spot the fat in foods. For example, commercially prepared baked goods such as pies, cakes, and cookies are common sources of "hidden fats." Although we may think of them only as "sweets," they are often prepared with butter or hydrogenated oils that provide hefty doses of saturated or *trans* fatty acids as well.

The Importance of Fat in the Body

We select foods rich in fat because fat provides sensory qualities that make these foods appealing. Once taken into the body, these qualities are no longer useful. Instead, other qualities of fat come into play, and these other qualities can create problems for us.

The body uses the fatty acids supplied in dietary fat primarily to provide energy. Some fatty acids have other uses as well. The body uses omega-6 fatty acids, for example, to produce hormones called prostaglandins. Prostaglandins regulate a wide range of functions, including breathing, circulation, salt excretion, conception, and labor. The body uses other fatty acids to make the protective coating, or membrane, that surrounds every body cell.

When you provide your body with more energy than it can use right away, it packages that energy into fat and stores it. The energy your body uses and stores comes from fuels in the foods you eat. Fats and carbohydrates are the primary energy-yielding fuels, but under some limited circumstances protein can also be used for energy. Alcohol is another fuel that can be used by the body.

The amount of energy obtained from a particular food is represented by the number of calories it produces when it is burned in the body. Foods high in calories provide more energy than low-calorie foods. When you derive excess energy from food, that extra energy is stored in the body as fat, regardless of whether the calories came from dietary fat, carbohydrate, or protein.

We all need some stored fat to provide our bodies with energy at times when we're not eating. Body fat is especially important as a source of energy at night, because vital functions such as breathing and circulation require energy even while we're asleep. And women acquire additional fat during pregnancy to support the fetus and placenta and to provide adequate energy for milk production following delivery.

Besides serving as stored energy, body fat also has several practical purposes. For one, a cushion of fat distributed at strategic places throughout the body protects the heart, lungs, kidneys, and other organs from injury. And a layer of fat just below the skin provides insulation that helps to diminish heat loss.

Women have more body fat than men do. A certain amount of fat tissue in women is necessary to initiate and maintain menstruation. The increase in body fat appears in adolescence and is a natural physical consequence of maturation.

The amount of fat in your body varies, depending on how much energy your body has stored. Only when an adult continually consumes more calories than the body needs for vital functions, daily activities, and exercise does body fat begin to accumulate, causing weight gain. Besides detracting from physical appearance and causing psychological distress, excessive body fat is also harmful to your health. Heart disease, diabetes, and high blood pressure are but a few of the negative health risks of being seriously overweight.

The Need for Fat in the Diet

Some fat in the diet is not only desirable but necessary for good health. Linoleic acid is considered an essential fatty acid because deficiency symptoms develop if enough is not consumed. Dermatitis, which is a type of skin rash, develops in adults who do not get enough linoleic acid. Infants and children who do not consume enough linoleic acid in foods will not grow normally. More serious problems may develop if the amount of linoleic acid consumed is so low that the body cannot produce enough prostaglandins.

The amount of linoleic acid required in the diet each day can be supplied in a tablespoon of vegetable oil. We can easily get enough of this fatty acid by simply eating a variety of foods, because vegetable oils are widely distributed in the food supply. Whole-grain products and oil-based salad dressings are good sources of linoleic acid.

A small amount of fat is also needed in order for the body to absorb vitamins A, D, E, and K (called fat-soluble vitamins) from food or supplements. Fat also facilitates the absorption of beta-carotene, a yellowish-orange pigment found in plant foods that protects cells from damage caused by oxygen. (Beta-carotene is therefore referred to as an "antioxidant.")

Because linoleic acid is a polyunsaturated fatty acid, sources of polyunsaturated fats are the only fat-containing foods actually needed in the diet. Although monounsaturated and saturated fats can aid the absorption of fat-soluble vitamins and beta-carotene (just as polyunsaturated fats can), there is no special dietary requirement for either of these fats.

Chapter 2: Dietary Fat and Blood Cholesterol

News about cholesterol is popping up everywhere—on television, in newspapers and magazines, even in casual conversation. Sometimes the news is difficult to understand, sometimes it contradicts information you've heard elsewhere, and sometimes it's simply inaccurate.

Quite a bit of this confusion centers around the term *cholesterol* itself. Experts have been highlighting the link between cholesterol and heart disease, so many people have jumped on the bandwagon to try to cut cholesterol out of their diet. Although that's not necessarily a bad course of action, there's an important element missing in the equation. While cholesterol is found in certain foods, it is also found in the human body, especially in the blood. It is the cholesterol in our blood, referred to as blood cholesterol, that scientists, doctors, and nutritionists are most concerned about. The level of cholesterol in your blood, far more than the level in your diet, affects your risk of heart disease. And while eating foods that are rich in cholesterol may affect your blood-cholesterol level, eating a diet that is high in saturated fat can cause a much greater increase in your blood-cholesterol level, especially if your diet is also rich in cholesterol. No other dietary factor increases blood cholesterol as much as a high intake of saturated fat. (*Trans* fatty acids may also raise blood cholesterol by about half as much as saturated fat does.) And that elevation in blood cholesterol appears to increase your risk of heart disease.

The links between diet, blood cholesterol, and heart disease are complex. To help you understand them, this chapter discusses in greater detail how dietary fat, and especially saturated fat, affects your blood-cholesterol level.

What Is Cholesterol?

Cholesterol is a white, odorless, fatlike substance that is a basic ingredient of the human body. It is one of a group of substances known as lipids, which do not dissolve in water. Every cell in the body is wrapped in a protective covering, or membrane, composed partly of cholesterol. Indeed, cholesterol is so essential to our health and well-being that our bodies have the ability to manufacture it, guaranteeing that we always have a readily available supply.

Cholesterol is also found in many foods, although you can't taste it or see it on your plate. All animals have the ability to produce cholesterol, and all foods from animal sources—such as milk, eggs, cheese, butter, and meat—contain cholesterol. Plants, on the other hand, do not manufacture cholesterol, so plant foods, such as cereal grains, nuts, fruits, vegetables, and vegetable oils, do not contain cholesterol.

How Does Your Body Use Cholesterol?

As a vital part of the body's chemistry, cholesterol is used to produce the steroid hormones required for normal development and functioning. These include the sex hormones estrogen and progesterone in women and testosterone in men. These hormones give women and men the physical traits that are characteristic of their sexes; they also play a role in reproduction. Other steroid hormones produced from cholesterol are cortisol, which is involved in regulating blood-sugar levels and defending the body against infection, and aldosterone, which is important for retaining salt and water in the body. The body can even use cholesterol to make a significant amount of vitamin D—the vitamin responsible for strong bones and teeth—when the skin is exposed to sunlight.

Cholesterol is also used to make bile, a greenish fluid that is produced by the liver and stored in the gallbladder. The body needs bile to digest foods that contain fat. Bile acts as an emulsifier—it breaks down large globules of fat into smaller particles so they can mix better with the enzymes that digest fat. Once the fat is digested, bile helps the body to absorb it. The presence of bile in the intestines is required before cholesterol can be absorbed from foods.

The body also needs bile in order to absorb vitamins A, D, E, and K (referred to as fat-soluble vitamins) from food or supplements.

Balancing Cholesterol in the Body

Your body has the ability to make all the cholesterol it needs for these various functions. A diet that contains animal products, however, also supplies cholesterol to the body. In an effort to balance these two sources of cholesterol, your body adjusts the amount it produces each day. For example, your body gets a substantial dose of cholesterol from the diet—dietary cholesterol—when most of the foods you eat come from animal sources, so the body slows down its production of cholesterol. On the other hand, when most of the foods you eat come from plant sources, your body manufactures more cholesterol in order to meet its needs.

Your body can also eliminate some excess cholesterol through bile. Whenever bile is released into the intestine, a portion of it is absorbed back into the body to be used again. The remaining bile is excreted in the feces. To keep the cholesterol balance, the body can dissolve excess cholesterol in the bile. It can also convert more cholesterol into bile acids so the cholesterol is excreted with the feces.

Cholesterol in the Blood

Some cholesterol is always present in the blood because blood helps to transport cholesterol through the body. As mentioned earlier, cholesterol is a lipid, so it doesn't mix with water. Blood is made up of a substantial amount of water. Therefore, in order to move the cholesterol through the bloodstream, the body wraps the cholesterol in proteins, forming lipoproteins. Lipoproteins surround cholesterol and prevent it from coming in contact with the blood. The lipoproteins glide through the bloodstream like microscopic submarines carrying cargoes of cholesterol to destinations in the body.

Two types of lipoproteins play a major role in transporting cholesterol. Low-density lipoproteins, or LDLs, carry cholesterol to the body's cells, where it can be stored, woven into the covering or membrane of the cell, or used to make vitamin D or steroid hormones. High-density lipoproteins, or HDLs, are thought to carry cholesterol from the cells back to the liver so it can be removed from the body in the bile. A third type of lipoprotein, called a chylomicron, is responsible for picking up dietary cholesterol from the intestines after it has been absorbed from food during digestion.

The amount of cholesterol in the blood can be referred to as either serum cholesterol or plasma cholesterol. The plasma is the watery part of the blood that remains after the blood cells are removed. The serum is the watery part of the blood that remains after both the blood cells and the clotting factors are removed. For simplicity's sake, in this book we refer to cholesterol in the blood simply as blood cholesterol. The level of cholesterol in your blood is expressed in "milligrams per deciLiter," or "mg/dL," which indicates the weight of the cholesterol found in one deciLiter of blood. (See Chapter 4 for more on blood-cholesterol testing.)

Blood-cholesterol tests usually measure the total amount of cholesterol in your blood. However, your blood can also be tested to see how much of that cholesterol is contained in the form of HDLs and how much is in LDLs. In the future, something called an apolipoprotein may also be routinely measured. Apolipoproteins are the protein portions of lipoproteins; they are alphabetically designated as A, B, C, or E. Scientists are currently studying these subunits of lipoproteins to see what additional information they can provide about the body's blood-cholesterol levels.

The Importance of Blood-Cholesterol Levels

If cholesterol is normally present in your blood, why should you worry about it? The reason is that the total amount of cholesterol in your blood reveals how efficiently your body is using and managing cholesterol. Excessive cholesterol in your blood may mean that something is going wrong with your body's balancing mechanism.

When more of the cholesterol in your blood is being carried by HDLs, there is less danger of cholesterol accumulating in the body; the HDLs, after all, are responsible for taking that excess cholesterol to the liver so it can be excreted in bile. That's why HDLs are often referred to as "good" cholesterol. If LDLs are carrying more of the cholesterol, the balance is tipped in favor of cholesterol remaining in the body. LDLs, therefore, are often referred to as "bad" cholesterol.

In 1985, Joseph Goldstein and Michael Brown won the Nobel Prize for Medicine and Physiology for their pioneering work with LDL cholesterol. Their research explains how LDLs exchange cholesterol with the cells of the body.

They found that only certain types of cells could accept cholesterol from LDLs. These cells have special structures called receptors, located on the surface of their membranes, that are responsible for pulling in the cholesterol from the LDLs. A large number of these receptors are found on the surface cells of the liver; the rest are found on a variety of other cells in the body. When these cells have taken up all the cholesterol that they can manage, the number of receptors shrinks to decrease the amount of cholesterol entering the cell. Any extra LDL cholesterol not taken up by the receptors then remains in the blood.

This is where the danger to your heart lies. The LDLs take the unused cholesterol and deposit it in the walls of your arteries (the vessels that carry oxygen-rich blood to the cells of the body). This excess cholesterol can accumulate to such an extent that it narrows the arteries. As this process continues, the narrowed artery is more likely to become obstructed by a clot, which in turn would block the flow of blood. Once the artery is blocked, the cells that depend on that blood flow for oxygen will die. If the blockage occurs in the arteries that supply the heart—the coronary arteries—some of the heart's cells die and a heart attack occurs.

How Do Blood-Cholesterol Levels Get Too High?

You may wonder how blood-cholesterol levels get high enough to cause all that damage. After all, the body has a mechanism to balance cholesterol levels. If too much dietary cholesterol is consumed, the body decreases the amount it produces. The body can also jettison some excess cholesterol into bile leaving the body.

The answer lies partly in nature and partly in nurture. Heredity plays a role in how efficiently the body handles its cholesterol. Despite how naturally well-equipped we might be, the way we live our lives—particularly our dietary habits—can eventually lead to a problem with too much cholesterol.

When Biology Is Destiny

Some people with high levels of blood cholesterol have inherited a disorder called familial hypercholesterolemia. As Goldstein and Brown discovered, this disorder affects the receptors on the cells that are responsible for accepting cholesterol from LDLs. Individuals with familial hypercholesterolemia have too few receptors, no

receptors, or receptors that do not work properly, and these conditions allow cholesterol to accumulate in the blood. This disorder can be detected early in childhood and accounts for less than one percent of all cases of high blood cholesterol. Still, if left untreated, people with familial hypercholesterolemia often die of heart disease before the age of 50.

The Fat Connection

In the United States, blood-cholesterol levels tend to rise progressively with age. For many, this is probably due to dietary and lifestyle habits acquired over time. The body's mechanism for balancing cholesterol—passed down from our ancestors over a period of hundreds of thousands of years—is simply not designed to handle the challenge of our modern lifestyles.

Unhealthy habits such as overeating, a lack of regular exercise, and smoking all take a toll on the delicate balance of cholesterol in our bodies. The three dietary factors that are chiefly responsible for the mildly to moderately elevated blood-cholesterol levels seen in the United States are saturated fats, dietary cholesterol, and excessive total calories. *Trans* fatty acids may also contribute to high cholesterol levels if large amounts of hydrogenated or partially hydrogenated fats are eaten. And some experts feel that insufficient dietary fiber may play a role. But by far the most important of these factors is the amount of saturated fat in the diet.

Fat is a big part of the modern American diet. In fact, on average, 37 percent of the calories we eat daily come from dietary fat. Most of this fat is saturated fat derived from animal products, outweighing the fat derived from plant products by almost two to one. The large number of animal products we eat also contributes about 400 to 500 milligrams (mg) of dietary cholesterol daily. Compared with many countries around the world where heart disease is much less common, the consumption of this much fat and cholesterol is unusual.

We have not always eaten like this. It is important to remember that for many hundreds of thousands of years our ancestors survived on diets that consisted mostly of plant-based foods such as nuts, roots, and berries. Because of their largely plant-based diet, they consumed three to four times more dietary fiber than most Americans eat nowadays. Even though from time to time they may have eaten large amounts of meat, the meat came from game animals that were much leaner (and thus had a smaller percentage of fat) than the grain-fattened domestic animals that provide most of our meat today. Fat-rich dairy products that are so common today were relatively unknown until fairly recently in the history of our species.

It has only been in modern times that the saturated fat content of our diets has increased substantially, while the fiber content has decreased. Dating back to the eighteenth century, Americans have prized fried foods, meat, and dairy products. And long before the advent of fast foods, animals were bred to have a high ratio of fat to lean. Even milk cows were bred to produce high-fat milk.

Technology has also brought about food processing, creating new food products rich in saturated fats and *trans* fatty acids. Examples include commercially prepared baked goods, snack foods, and candies. Fast-food restaurants have also become commonplace. A single meal at one of these establishments can easily provide half the amount of dietary fat that is usually consumed in an entire day, and much of this fat is saturated. Given how recently in human history these new food choices and eating habits have developed, it is no wonder that our bodies have difficulty managing the high levels of total fat and saturated fat in the modern diet.

No other substance has as great an impact on the cholesterol balance within the body as saturated fat. To understand how saturated fat affects blood-cholesterol levels, we must first look at how fat makes its way through the body.

Fat in the Blood

Like cholesterol, some fat is normally found in the blood; it travels through the bloodstream to get from its food sources and body stores to the cells that use it. Fat also needs lipoproteins to carry it through the bloodstream. To illustrate how important these lipoproteins are for fat transport, drop a tablespoon of oil or a pat of butter into a glass of water and watch what happens. The fat and water repel each other. This reaction makes transport of fat through blood difficult. When fat is encased in a lipoprotein that prevents it from mixing with blood, however, it can move effortlessly through the bloodstream.

Although all lipoproteins carry some triglycerides (fat molecules), the chylomicrons and the very-low-density lipoproteins (VLDLs) are the primary movers. Each one transports triglycerides from a particular source.

When dietary fat is digested in the body, the fatty acids are released and then packaged into triglycerides in the intestines. The chylomicrons pick up these triglycerides, along with dietary cholesterol, and transport them through the blood to the muscle cells and fat cells. An enzyme residing on these cells breaks down the chylomicrons so the fatty acids can enter the cells. The dietary cholesterol and any remaining fatty acids are left behind in the remnant, which makes its way to the liver. The enzyme works quickly: Within five minutes it can clear from the blood half the triglycerides absorbed from a meal. Within a few hours after a meal the enzyme has removed all the chylomicrons from the blood.

When your body makes its own fat in order to store extra calories from food, a different lipoprotein takes care of transportation. The VLDLs carry the fat that is made in the liver, along with cholesterol, to the cells where the fat is stored. Once the VLDLs have dropped off their triglycerides, they contain mostly cholesterol and become LDL molecules.

In order to have your blood triglyceride level measured, you have to fast for 12 hours. This allows enough time for the chylomicrons to be cleared from the blood. Once the chylomicrons are cleared, a blood test will show how much triglyceride is circulating in your blood. A simple formula can then be used to determine how much of that triglyceride is being carried in VLDLs. The level of triglycerides carried in VLDLs is important because, as we mentioned, once the VLDLs drop off their triglycerides, they are transformed into cholesterol-laden LDLs. High levels of triglycerides in blood measured after an overnight fast are especially significant if levels of blood cholesterol are also high.

How Dietary Fat Affects Blood Cholesterol

The relationship between dietary fat and blood cholesterol is a close one. Not all sources of fat have the same impact on blood cholesterol. Saturated fat is more of a culprit in disturbing the body's cholesterol balance than unsaturated fat. For reasons not well understood, saturated fats suppress the production of LDL receptors, which are responsible for pulling cholesterol out of the bloodstream. As a result, less LDL is bound and used by the cell, so the total amount of cholesterol in the blood rises.

In contrast, polyunsaturated fats, when they replace saturated fats in the diet, tend to lower total cholesterol levels. This is an important qualifier to keep in mind. Adding large amounts of polyunsaturated fats to your diet without removing saturated fats increases your total fat and calorie intake. What's more, scientific experiments in which people were given formulas containing different proportions of saturated and unsaturated fats in carefully measured amounts show polyunsaturated fats are only half as effective at lowering cholesterol levels as saturated fats are at raising it. In other words, you can't eat all the saturated fats you want and then expect to make up for it by piling on the polyunsaturated fats. Another reason to eat polyunsaturated fats in moderation is that while polyunsaturated fats help to lower levels of LDL, they also have the effect of lowering levels of HDL—although to a much lesser extent.

Early experiments led many researchers to conclude that monounsaturated fats had no effect at all on blood cholesterol. More recent evidence has challenged this contention. For example, a diet high in monounsaturated fats from olive oil or other plant sources (such as beans and nuts) is now believed to be responsible for the lower blood-cholesterol levels found in people living in Mediterranean countries. This new evidence indicates that monounsaturated fats lower total blood-cholesterol levels by lowering LDLs without lowering HDLs. A diet high in monounsaturated fats from meat, on the other hand, does not have a beneficial effect because such a diet also adds saturated fat, which cancels any benefits.

The total amount of fat in your diet can also have an important, although more indirect, influence on how your body handles cholesterol. A diet rich in polyunsaturated fats or monounsaturated fats has not been shown to adversely effect blood cholesterol in the way that a diet high in saturated fats does. However, since a gram of fat provides over twice the number of calories (nine) as a gram of protein or carbohydrate (four each), a high-fat diet is likely to be high in calories. Excessive calorie intake, especially when accompanied by an inactive lifestyle, can lead to obesity. And obesity can affect the levels of cholesterol and other fats in the blood. In some cases, such excess weight raises total blood cholesterol; in most cases, however, it lowers the level of protective HDLs and increases the level of triglycerides in the blood. Recent research seems to indicate that a combination of low HDLs and high triglycerides can increase the risk

of heart disease. In addition, while it is possible to consume a high-fat diet that consists mainly of unsaturated fats (such as the Mediterranean diet), the high-fat diet commonly consumed in the United States tends to be high in saturated fats, which can increase blood-cholesterol levels.

What About Dietary Cholesterol?
Dietary cholesterol also affects blood-cholesterol levels by suppressing the production of LDL receptors. The impact of dietary cholesterol is less than that of saturated fat because of the body's feedback mechanism, which slows cholesterol production when amounts in the diet are large. The degree to which dietary cholesterol affects blood cholesterol seems to depend on how much total fat and saturated fat are eaten along with it. An important point to emphasize is that there is much variability among individuals in terms of how a change in dietary cholesterol affects blood-cholesterol levels.

The balance between dietary cholesterol and cholesterol manufactured by the body is best when moderate amounts of saturated fat are consumed. It would be difficult, however, to consume a high-cholesterol diet that wasn't also high in saturated fat. Foods rich in cholesterol are typically rich in saturated fat as well. (The only foods that contradict this rule are shellfish, such as lobster and shrimp, which are rich in cholesterol but have a high content of polyunsaturated rather than saturated fat.) So, even if your body could adjust its cholesterol balance to accommodate a high-cholesterol diet, the large amount of saturated fat that accompanies the cholesterol in food would again upset the balance.

The richest sources of dietary cholesterol are egg yolks. They contribute more than 35 percent of the cholesterol in the American diet. (A single egg yolk provides about 213 mg of cholesterol.) Additional sources of cholesterol that are also rich in saturated fat include beef, lamb, pork, and veal. Butter, cheese, cream, traditional hot dogs, ice cream, most luncheon meats, sausages, and whole milk contain large amounts of fat, saturated fat, and cholesterol as well.

Commercially prepared baked goods, candy, and processed snack foods are frequently overlooked sources of considerable fat, saturated fat, and cholesterol. These "treats" are often made with palm oil, coconut oil, or partially hydrogenated vegetable oils because these oils add flavor and are often cheaper than less saturated oils.

13

Chapter 3: Dietary Fat, Blood Cholesterol, and Heart Disease

These days it seems as though everywhere you turn, someone is telling you to change your diet. Food manufacturers claim that by switching to their product you can live a healthier life. The news media continually run stories about the correlation between a poor diet and heart disease. But do you really need to worry about heart disease? Do your food and lifestyle choices really have that much to do with the health of your heart?

The answer to both of these questions is a resounding YES. Cardiovascular disease—disease of the heart and blood vessels—continues to be the major health problem in the United States today. According to the American Heart Association (AHA), it remains the nation's number one killer, claiming a new victim every 34 seconds, on average. The cost to the nation in 1994 was estimated at $128 billion, a total that includes charges for physician, nursing, hospital, and nursing-home services along with medication and the value of time lost from work. In 1991, the most recent year for which such statistics are available, cardiovascular disease was considered the cause of more than two out of every five deaths in this country.

The leading kind of cardiovascular disease is coronary heart disease (CHD). It occurs when the arteries that supply blood to the heart muscle are either critically narrowed or clogged by fatty deposits and blood clots. If a clot completely cuts off the blood supply to the heart, a heart attack occurs and part of the heart muscle dies. The AHA says that heart attacks strike 1.5 million Americans each year and kill more than half a million of them. What's more, nearly half of all heart attacks occur in people who are under the age of 65.

The good news is that coronary heart disease can often be prevented and controlled through changes in lifestyle. Until the mid-1960s, the death rate from coronary heart disease increased steadily. Since the late 1960s, however, that rate has taken a downward turn. Indeed, from 1976 to 1985, the death rate from coronary heart disease fell nearly 24 percent. According to one researcher's estimates, about 40 percent of that decline may have been due to striking medical advances such as coronary care units, bypass surgery, use of new cardiac drugs, and the lowering of blood-pressure levels by medication. A nationwide reduction in blood-cholesterol levels may have accounted for about 30 percent of the decline, and a decrease in cigarette smoking may have accounted for about 24 percent. In other words, more than 50 percent of the reduction in coronary heart disease may have been due to lifestyle changes. While it is difficult to determine precisely how much of the decrease is due to each of these factors, it is clear that changes in lifestyle can affect heart-disease risk.

Although Americans have steadily changed their dietary habits, this effort has only recently received national attention. Part of the delay in spreading the word was due to the fact that doctors didn't agree on whether blood cholesterol really played a role in coronary heart disease. Thus it is not surprising that as late as the mid-1980s, neither physicians nor their patients knew much about the cholesterol issue.

Still, word does appear to be getting out. Largely due to the efforts of the AHA and the National Cholesterol Education Program (NCEP), an increasing number of Americans are aware of their cholesterol level and the dietary factors that influence it. The information in this book will help you join their ranks.

What Is Atherosclerosis?

Atherosclerosis is the condition in which the inner layers of the artery wall, known as the intima, become thick and irregular due to deposits of fats (mainly in the form of cholesterol and another fat called a phospholipid) and other substances. When these deposits occur in the arteries that supply blood to the heart, the condition is called coronary atherosclerosis. As the buildup grows, the artery narrows and the flow of blood to the heart muscle is reduced. Like any other muscle, the heart needs blood to provide it with oxygen. When that blood flow is reduced or completely blocked, some of the cells in the heart muscle can suffocate and die.

Atherosclerosis does not occur overnight. In most cases, the fatty buildups that can clog the artery develop "silently" over decades. Pathologists divide the telltale signs of atherosclerosis into two major types: the earliest deposits, called fatty streaks, and the advanced deposits, called plaques.

Fatty streaks, which contain about 25 percent fat, can be seen even in the arteries of teenagers. During the development of fatty streaks the cells that line the arteries are stimulated to take in more cholesterol than they can handle. Although this process is not completely understood, it may begin when damage occurs to the endothelium, the thin layer of cells lining the inside of the artery.

Several factors are suspected of causing this damage, including cigarette smoking and high blood pressure. The key process, however, is a chemical change in LDL whereby LDL is oxidized. Oxidized LDL is damaged LDL that can stimulate the process of atherosclerosis in several ways. First, oxidized LDL is toxic to the walls of the arteries and encourages further injury. Second, it sends out chemical distress signals that cause more blood cells—called monocytes—to flock to the artery. The monocytes can then penetrate the endothelium and become cholesterol-laden scavenger cells. The scavenger cells themselves are able to more easily ingest this oxidized or damaged LDL and swell with cholesterol.

This sets up a vicious cycle in which the response of the body to this injury both starts and continues the process of building the cholesterol-engorged plaques. The earliest visible deposits are called fatty streaks, which are present to some extent in all of us, even youngsters. But fatty streaks alone do not obstruct the flow of blood and do not cause heart disease. They become a problem in people who have a diet high in saturated fat and dietary cholesterol, which causes the fatty streaks to grow into the clinically important, cholesterol-rich plaques.

Plaque is the hallmark of coronary atherosclerosis. It forms as more and more cholesterol is deposited at the site of the fatty streak. A simple plaque can also grow into a complicated one when calcium accumulates and hardens the plaque and when blood clots develop. Clots are a particularly feared complication because if the cap or covering of the fibrous plaque tears or ruptures, heavy bleeding occurs. This causes a local clot called a thrombus, which can obstruct the artery, cut off the flow of blood to the heart muscle, and lead to a heart attack (also known as a coronary thrombosis).

When the plaque grows more slowly it may eventually reduce blood flow through the coronary arteries. If an artery is narrowed to 30 percent or less of its normal diameter, the situation is clinically described as angina, a pain or discomfort in the chest. Angina usually occurs during a time of exertion, when the heart requires more oxygen than it needs while the body is at rest. Not all of those who suffer from threatening heart disease experience the relatively mild warning of angina, however. Angina is the most common early sign of heart disease among women. Among men, the first symptom is often a full-blown heart attack—which could be fatal. A heart attack occurs when the blood supply to a portion of the heart is completely cut off: The cells in that area of the heart die. If enough of the heart is affected, the victim dies.

Fatty streaks, however, do not always grow into cholesterol-laden plaques. They do tend to progress to plaques in people who have a high blood-cholesterol level caused either by genetic factors or diet. There is strong evidence based on animal experiments and human clinical trials that blood cholesterol plays a key role in both the start-up and the ongoing process of plaque formation called atherosclerosis.

Does Blood-Cholesterol Level Identify Those at Risk?

There is wide agreement that the higher the level of blood cholesterol, the greater the risk of coronary heart disease. This relationship was first underscored by the pioneering Framingham Heart Study. Since 1948, the study has monitored 5,209 men and women in Framingham, Massachusetts, for the development of coronary heart disease. Data from this and other studies was compiled in a report, which showed that the risk for coronary heart disease increases as blood-cholesterol level rises, especially as it rises past 200 mg/dL (milligrams per deciLiter). One important finding was that with advancing age, there was less of a difference in the likelihood of heart attack between those with the highest blood-cholesterol levels and those with the lowest. A likely explanation for this is that since blood-cholesterol levels rise with age, there are simply more people who have a high level of blood cholesterol. Therefore, even the lower levels remain high enough to put those individuals at risk for coronary heart disease.

Recent follow-up data from a study of 361,662 men, called the Multiple Risk Factor Intervention Trial (MRFIT), have expanded our understanding of the link between blood-cholesterol levels and heart disease. This very large study demonstrated clearly that there is no minimum level of blood cholesterol at which heart disease risk begins. It is clear those at highest risk appeared to have levels above 240 mg/dL, while those at lowest risk had values below 200 mg/dL. Yet even those subjects with the lowest levels were not completely without risk. The data also emphasized that higher values for blood cholesterol compound the risk of coronary heart disease at an ever-increasing rate (similar to the way interest is compounded in a savings account). Indeed, half of the deaths due to coronary heart disease occurred in subjects whose blood cholesterol was above 253 mg/dL.

A closer look at the results of the study also appeared to show that certain habits could greatly increase a person's overall risk. For example, a smoker whose cholesterol level is below 181 mg/dL appears to have the same risk of coronary heart disease as a nonsmoker with a cholesterol level almost 60 points higher. The same holds true for an individual who has high blood pressure, another known risk factor for coronary heart disease. What's more, a person who has a low blood-cholesterol level (under 182 mg/dL) but who smokes and has high blood pressure actually has the same risk for coronary heart disease as does a nonsmoker with normal blood pressure and a high blood-cholesterol level (246 mg/dL or more). In other words, other risk factors can turn a low-risk cholesterol level into a high-risk condition.

The effect of these other risk factors is particularly important if your blood-cholesterol level is in the 200 to 239 mg/dL range, known as the "borderline-high" range, or higher. When two or more risk factors are present and the cholesterol level is in the borderline range, the risk for heart disease doubles. However, in the complete absence of other risk factors—such as cigarette smoking, high blood pressure, and diabetes—the MRFIT results show that the overall risk of coronary heart disease for men is not increased markedly even at cholesterol levels as high as 200 to 239 mg/dL.

Thus, in order to understand a person's risk of coronary heart disease, you have to look at more than just blood cholesterol. You need to take into account other risk factors that could turn a seemingly innocent cholesterol level into a killer. A reasonable list of risk factors includes:

- age: males aged 45 and older and women aged 55 and older (along with women who experienced a premature [before age 45] menopause and did not receive estrogen-replacement therapy);
- high blood pressure: equal to or greater than 140/90 or on medication for high blood pressure;
- current cigarette smoking;
- low HDL-cholesterol level: less than 35 mg/dL;
- diabetes mellitus: women with diabetes have the same risk as men;
- family (parent, sibling, or child) history of premature coronary heart disease: men before age 55 and women before age 65;
- obesity (not really a separate risk factor in itself, but it brings about an increased risk of coronary heart disease indirectly by promoting hypertension, diabetes, and elevated blood cholesterol).

See Chapter 4 to learn more about how these factors can affect your risk. Of course, individuals with evidence of coronary artery disease and those who have other forms of vascular disease have the highest risk of suffering from unstable angina or a heart attack.

What Do LDL and HDL Measurements Tell Us?
Measuring lipoprotein levels in the blood can also provide useful information about a person's risk of coronary heart disease. For instance, a person who has a high total blood-cholesterol level usually has a high level of LDLs. Several studies, including work done at Framingham, have shown that a high level of LDLs is an independent risk factor (a habit, trait, or condition that is associated with an increased

chance of developing a disease, regardless of whether other predisposing traits or conditions are present) for coronary heart disease. When scientists looked at the arteries of young people who had died from causes other than heart disease, they found that the victims who had had high levels of LDL cholesterol also had more fatty buildup in their arteries.

Further evidence of the role of LDLs comes from studies of the Pima Indians. Although obesity and diabetes are common among members of this group, they have low total cholesterol levels, low LDL levels, and low rates of coronary heart disease.

Studies of families with an inherited defect that causes high LDL levels also implicate LDLs as the key to risk of coronary heart disease. In a study of 116 families with familial hypercholesterolemia (inherited high blood cholesterol) conducted by the National Institutes of Health, family members who had the defect not only had a higher risk of coronary heart disease than unaffected family members, but their coronary heart disease occurred an average of 20 years earlier.

Finally, studies of both diet and drug therapy show that lowering LDL levels decreases the risk of coronary heart disease. Thus, if you want to lower your risk of heart disease, lowering your level of LDLs is the place to start.

Measurement of your HDL level is another powerful tool in assessing your risk of coronary heart disease. In the early 1950s, scientists realized that patients with coronary heart disease had low levels of HDLs. A study done in 1966 found that men with low levels of HDL-2, a cholesterol-rich portion of HDL, were more likely to develop coronary heart disease. (The test used to measure levels of HDL-2 is a specialized laboratory test that isn't available commercially.) There are no comparable studies for women, but limited data suggest that the level of LDL cholesterol is important as a risk factor for women. At the same time, levels of HDL cholesterol and triglycerides may be more important as predictors of risk for women than for men.

Beginning in 1968, as part of the Framingham study, 2,815 men and women ages 49 to 82 had both their lipoproteins and fasting lipids measured. The men and women who had low levels of HDL cholesterol (less than 35 mg/dL) had eight times the risk of coronary heart disease as did those who had HDL levels above 65 mg/dL. A 12-year follow-up showed that the group that had HDL levels below 53 mg/dL experienced 60 to 70 percent more heart attacks than the group with higher levels of HDL. In addition, the researchers found that low HDL levels could predict the risk of heart attack in people who had the lowest total cholesterol levels.

These studies highlight the importance of HDL levels in understanding your risk of heart disease. The link between HDLs and coronary heart disease has been strengthened by a number of clinical trials. These show that regression, or decreased narrowing of a blood vessel, occurred in those cases where LDL cholesterol not only fell, but HDL cholesterol rose. Yet interpretation of HDL-cholesterol levels is difficult at times because those on a low-fat diet (such as vegetarians) have lower HDL levels. The key point is that vegetarians have even lower LDL-cholesterol levels. In fact, when Tarahumara Indians, who have a low rate of heart attack, were fed a high-fat Western diet, their HDL-cholesterol levels rose, but their LDL levels rose even more. The lesson? Clearly you can't look at HDL cholesterol without also considering what happens to LDL cholesterol.

Scientific research appears to show that blood-triglyceride level, unlike blood-cholesterol level, does not independently predict risk of heart disease in the general population, although it did have predictive value for older women in the Framingham study. Doctors do not find large amounts of triglycerides in the plaques that clog arteries. Still, people who have survived heart attacks often do have high blood-triglyceride levels. A high triglyceride level, therefore, may indicate that you have another trait that increases your risk of coronary heart disease or it may simply tend to occur when proven risk factors are present, such as low HDLs or high LDLs.

You may also hear about tests that measure the specific types of proteins that your HDLs and LDLs contain, which are called apolipoproteins. Some recent data has linked two apolipoproteins—apo B and apo A-I—to coronary heart disease, and measuring these proteins may give doctors a clearer idea of a patient's risk. For example, some people who have normal levels of LDL may have higher-than-normal levels of apo B (usually there's only one apo B molecule on each LDL). This higher level may indicate greater risk, and it would not have been detected with standard LDL testing. Similarly, low levels of apo A-I, the apolipoprotein found on HDL, seem to indicate a greater risk of coronary heart disease in some patients whose HDL levels alone don't indicate greater risk.

Preliminary research also appears to indicate that a genetic difference in a form of apo E, a key protein in the metabolism of LDLs, may predict a person's risk for coronary heart disease. For example, people who have the apo E form appear to have higher LDL levels and develop coronary heart disease earlier than those with other forms.

Researchers have also found a way to measure Lp(a), a cholesterol-rich lipoprotein that is associated with a tendency toward clotting (thrombosis) and enhanced atherosclerosis. High levels of Lp(a) seem to indicate an increased risk of coronary heart disease in men and women. Although some researchers have noted that niacin or estrogen therapy can reduce Lp(a) levels, there are no good studies proving that using Lp(a) as a target is worthwhile. In fact, recent research suggests that in those men who had LDL cholesterol lowered substantially through diet and medication, Lp(a) was no longer a good indicator of risk.

Does Diet Identify Those at Risk?

Animal studies have provided us with a good deal of information about diet and coronary heart disease. For example, diets that are rich in saturated fats and cholesterol have caused atherosclerosis in many animal species, including primates (such as monkeys, apes, and similar life forms). And when attempts have been made to lower blood cholesterol, the plaques have regressed, or grown smaller. But these studies need to be viewed carefully because, for one thing, animals have a different range of lipoproteins than humans. In addition, unlike blood cholesterol in animals, there's a limit to how high a human's blood cholesterol can go due to dietary excess. In other words, in order to reach extremely high levels of blood cholesterol, a human requires a poor diet and faulty genes. Despite these differences, however, the animal studies have provided useful information. Studies in humans seem to support the link between an increased risk of coronary heart disease and a diet that is high in cholesterol and saturated fat.

Studies of coronary heart disease in different populations with different diets have generally shown that those with the most extensive heart disease have elevated levels of blood cholesterol and often indulge in diets rich in saturated fats and cholesterol. The Seven Countries Study, for example, was a landmark study of over 12,000 men from 18 diverse populations ranging in age from 40 through 59. Researchers found a strong correlation between dietary saturated fat, blood-cholesterol levels, and coronary heart disease. The results showed that, on average, western countries such as Finland, the Netherlands, and the United States had the highest intakes of saturated fat and the highest cholesterol levels. The Finns, who ate the most saturated fat, had the highest average blood-cholesterol levels and the highest rates of coronary heart disease. The Japanese, on the other hand, consumed the least amount of saturated fat, had the lowest levels of blood cholesterol, and had the lowest rates of coronary heart disease.

These results are supported by studies such as the International Atherosclerosis Project, which evaluated autopsy results from over 23,000 persons from 14 countries. This study showed that those individuals who had consumed more fat had more severe atherosclerosis. The researchers also noted that those individuals with the most advanced plaques came from populations with the highest average blood-cholesterol levels.

A more recent study compared the plaques in the arteries of men from Tokyo and New Orleans. The results showed that white men in New Orleans had approximately three times as much plaque in their coronary blood vessels as did the subjects monitored in Japan.

You may wonder whether the differences between populations are caused by heredity. Perhaps the Japanese have a low risk of coronary heart disease because of their genes. An eye-opening study explored this link. The Ni-Hon-San Study examined the dietary habits of Japanese living in Japan, Hawaii, and San Francisco in relation to their history of coronary heart disease. This allowed the researchers to see whether the Japanese diet or the Japanese genetic makeup was more important in determining their cholesterol levels. The Japanese who lived in Japan, where the traditional diet is low in saturated fat, had the lowest death rates from coronary heart disease. The Japanese who lived in Hawaii, where their diet consisted of traditional Japanese as well as western fare, had higher death rates from coronary heart disease. The Japanese who lived in San Francisco, however, ate a mostly western diet—meaning one that is high in fat and cholesterol—and of the three groups they had the highest death rate from coronary heart disease.

Population studies like these also provide us with information about dietary factors other than saturated fat. For example, studies of the diet of people living in the Mediterranean area, including the island of Crete, suggest that a high intake of monounsaturated oil may have a protective effect. The average blood-cholesterol level in this area—while somewhat lower than the averages in countries such as the United States—is not as low as would be expected considering the lower rate of heart disease found there. It's possible, therefore, that the high intake of olive oil (a monounsaturated fat) in this region may play a role in warding off heart disease.

A study in the village of Zutphen, Netherlands, gave us two more lessons about diet and coronary heart disease. First, regular fish intake was found to provide some protection against coronary heart disease in the men of this village. In addition, their intake of dietary cholesterol predicted their rates of coronary heart disease as shown after 20 years had elapsed.

Further support for the link between diet and heart disease comes from studies in which some of the participants were placed on special diets (this type of study is called a clinical trial). The Oslo study, for example, looked at 1,232 men aged 40 through 49 with normal blood pressure, no symptoms of coronary heart disease, and cholesterol levels of 290 to 380 mg/dL. These men were randomly placed into two groups: One group received advice on diet and smoking; the other received no advice. After a five-year period elapsed, the group that received the advice showed a 13-percent decrease in blood cholesterol, a decline in smoking, and a 47-percent decline in incidence of sudden death and heart attack. Moreover, it appeared that the dietary-induced decline in blood cholesterol, not the decrease in cigarette smoking, played the major role in reducing the number of heart attacks.

The effects of a vegetarian diet on 39 men who had both high blood-cholesterol levels and angina (chest pain) were considered in the Leiden Study. Before beginning the diet, and then two years later, the men were tested using coronary angiography. (Coronary angiography is an X-ray examination of the flow of blood through the coronary arteries. The blood becomes visible to X rays after the injection of a special dye. The image obtained is called an angiogram, but this term is sometimes loosely used to refer to coronary angiography.) The vegetarian diet resulted in lower body weight, lower blood pressure, lower total cholesterol, and a healthier ratio of HDL to total cholesterol. The angiograms showed that in almost half of the subjects the atherosclerosis had not progressed and that the size of the blockages correlated with the ratio of total cholesterol to HDL cholesterol. In other words, the plaques had not grown in the patients whose ratio of total cholesterol to HDL cholesterol was in the desirable range (less than 6.9). On the other hand, those who had an unfavorable ratio of total cholesterol to HDL cholesterol showed significant progression of their coronary heart disease.

Despite this impressive array of information about the effects of diet on coronary heart disease, some skeptics don't seem to be impressed with the benefits of a diet to lower cholesterol for the general population. Researchers in Boston, for example, looked at Framingham and other studies and calculated how much extra life persons aged 20 to 60 could gain by adhering to a cholesterol-lowering diet. They found that for persons who are already at low risk, the gain in life expectancy was just three days to three months for a lifelong program of cholesterol reduction. For persons who are at high risk, the gain from such a program ranges from 18 days to 13 months. However, these estimates, and some of the assumptions on which they were based, have been disputed by researchers at the National Heart, Lung, and Blood Institute. And even the Boston researchers themselves recognized that their calculations didn't take into account the other benefits that can accrue from a change to a healthier diet. For instance, diet modification may delay or prevent angina and nonfatal heart attacks. So even if these calculations are correct, the chance to live healthier in your later years without the discomforts, restrictions, and costs of coronary heart disease seems well worth the minor inconveniences of adopting a healthier diet.

Does Lowering Blood Cholesterol Reduce Risk?

We've looked at studies that link a diet that is high in saturated fat and a high blood-cholesterol level to the development of coronary heart disease. Several other studies, however, have taken up the specific question as to whether or not lowering levels of blood cholesterol actually reduces a person's risk of coronary heart disease. All the subjects in these studies were placed on cholesterol-lowering diets, but some of them were also given drugs designed to reduce cholesterol levels. Those who didn't receive drugs were given a placebo so no one (neither the researchers nor the subjects) could tell who was getting the real thing.

A decade ago, two important studies, the Lipid Research Clinics Coronary Primary Prevention Trial and the Helsinki Heart Study, found that lowering cholesterol would reduce the number of deaths from heart disease by significantly reducing both heart attacks and deaths from heart attacks. But the studies were not large enough to determine whether total mortality (death from all causes) would be improved by an aggressive cholesterol-lowering strategy that included diet and drug therapy.

By the end of 1995, after almost 20 years of clinical trials, two large studies had firmly established that lowering cholesterol reduces rates of heart attack, both for those who already suffer from coronary disease and for those at high risk of coronary disease. The first was the Scandinavian Simvastatin Survival Study (4S), which recruited patients from clinical centers throughout Scandinavia. The study group included 4,444 men and women, aged 35 to 69, who had cholesterol levels between 212 and 309 mg/dL. All had coronary heart disease with stable angina, a previous heart attack, or both. Half of the subjects, the placebo group, were given diet and a placebo. The other half received simvastatin, a cholesterol-lowering drug from a class of drugs called HMG-CoA reductase inhibitors, or statins. Initially, 20 mg of simvastatin was given. If cholesterol levels did not fall to below 200 mg/dL, the dosage was increased to 40 mg.

The results were striking. After only 5.4 years, it was clear that those who were randomly chosen to receive simvastatin and diet had the safer and more effective therapy. The simvastatin group had a 35 percent reduction in LDL cholesterol, and deaths from coronary disease were reduced by 42 percent as compared to the placebo group. In addition, there was a reduced need for procedures such as angioplasty or coronary artery bypass surgery. The treatment was remarkably safe, as deaths from all causes, not just heart disease, were reduced by 30 percent in the simvastatin group.

The second study was the West of Scotland Study. This was an appropriate area in which to conduct research because the men living in the west had a substantially increased risk of coronary artery disease compared to other areas of Scotland. The study group consisted of 6,565 men ranging between 45 and 64 years of age with high cholesterol but without a history of heart attack. This gave the study enough statistical significance to show whether lowering cholesterol would be both safe and effective in this high-risk group. Half the subjects received diet therapy and pravastatin (another member of the statin family of drugs); the other half received diet therapy and a placebo. To avoid bias, neither the researchers nor the subjects knew what treatment was given to each individual subject.

After an average follow-up period of 4.9 years, the results were analyzed. In the pravastatin group, cholesterol levels dropped by 20 percent, and the all-important LDL component fell by 26 percent. Compared to the group that received the placebo, the group that received pravastatin experienced a highly significant 31 percent reduction in coronary events (heart attacks or deaths from coronary heart disease). Most important, there was no increase in the number of deaths brought about by causes other than heart disease. On the contrary, relative to the placebo group, the pravastatin group experienced a 22 percent reduction in the risk of death from any cause.

Thus, research has shown that substantial lowering of LDL cholesterol is of proven benefit in reducing the risk of coronary heart disease. It should be emphasized that there is more urgency in treating those who already have coronary disease. That is also the group in which the greatest benefits can be seen. Yet for both those with coronary disease and those at high risk who have not had a heart attack, taking powerful drugs like the statins should not be the only intervention. Treating other risk factors such as smoking, reducing fat (especially saturated fat) in the diet, maintaining ideal weight, and exercising on a regular basis are critically important to overall heart health. Remember that a healthful diet is an important anchor of treatment to lower cholesterol; even when medications are prescribed, a dietary regimen that is low in saturated fat and cholesterol must be maintained.

While no study looking only at HDL cholesterol has been carried out with human subjects, the wealth of available evidence suggests that raising your HDL-cholesterol level as well as lowering your LDL level reduces your risk even further. And the best way to raise HDLs is to stop smoking, exercise regularly, and lose excess weight.

Many people ask how long it takes for the benefits of lowering cholesterol to become apparent. Do you have to wait four to five years—as in the studies cited above—to enjoy a benefit? The greatest benefit from substantial cholesterol lowering through diet and drug therapy is probably caused by stabilization of the lipid-filled plaques, preventing them from rupturing (rupture of the plaque leads to an overlying clot of blood that interrupts blood flow and can lead to a heart attack). Benefit from plaque stabilization probably occurs after one to two years of therapy.

Researchers have also shown that in the presence of high cholesterol levels and other risk factors, blood vessels begin to lose the ability to dilate in response to various stimuli. This altered response occurs before the usual changes of atherosclerosis are seen. Importantly, reduction of cholesterol levels with diet alone or with diet and medication have been shown to reverse these changes. This improvement in the tone of blood vessels may account for improvement in symptoms noted by some patients within the first month or two of cholesterol-lowering therapy, well before any reduction in the cholesterol plaque could possibly have occurred.

Can Lowering Blood Cholesterol Slow the Progression of Heart Disease?

The studies discussed in the previous section looked at the ability of cholesterol-lowering therapy to delay or reduce heart attacks. Other studies actually monitored the plaques—through coronary angiography—to see if treatment could slow or stop their growth and perhaps even cause them to diminish, or regress.

One such study, called the Cholesterol Lowering Atherosclerosis Study (CLAS), looked at men aged 40 through 59 who did not smoke and who had blood-cholesterol values averaging about 245 mg/dL. The subjects were evaluated after they had gone through coronary bypass surgery, in which the surgeon removes a blood vessel from the leg or chest and uses it to reroute blood around a blocked coronary artery. The treatment group was given a diet to lower cholesterol, niacin, and colestipol. This regimen, on average, lowered their total cholesterol levels to 180 mg/dL, lowered their LDL levels to 97 mg/dL, and raised their HDL levels to 61 mg/dL. Two years after surgery, the men underwent a second angiogram. The results showed that in the treatment group significantly fewer plaques pro-

gressed and fewer new plaques formed in arteries that had not been bypassed. Overall, atherosclerosis had actually regressed in 16.2 percent of the treatment group compared to only 2.4 percent of the placebo group.

Findings from the CLAS trial suggested that even dietary therapy alone could slow the progress of coronary heart disease somewhat. In the group assigned to diet and placebo, those whose coronary heart disease worsened during the trial ate a diet in which, on average, 34 percent of the calories came from fat. On the other hand, those whose coronary artery disease did not progress consumed a diet that was much lower in fat—only 27 percent of their calories came from fat.

The possibility that dietary therapy could reverse the narrowing of the arteries due to cholesterol-laden plaque was demonstrated by Dr. Dean Ornish and colleagues and reported in 1990. They showed that in a small and highly select group of men who had coronary heart disease (as proven by angiography), a strict program consisting of a ten-percent-fat vegetarian diet, aerobic exercise, and stress management could result in a slight regression of plaques in the treatment group as compared to a control group. There was also less angina in the treatment group. Women also benefited from making the lifestyle changes in the Ornish program.

Thus, studies of people who already have coronary heart disease offer clear-cut evidence of the benefit of lowering blood cholesterol. Indeed, nearly twenty angiographic studies involving both coronary and carotid arteries (carotid arteries are blood vessels in the neck that supply blood to the brain) consistently show that lowering LDL cholesterol and raising HDL cholesterol are associated with more open arteries due to less progression of plaques. The AHA has emphasized the key role of lowering LDL cholesterol substantially in those who already have coronary disease: The goal is 100 mg/dL or less. This has been called secondary prevention. In fact, lowering cholesterol with diet and, if needed, drug therapy, is an essential part of the medical approach to coronary disease.

Understandably, many people wonder if lowering cholesterol can take the place of coronary bypass surgery or angioplasty. They should understand that there may not be enough time for stabilization of plaque to occur by means of lowered cholesterol. This is particularly true in patients with unstable plaques who also have a significant amount of heart muscle in danger of being lost due to one or more clogged coronary arteries. In such cases a cardiologist may recommend bypass surgery or angioplasty to open critical blockages. Even when subcritical blockages are involved (when only 30 to 50 percent of the vessel is blocked), aggressive treatment to lower LDL levels should be undertaken because such blockages could rupture or progress to a critical level in the future. Cases that do not respond to the usual drug and dietary therapy should be referred to a lipid specialist.

Can You Lower Blood Cholesterol Too Far?

When it comes to lowering your blood cholesterol, can you take a good idea too far? Some concern about this possibility was raised several years ago when very low levels of blood cholesterol were found in a number of men who developed colon cancer. At about the same time, observations were made that people with very low blood-cholesterol levels had a higher risk of dying from cancer. Upon closer scrutiny, however, medical researchers found that the low blood cholesterol in these individuals was actually a result of the cancer, not the cause of it. Because cancer can often go undetected for many years, the consequences of the disease can sometimes be seen before the disease itself is actually diagnosed. So when cancer is detected, it may already be advanced into late stages. As a result, it can appear that the consequences developed before the disease; thus the consequences are mistakenly suspected of causing the disease.

To date, a study designed specifically to test the suspicion that low blood cholesterol causes cancer has not been done. However, helpful information has been gained by identifying people who have participated in dietary studies designed to lower blood cholesterol to prevent coronary heart disease and looking at whether they develop cancer more frequently than a similar group of people who have not participated in such a study. When this was done for over 4,000 people between the ages of 40 and 89, cancer was not found to be more common in those who had lowered their blood cholesterol through dietary means. As a matter of fact, according to the Committee on Diet and Health of the National Academy of Sciences, low risk of coronary heart disease, as reflected by low blood-cholesterol levels, is typically associated with a low risk of cancer.

Healthy people do not have to worry that their blood-cholesterol levels will fall too low because, as described in Chapter 2, the body has a built-in system for checking this. When blood-cholesterol levels drop to a critical level, the liver simply manufactures additional cholesterol. As long as you do not interfere with this feedback mechanism by eating a diet that is high in saturated fat, and as long as you do not have an inherited disorder that interferes with how your body handles cholesterol, your level of blood cholesterol automatically stabilizes at a point that is healthy for you.

Chapter 4: Blood-Cholesterol Testing

Getting your blood cholesterol tested can give you an idea of how your diet—especially your intake of saturated fats and cholesterol—is affecting your risk of coronary heart disease. Then, when you make diet and lifestyle changes to lower your risk of heart disease, blood-cholesterol testing can give you an idea of how well you are doing.

It is estimated that more than 100 million cholesterol tests are done annually. That number is expected to increase, thanks to the National Cholesterol Education Program (NCEP), which has launched a massive campaign to educate both patients and physicians about the importance of keeping tabs on blood cholesterol. Using the NCEP's criteria, it is estimated that 36 percent of all adults aged 20 to 74 years are candidates for medical advice and intervention for high blood-cholesterol levels.

While the number of cholesterol tests is expected to increase, the follow-up that should go along with such testing may be lagging behind. This unfortunate situation was highlighted by a recent survey of cardiology practices in New York City. According to the survey, at the time of angiographic study (a type of X ray that helps determine the extent of blockage in arteries), only 17 percent of patients with abnormal lipid levels were being actively treated. Incredibly, after one to two years of follow-up, the percentage of patients treated increased only to 35 percent.

It is important to keep in mind that knowing your blood-cholesterol level is only the first step in lowering your risk of coronary heart disease. If testing shows that your blood cholesterol is at an undesirable level, you and your doctor must take steps to get it under control. If it is at a desirable level, you must continue to be vigilant about diet and lifestyle to help keep it there.

What Is a Cholesterol Test?

From the consumer standpoint, a cholesterol test is a simple blood test that's nearly painless and fairly inexpensive. In a doctor's office or at a hospital, a small amount of blood is drawn into a test tube and sent to a laboratory for analysis. The test result is then sent back to your doctor, who informs you of the numerical value. The numerical value indicates the weight, in milligrams, of the cholesterol contained in one deciLiter of your blood (mg/dL).

New technology has also made large-scale cholesterol screening possible. Cholesterol screening programs use portable machines that deliver results in less than ten minutes, using blood drawn by pricking the patient's finger. The programs offer many Americans the convenience of having their cholesterol checked in such places as shopping malls and workplaces. However, if the result from a cholesterol check done through a screening program is above the desirable range, the individual needs to see a physician for retesting and evaluation.

Most often, a blood-cholesterol test measures the total amount of cholesterol in your blood. Your blood-cholesterol level, however, is not the only factor you need to take into account when considering your risk of heart disease. It is best to discuss all of your risk factors with your doctor.

All adults over age 20 should have both total cholesterol and HDL cholesterol measured. Ideally, this test should be performed along with an evaluation of the subject's coronary risk (overall risk of experiencing unstable angina or a heart attack). This is very important—abnormalities in total cholesterol and HDL cholesterol are viewed as more significant in those at higher risk than they are in those at lower risk. If total cholesterol is over 200 mg/dL, or if HDL cholesterol is under 35 mg/dL, then your doctor may request your blood be analyzed further to determine your level of LDL cholesterol. Measurements of levels of HDL and LDL cholesterol provide the two most important cholesterol-carrying components, or fractions, in determining coronary risk.

As mentioned earlier, LDL is the fraction that raises your risk of coronary heart disease, so you want your LDL cholesterol level to be low. HDL is the fraction that lowers your risk of coronary heart disease, so you want your HDL cholesterol level to be high. LDLs, HDLs, and another fraction called very-low-density lipoproteins, or VLDLs—which are rich in triglycerides (fat)—all carry cholesterol in the blood. The sum of the cholesterols on each of these lipoproteins, LDL + HDL + VLDL, equals total blood cholesterol. Total cholesterol, HDL cholesterol, and triglycerides can be measured directly. To calculate the level of VLDL cholesterol, the total amount of triglycerides is divided by five, since a VLDL carries roughly five times as much triglyceride as cholesterol. To figure out the LDL level, the amounts of HDL cholesterol and VLDL cholesterol are subtracted from total cholesterol. Often your doctor will request measurements of specific cholesterol fractions when a previous test showed you had a total cholesterol level above the desirable range.

What Are Cholesterol Ratios?

Many patients find it hard to keep the various fractions of cholesterol straight in their minds. LDL values easily get confused with HDL values. Thus, many physicians find it easier to provide their patients with a simple ratio of total blood cholesterol to HDL or of LDL to HDL.

These ratios are strong predictors of coronary heart disease. In the Framingham study, for instance, the ratio of total cholesterol to HDL and the ratio of LDL to HDL were found to have the strongest associations with coronary heart disease. The researchers suggested that a total cholesterol-to-HDL ratio greater than six and an LDL-to-HDL ratio greater than four indicated a high risk for coronary heart disease.

Although these ratios are simple ways of summarizing a lot of confusing data, important information is lost if the specific values that make up the ratios are not looked at individually. Indeed, the NCEP does not use ratios in its recommendations specifically because it considers the fractions to be independent risk factors for coronary heart disease. Therefore, you need to ask for the individual values if they are not provided to you.

It is useful to know which of the components of the ratio are abnormal in order to direct appropriate treatment. The factors that affect LDLs are often very different from the ones that affect HDLs. For instance, in some patients, a high level of LDLs responds well to a diet low in saturated fat and cholesterol, while a low HDL level may be improved when the patient quits smoking, starts an aerobic exercise program, or loses weight. LDLs and HDLs are both affected by medications, but often different ones. In addition, an analysis of ratios appears to be of little value in individuals who have extremely low HDL or very high LDL levels.

Finally, measurements of HDL cholesterol can vary three times as much as total cholesterol measurements, even when they're performed at the best laboratories. This can cause potentially serious problems if these measurements are used to predict risk and prescribe treatment. For instance, consider the patient whose HDL level falls in the 30- to 40-mg/dL range: A ten-percent testing error in one direction can put that person in the high-risk group, while a ten-percent error in the other direction can put that same individual in the low-risk group.

Who Should Undergo Cholesterol Testing?

The NCEP Adult Treatment Panel Report suggests all adults aged 20 and over have a nonfasting total cholesterol test as well as an HDL test to see if they have a blood-cholesterol level high enough to warrant further evaluation. The guidelines advise the test be performed again at least once every five years. How often you should have your level checked depends on the results of that first test (see "What Do My Results Mean?").

Ensuring Accurate Test Results

New technology and increasing awareness of cholesterol's role in heart disease may soon make blood-cholesterol testing in your doctor's office as common as blood-pressure measurements. Yet there's still some concern about how accurately the test results reflect a person's true cholesterol level.

A variety of factors can influence the accuracy of your test results, ranging from the effectiveness of the machine used in analyzing your blood to the time of year you have the test performed. Until very recently, most blood samples were analyzed by large clinical laboratories staffed with certified technicians. Due to a lack of uniform standards, however, the results from these laboratories have been shown to vary considerably. For example, in 1985, the College of American Pathologists sent a sample specimen of blood to more than 5,000 laboratories in the United States to have it analyzed for blood cholesterol. The answers that came back ranged from 193 to 379 mg/dL. According to the Centers for Disease Control (CDC), the correct value was 263 mg/dL. Fortunately, this undesirable situation is being remedied by the NCEP's Laboratory Standardization Panel. In the meantime, to ensure quality results a good first step is to ask your doctor if the laboratory doing your analysis is standardized.

In addition to laboratory analysis, newer desktop cholesterol analyzers are also being used. Each type employs a different technology to analyze blood cholesterol. These machines make widespread cholesterol screening possible, but they also increase the likelihood that results will vary. For example, unskilled operators may report results that are less accurate than those reported by more experienced operators.

Biologic factors must also be taken into account. They include age, sex, seasonal variation, recent diet and weight changes, recent alcohol intake, exercise, family history of cholesterol disorders, other illnesses that affect blood-fat levels, pregnancy, and medications.

Your age and sex influence your blood-cholesterol level. In childhood, females have higher cholesterol values. Males actually show a significant decline during adolescence, when testosterone starts flooding their bodies. Adult males over the age of 20 generally have higher levels of cholesterol than females. Once they reach menopause, however, women have higher cholesterol levels than their male counterparts.

Seasonal variation has been shown to affect cholesterol values. In one study, the cholesterol levels of subjects who were not receiving treatment were an average of 7.4 mg/dL higher in December than in June. The reasons for this are still unknown.

Your cholesterol levels are also clearly affected when you consume too many calories or increase your intake of saturated fat and cholesterol. Excess alcohol intake raises your triglyceride levels and HDL levels. To ensure your test results are consistent, you need to have the test performed after you've maintained your usual diet and weight for at least two weeks. In other words, you don't want to have your cholesterol tested the day after Thanksgiving.

Engaging in vigorous exercise just before your blood test can temporarily lower your cholesterol and triglyceride values. It's wise, therefore, to avoid intense workouts the day before you take the test. (On the other hand, a program of regular, vigorous exercise can have a longer-lasting beneficial effect by raising HDL and lowering triglyceride levels.)

A personal or family history of certain diseases can also affect your results and treatment. For example, a family history of elevated lipids is important because genetic forms of high blood cholesterol often do not respond fully to diet therapy. Yet these disorders increase your risk of heart disease by exposing you to lifelong elevated cholesterol levels. Your doctor needs to consider these points when interpreting your test results. Likewise, a severely elevated cholesterol level (more than 280 mg/dL) that suddenly appears later in life may be caused by a disease that requires treatment before the cholesterol level can be lowered. Hypothyroidism (due to insufficient amounts of thyroid hormone) is a common secondary cause of elevated cholesterol levels. This disease can be diagnosed by a blood test. People with poorly controlled diabetes also tend to have high blood-cholesterol levels. Other less commonly found causes include nephrotic syndrome (a kidney disease), obstructive liver disease, and, in rare instances, dysgammaglobulinemia (a disorder of the immune system) and porphyria (a group of metabolic disorders).

Cholesterol values also rise progressively during pregnancy and often take several months to a year to return to prepregnancy levels. It's important for your doctor to know if you could be pregnant, since high cholesterol caused by pregnancy is only temporary and does not warrant treatment—especially drug therapy.

Situational factors must also be considered when your cholesterol values are interpreted. Situational factors that can affect lipid testing include fasting, your posture for the 30 minutes before the blood is drawn, recent surgery, and recent illnesses such as heart attack and infection.

If you're having your blood screened to see if your total blood-cholesterol level is high, you don't need to fast before you have the test done. Recent food intake has a very small effect on these results. On the other hand, if you're going to have your HDL and triglyceride levels measured and your LDL level calculated, then you need to fast for 12 to 16 hours before the test.

Even your posture before the blood test can affect the values obtained. A blood sample drawn after you've been sitting for 30 minutes shows a higher cholesterol level than a sample drawn when you're lying down. This difference comes into play if you have one test done in a screening program (where you may have been standing or sitting just prior to the test) and a follow-up test performed in a hospital setting (where you may have been lying down before the test).

Finally, it's widely recognized that cholesterol values fall and triglyceride values rise after a heart attack, major surgery, or extensive burns. After a major vascular event such as a heart attack or stroke, physicians should wait at least eight weeks before performing cholesterol measurements. This allows the patient to be on a steady diet and reach a stable weight when the measurements are made.

Practically speaking, there are a few steps you can take to help reduce nonlaboratory errors. Before you have the test done, ask yourself if your diet, exercise patterns, medications, and health have been stable for the past two or three weeks. If the answer is yes, then proceed with the test. If the answer is no, then it may be best to delay the test until these factors have been consistent for at least two weeks. If you're unsure, it would be wise to average the results of two separate tests for cholesterol and triglycerides taken within a one- to six-week period (the NCEP recommends a second test in any case if the result of the first test is over 200 mg/dL). This average can then be used in deciding whether further tests and treatment are in order. Using two measurements, there's a 90 percent chance that the average is within 9.3 percent of your true cholesterol level; using three tests, the average is likely to be within 7.6 percent of your true cholesterol level. The NCEP Adult Treatment Panel cautions that if the results of two tests for either total cholesterol or LDL level are not within 30 mg/dL of each other, you should have a third test done and use the average of the three. An accurate cholesterol value allows your doctor to prescribe adequate dietary or drug treatment.

Recently, physicians have pointed out that having several cholesterol tests done allows the patient to see the natural biologic variability inherent in these measurements. It encourages patients to avoid thinking of the cutoffs separating borderline and normal as rigid since, in reality, the difference in risk between a cholesterol level of 202 and one of 198 is minor.

What Do My Results Mean?

The NCEP has established guidelines to help you and your doctor interpret your cholesterol test results and decide how to handle them.

Classification Based on Total Blood Cholesterol	
<200 mg/dL	Desirable Blood Cholesterol
200–239 mg/dL	Borderline-High Blood Cholesterol
≥240 mg/dL	High Blood Cholesterol

If your test results show that you have a high blood-cholesterol level or a borderline-high blood-cholesterol level, you must undergo a second test, performed by your doctor, to confirm it. This is especially important if your cholesterol falls in the borderline range of 200 to 239 mg/dL. This is the cut-off range used to decide whether an individual needs to be evaluated further. If the results of the two tests differ by more than 30 mg/dL, you should have a third test done. The average of the test results can then be used as your initial baseline cholesterol value. In the time between tests, make an effort not to change your eating habits. You want the results of the tests to accurately measure your cholesterol values when you're on your usual diet.

Research has shown that at a blood-cholesterol level of 240 mg/dL, the risk of coronary heart disease begins to rise sharply. Yet the daily experience of physicians and the decades-long experience of researchers is that your risk of coronary heart disease at any level of cholesterol depends on your clinical risk profile as well. This profile takes the following factors into account:

- age: males aged 45 and older and women aged 55 and older (along with those women who experienced a premature [before age 45] menopause and did not receive estrogen-replacement therapy);
- high blood pressure: equal to or greater than 140/90 or on medication for high blood pressure;
- current cigarette smoking;
- low HDL cholesterol: less than 35 mg/dL;
- diabetes mellitus: women with diabetes have the same risk of heart disease as men;
- family history of premature coronary heart disease affecting either parents or other close relatives such as children or siblings: *premature* refers to heart attack or sudden death before age 55 in men and before age 65 in women;
- obesity (though not, strictly speaking, included as a risk factor, obesity is noted as a target for therapy, since it can contribute to

high blood pressure, elevated blood cholesterol or triglycerides, and diabetes).

If HDL cholesterol is 60 mg/dL or more, it is considered a negative risk factor in that it should be subtracted from the total number of risk factors. Thus, a premenopausal woman with a family history of premature coronary heart disease and hypertension, or high blood pressure, who has an elevated HDL cholesterol reading of 70 mg/dL is considered to have only one risk factor, since the high HDL cholesterol lowers the total from two risk factors to one.

Of course patients with evidence of coronary heart disease—such as a positive stress test, angina, heart attack, angioplasty, or vascular (blood vessel) disease of the extremities or brain—are considered at the highest risk of suffering from angina or another heart attack.

The new NCEP guidelines urge physicians to measure total cholesterol as well as HDL cholesterol as part of the initial screening process. This is done so that the physician doesn't miss the person with a low HDL cholesterol and a family history of premature heart disease. Thus, the initial lipid screening tests consist of a nonfasting-cholesterol and HDL-cholesterol test as well as an assessment of the nonlipid risk factors for coronary heart disease.

Those with a total cholesterol under 200 mg/dL and an HDL cholesterol of 35 mg/dL or more need only general education on diet, physical activity, and risk-factor reduction and are urged to repeat the tests for cholesterol and HDL within five years. For those with a borderline-high cholesterol level of between 200 and 239 mg/dL and an HDL level of 35 mg/dL or more along with fewer than two risk factors, the above general information is provided and the patient should be reevaluated in one to two years. The most intensive evaluation is offered to those with either a high level of blood cholesterol (240 mg/dL or more) or an HDL cholesterol of less than 35 (without regard for how high the total cholesterol value is). These individuals should have a lipoprotein analysis that follows a 9- to 12-hour fast. The lipoprotein analysis determines the LDL cholesterol, which is an important target for therapy if the risk of a coronary event is to be reduced.

Those with a desirable LDL cholesterol of less than 130 mg/dL need to have a repeat test of total cholesterol and LDL cholesterol within five years. Those with borderline-high-risk LDL cho-

lesterol of 130 to 159 mg/dL and fewer than two risk factors are put on a Step One diet to lower cholesterol (see Chapter 7) and urged to undertake regular physical activity. Their status is reevaluated annually. Those with a borderline-high-risk LDL cholesterol of 130 to 159 and two or more risk factors, as well as those with a high-risk LDL cholesterol of 160 or more, should undergo a more intensive evaluation.

Clinical evaluation is performed to see if your elevated level of LDL cholesterol or reduced level of HDL cholesterol is due solely to genetic causes or whether it is due, at least in part, to secondary causes such as diet, medication, or disease. To do this, your doctor will review your medical and family history and perform a physical examination; review any medications you take (including those either recently added, changed, or dropped); and determine whether or not you have inherited a form of high blood cholesterol.

Your doctor also will decide whether laboratory studies should be performed to rule out secondary causes of high blood cholesterol. They may include a blood or urine test to rule out pregnancy, a blood test to diagnose hypothyroidism, a urine test to rule out nephrotic syndrome, a fasting blood sugar test to see if diabetes is present, and liver function tests to see if there is evidence of obstructive liver disease. Tests to rule out dysgammaglobulinemia or porphyria may be required, but this is rare.

The evaluation and tests help your doctor understand the cause of your high blood-cholesterol level and determine how to go about treating it. Diet therapy is considered the cornerstone of therapy to control cholesterol. Drug therapy should be considered only when diet therapy has failed to lower your blood cholesterol to an acceptable level (or in those rare cases when a quicker and more drastic lowering is essential). Even then diet therapy must be continued. To monitor your progress in diet or drug therapy, your doctor will see to it that your cholesterol level is tested periodically.

On the other hand, those who already have coronary heart disease should start with two lipoprotein analyses taken one to eight weeks apart. Averaging the two values is considered the most careful way to begin. The goal for these individuals is an LDL-cholesterol level of 100 mg/dL or less. To achieve this, they will need an individualized diet, physical activity, and, in many cases, drug therapy.

Chapter 5: Dietary Fat and Cancer

Cancer is second only to heart disease in the number of lives it takes each year in the United States. Once thought to be a disease that was caused by chemicals in the environment and that primarily affected people with a genetic tendency, cancer is now considered to be more a disease of lifestyle. Smoking, drinking, and dietary habits are believed to be behind most of the cancers that develop in this country each year. In 1988, the *Surgeon General's Report on Nutrition and Health* concluded that more than 75 percent of all the cancers that occur in the United States could be prevented by changes in smoking behavior, alcohol use, and diet.

In 1980, two British scientists, Richard Doll and Richard Peto, compiled information from all over the world and identified the causes of cancer they considered avoidable. Among these causes are tobacco use, excessive alcohol consumption, and a diet that is rich in fat and lacking in whole grains, fruits, and vegetables. Since Doll and Peto published their findings, many studies have been done that support their research. What these studies suggest is that we could drastically reduce our odds of getting cancer simply by changing the way we typically eat and by making a personal choice to stop smoking and drink less. According to the estimates of Doll and Peto, more than one-third of all cancers might be avoided by making dietary changes.

The Surgeon General based the dietary recommendations of the 1988 report on this collection of information and on existing evidence about the dietary causes of heart disease. According to the Surgeon General, the top priority for dietary change to promote better health in this country is to reduce the amount of fat we eat. Cancer and coronary heart disease combined kill almost half of all Americans who die each year, and fat-rich diets are implicated in both diseases. Not every type of cancer is equally affected by the amount of fat in the diet. But the most common cancers in this country—breast, prostate, and colon—are strongly linked to high-fat diets.

What Is Cancer?

Although different forms of cancer can appear to be very different diseases, cancer is actually a group of related diseases. Some develop slowly over a period of years; others take off rapidly and symptoms appear within months. Some are readily treated and cured; others linger on despite rigorous treatment. All cancers do have one thing in common: They begin with normal cells that somehow have lost the ability to control their own growth. Cancer is a formidable disease because once it progresses to a certain stage, it is very difficult to control. And once it begins to spread, or metastasize, cancer is usually fatal.

All cancers have their start in cells in which the genetic material called DNA has been damaged, so the codes contained in the genes are not correctly read. This damage is called a mutation. DNA directs all the activities of the cell, so when the DNA is damaged or mutated, cells can no longer function normally.

The cell's DNA operates like a switch that tells the cell when to divide and when to stop dividing. Cells divide to increase their numbers. One cell splits into two, two cells split into four, four cells split into eight, and so on. Some new cells are needed so that growth can take place; other new cells are needed just to replace dead cells. When DNA is damaged, the switch malfunctions, and cells continue to divide well past the numbers needed. A mass of cells, called a tumor, then begins to form.

The cells that begin to accumulate in a tumor are actually different from the surrounding normal cells in the way they appear and behave. Differences in appearance can be detected under a microscope and are used in a test called a biopsy to decide whether a growth is benign (noncancerous) or malignant (cancerous). The most critical difference between these two kinds of growths is in the way they behave. Benign cell masses may grow very large, but they stay glued together in a closed area. Malignant cells, on the other hand, do not stick together; they readily peel off to be carried away by body fluids to other locations in the body. With crablike projections, malignant cells can also penetrate into the surrounding area of healthy cells, where they can do more damage. This feature of a malignant growth provides a name: Cancer comes from the Latin word for crab.

Blood is one means by which malignant cells can be transported to other parts of the body. The more common mode of transport is through the lymphatic system, a secondary circulation system connected to the bloodstream. The lymphatic system, attached by a series of relay stations called lymph nodes, plays a role in fighting off infections. Whether they arrive by lymph (the fluid in the lymphatic system) or by blood, the malignant cells spun off from the primary tumor plant themselves at a new place in the body. There they begin to grow into a secondary tumor, or metastasize. This is cancer in its deadliest form, because at this point controlling the spread of the disease is very difficult.

How Cancer Begins

The growth of malignant cells can begin with a small change in the DNA of a single cell. This change can be brought about by damage from chemicals or radiation or by mistakes made when cells divide. The damaging chemicals can come from pollutants in the environment or from the normal, life-sustaining activity of the cell, called metabolism. During metabolic activities, very unstable forms of oxygen called free radicals are made. These free radicals can damage DNA. Cells have the means to cope with free radicals and other chemicals before they can do much damage. Cells also have systems for repairing mistakes in DNA caused by activity they are unable to prevent.

Mistakes can also occur under ordinary circumstances during cell division. Every time a cell divides, new DNA must be made so the new cell is exactly the same as the old one. Otherwise, the new cell won't look or act the same as the old cell. Sometimes a mistake is made in the copying process. This happens in much the same way we might misspell a familiar word or absent-mindedly transpose digits in a phone number. These mistakes can be corrected by the repair systems in the cells.

These built-in repair systems can ordinarily handle the daily load of errors in DNA from normal exposures to chemicals or to free radicals made during metabolism. When these systems are overloaded by too many exposures at once or are weakened by improper maintenance, mistakes are repeated in a new generation of cells and the beginning of a tumor takes hold.

The Body's Surveillance System

The cell's repair systems are one means of defending against tumors. By correcting any mistakes in DNA, these defenses prevent the mutations in damaged DNA from taking hold and creating tumors. The body also has another line of defense, called the immune system. The immune system exists as a watchdog—it keeps a lookout for any substances that do not belong in the body. When this system is alerted to the presence of alien substances—like bacteria, viruses, and some proteins—it will seek them out and destroy them.

The immune system considers tumors to be aliens, too, because the damaged DNA in the tumor cells makes them different from normal cells. Most of the time, these cells can be detected and destroyed by the immune system. But there are times when tumor cells get away. This can happen when the cells are just too small to be detected. At other times, the immune system may be overtaxed by competing demands. Frequent illnesses and long-term stress are examples of competition for the attention of the immune system that can divert it from chasing down tumor cells.

Protection from the Culprits

If cancer begins with damage to DNA and progresses because this damage goes unrepaired, then the substances that cause the cancer must be involved at one or more steps along the way. Substances that inflict damage on DNA are called carcinogens. Substances that promote the growth of developing tumor cells are called promoters.

Most promoters operate by stepping up the speed at which cells divide. The odds of a mistake being made in the new DNA are enhanced when cells are dividing faster than they normally do. Not only are more mistakes likely to be made, but the repair systems of the cell can become overwhelmed by the increased error load. Another way promoters can encourage cells to grow is to provide them with the extra nutrition they need for that growth.

Avoiding carcinogens would seem to be the easiest way to protect ourselves from cancer because the damage they do is not easily reversed.

On some occasions they can be readily avoided, as when we avoid breathing cigarette smoke or when we use sunscreen before going out in the sun. But to completely avoid all carcinogens would mean giving up our modern technology entirely. Even then, we would still be exposed to the carcinogens that occur normally in nature. We would also have the free radicals produced naturally in our cells to deal with.

A better defense would be to concentrate on tackling the promoters of cancer while avoiding as many carcinogens as possible. We can also consume antioxidant vitamins to protect DNA from the damage caused by carcinogens and help support the systems that repair the damage. Because the body has built-in mechanisms for repairing much of the damage caused by carcinogens, it is actually the promoters that pose the greatest threat in the development of most common cancers. Keeping cells from dividing too fast by removing the promoters would give the repair systems the chance to fix the mistakes in the DNA (as long as the repair systems themselves are operating normally) before they could be repeated. Dietary fat acts primarily as a cancer promoter, especially for cancers of the breast, prostate, and colon. And it is in preventing the development of these cancers that a low-fat diet appears to be beneficial.

BREAST CANCER

A Killer Takes Its Toll

Breast cancer will confront one woman out of every nine in the United States this year. Many of these women will not survive the encounter. Breast cancer is more likely to strike after menopause, but it can strike women before this time of life as well. More white women suffer from this disease, but the incidence appears to be growing among black, Hispanic, and Asian women. Until recently, breast cancer killed more women each year in this country than any other cause. Today, as more and more women smoke cigarettes, lung cancer has surpassed breast cancer as the leading cause of death among women.

Hormones as Accomplices

Breast cancer has all the distinguishing features of cancer in general. But unlike some other common forms of cancer, such as those of the lung or skin, breast cancer may be affected, at least in part, by the body's own naturally produced hormones. Other cancers involving the reproductive organs of women—such as endometrial, uterine, and ovarian cancers—may also be affected by hormones. And, as you will see, hormones may play a role in prostate cancer in men. Colon cancer may also be affected by imbalances in the hormone insulin.

Estrogens, the steroid hormones primarily responsible for preparing a woman's body to bear children, may be involved in breast cancer. All estrogens do not appear to be equal in this respect, however. Estradiol is the particular form of estrogen that appears to be most strongly implicated in the development of breast cancer.

Estrogens, like other steroid hormones, affect the way cells behave by binding to receptors on the surface of the cells. When this happens in breast tissue, the DNA is given the message to increase the number of cells so breast tissue will grow. Such a response is normal when a young girl is developing at puberty. It also happens naturally each month in women of childbearing potential as the body prepares for the possibility of pregnancy. But if estradiol binds to receptors on cells with damaged DNA, the cells could multiply into a tumor. The extent of this effect depends on how much hormone is present. But even normal hormone levels can have a strong effect if there are more receptors than usual on the cell.

It may seem sinister that a substance as vital to the body as a hormone could actually do it harm. But estradiol is not the culprit; something else starts the process by damaging the DNA.

In some breast cancers, especially those that develop after menopause, estradiol may play only a minor role. For example, more women get breast cancer after menopause, when the ovaries are no longer producing estrogen. Since breast cancer appears to take 10 to 20 years to develop, it is possible that estradiol plays a role early in the development of such cancers, before the onset of menopause. In addition, women who take estrogens after menopause to protect themselves against osteoporosis or heart disease appear to be at the same risk for breast cancer as women who do not take estrogens. On the other hand, a drug called tamoxifen, which has an antiestrogen effect, works well to prevent recurrence of breast cancer in postmenopausal women.

Proteins found in soybeans may operate as antiestrogens as well. This may explain some of the differences in breast cancer rates between vegetarians and other groups consuming soy-containing diets compared with American women consuming their usual diets. So there clearly is much more to be learned about the link between estradiol and breast cancer.

Pinning Down the Culprits

The exact causes of breast cancer are not known. Genetics (heredity) may play a role. Breast cancer does tend to run in families. But women in the same family also share the same environment. In fact, most newly diagnosed cases of breast cancer are found in women who do not have any previous or family history of the disease.

Most cancers are believed to develop as a result of environmental influence. Although the word environment conjures up images of chemicals or pollutants in the air, water, or food, these substances are thought to account for only a small number of cancers. Diet—in particular dietary fat—is strongly linked to breast cancer.

Scientists have recently identified a gene that may be responsible for the high risk of breast cancer in some women. This gene, labeled BRCA1, is a tumor-suppressor gene that controls the normal development of breast cells. When there is a mutation of this gene, tumors are more likely to develop. Now that this gene has been identified, medical researchers are hopeful that a test may be developed to screen women who are at the highest risk of breast cancer. Such women, who stand to benefit most from preventive measures such as a low-fat diet, may then be identified early in life, when a greater chance exists that these measures can be successful.

More than 80 percent of women who develop breast cancer do not inherit the mutated BRCA1 gene and will not be identified by a screening test designed to detect it. Only about 5 percent of all breast cancers are purely genetic. This type of breast cancer is inherited by a woman through the transmission of a single gene directly from her mother. Another 13 percent of women may inherit their cancer through genes that are passed along through several generations: from their paternal grandmothers through their fathers, for instance.

A theory that may help to clarify the differences between these three types of breast cancers has been espoused by Susan Love, M.D., a surgeon and leading expert on the disease. Her theory proposes that the development of breast cancer probably involves two mutations of BRCA1. Some women inherit their first mutation and need only one more to initiate their cancer. A high-fat diet may be involved at this step. For the much larger numbers of women who do not inherit an already mutated gene, two assaults would be necessary to initiate their cancer. The first is probably hormonal, but the second comes from something in the environment, possibly a high-fat diet. This difference in the number of mutations required may explain why women with genetic cancer develop their disease earlier in life (before menopause) than women who do not inherit it (after menopause).

A recent discovery linked to the BRCA1 gene may offer hope for the majority of women who do not appear to directly inherit the disease. For these women, a protein produced by the BRCA1 gene may be misplaced within breast cells so it cannot function appropriately to control cell growth in breast tissue. Women with the genetic form of breast cancer produce a defective form of the protein. The discovery of a misplaced but otherwise normal protein may enable scientists to develop tests to determine how advanced the cancer is. This could lead to more effective means of treatment.

Because hormones are associated with the development of breast cancer, the timing of events that involve a significant change in hormone levels—such as the age at which a female gets her first menstrual period and the age at which she gives birth to her first child—may also affect a woman's risk of developing breast cancer. If a female has her first menstrual period before she is 12 years old or bears her first child late in life, her odds of getting breast cancer may be increased. Women who have never given birth may also have a greater likelihood of getting this disease. But these factors alone should not be cause for alarm. Breast cancer is a complicated disease that depends on a variety of factors for its development.

The process leading to breast cancer requires the involvement of several culprits. For example, in cultures where diets are rich in fat and calories, young girls reach puberty at an earlier age than in cultures where less fat is eaten. Until every culprit involved in breast cancer is identified, women should take steps to protect themselves in any way they can.

How Dietary Fat Is Implicated

Of all the elements in our diet that could be involved in breast cancer, the only one consistently supported by most of the evidence is dietary fat. When laboratory mice are fed a diet high in fat, they develop more mammary tumors (the animal equivalent of breast cancer) than mice given low-fat diets. These mice also have to be exposed to some cancer-causing agent. It doesn't matter whether the mice have been eating the high-fat diet all along or whether they are placed on the diet only after exposure to the carcinogen. Those that eat more fat develop more tumors once exposed to the carcinogen.

We have learned much about the link between dietary fat and breast cancer from animal studies such as these. For example, we know that fat itself is usually not the agent that causes cancer—in most cases, it does not actually damage DNA. Instead, fat appears to act primarily as a promoter of cell growth, including the growth of cells that have damaged DNA. And because it is a promoter, its effects can be readily reversed. Indeed, when the amount of fat presented to the cells is reduced, the fat's effects are weakened and may even be eliminated.

Fat encourages cells to grow by providing a rich source of energy for them. It may also raise the levels of estrogens produced by the body. Estradiol levels fall when women switch from high-fat to low-fat diets. (Remember that breast cells may be encouraged to grow when estradiol binds to their receptors.)

It is possible that fat may have a carcinogenic effect as well, although the evidence for this is not as strong as the evidence supporting fat as a cancer promoter. Fat may act as a carcinogen by combining with oxygen to form a special kind of free radical called a lipid peroxide. This compound can damage DNA.

Only one fat component—linoleic acid—has been shown to have a carcinogenic as well as a promoting effect when fed in large amounts to laboratory animals. Linoleic acid is a polyunsaturated fatty acid that is essential for health. The body cannot manufacture this fatty acid, so the diet must provide it. Vegetable oils, such as corn and soy oil, are the primary sources of linoleic acid. Linoleic acid is required for growth and for healthy skin as well as for the production of a group of hormones called prostaglandins, which are responsible for regulating functions of the heart, blood vessels, kidneys, lungs, nerves, and reproductive organs. While the body needs some linoleic acid for health, it is also the most common free-radical former of all the natural substances in the human body. That is why placing limitations on the total amount of fat in the diet, including both saturated and polyunsaturated fats, may be beneficial in helping to protect against cancer.

While only unsaturated fats are capable of forming free radicals, saturated fats may raise the level of another cancer-causing substance by raising blood cholesterol. Oxygen is drawn to cholesterol just as it is drawn to unsaturated fats. The union of cholesterol with oxygen produces a compound that causes cancer in laboratory mice. This compound has also been found in the breast fluid of women who eat high-fat diets.

Fat may also affect the development of cancer by shutting down the immune system. When fat consumption is high, excess polyunsaturated fats (especially those that provide linoleic acid) could cause more prostaglandins to be made. Prostaglandins normally temper the immune system to keep it from being too aggressive, for an overly active immune system can cause problems such as allergies or other diseases. But if too many prostaglandins are made, the immune system might be weakened and therefore wouldn't be able to carry out its surveillance tasks very effectively. The omega-6 fatty acids found in vegetable oils are the ones most likely to cause this problem. Omega-3 fatty acids in fish oils, on the other hand, may actually prevent this from happening.

Tracking Down the Evidence

The evidence implicating dietary fat's role in breast cancer has been steadily accumulating over the past twenty years. Animal studies have been useful in showing us that fat is involved and how fat acts in this process. In humans, the connection between dietary fat and breast cancer is more difficult to demonstrate. Since it takes much longer for cancer to develop in humans, we would have to try to determine what foods breast cancer victims were eating 10 or 20 years earlier, when the cancer first began to develop, in order to link fat intake to breast cancer.

Another approach is to look at the average amount of fat consumed by women living in different countries around the world and then to compare these levels with the average number of deaths from breast cancer in each country. In 1975, one of the first such studies looked at fat consumption in over 30 countries and found that more women died from breast cancer in countries where the most fat was consumed. At the time of that study, American women were getting about 40 percent of their total calories from fat; the United States also had one of the five highest death rates from breast cancer in the world. Other studies have pointed in the same direction. Childbearing practices did not seem to have as great an impact on breast cancer rates as did the intake of dietary fat.

The most interesting kinds of studies have looked at how patterns of breast cancer change when women from one country move to another. Breast cancer, for example, is less common in Japan than in the United States. But when Japanese women move to the United States, they eventually adopt the lifestyle of American women. When this happens, breast cancer becomes almost as common as it is among American women. What's more, the American-born daughters of these Japanese women have higher cancer rates than do their immigrant mothers. Because Japanese women in the United States share a similar genetic background to women still living in Japan, the most likely explanation for the difference in breast cancer rates involves some difference in the environment.

Like the United States, Japan is a modern, industrialized nation, so Japanese women are not likely to be exposed to fewer cancer-causing chemicals than are American women. But the typical Japanese diet differs dramatically from the typical American diet. The Japanese get about 20 percent of their total calories from fat—the lowest level of fat consumed in any developed country of the world. Americans typically consume about twice as much fat. Even among American women, those who eat a traditional vegetarian diet (who presumably consume less fat) have a lower rate of breast cancer than do those who eat meat (who presumably consume more fat).

But not all the evidence has implicated fat in the breast cancer story. For example, in a study of female nurses in which the subjects were grouped according to how much fat they ate, breast cancer was not less common in the group with the lowest intake. However, since these women were all Americans, most of them typically consumed about 30 to 40 percent of their total calories as fat. Many experts believe that fat intake has to be much lower than 30 percent of total calories—more like the 20 percent consumed by Japanese women—before any protection against breast cancer becomes evident.

Other Facts to Consider

It may not be only the amount of dietary fat but the food sources of that fat that make a difference in terms of breast cancer risk. Breast cancer is usually more common in countries where more meat is consumed. For example, in Mediterranean countries, the amount of fat eaten is comparable to the amount eaten in the United States, but the fat in the Mediterranean diet comes largely from olive oil. In the United States, it comes from meat and vegetable oil. The breast cancer rate in Mediterranean countries is lower than the rate in the United States, though still higher than the rate in Japan. Another example is provided by the Greenland Eskimos, who also eat a lot of fat, but their fat comes mainly from fish. Breast cancer is not very common among Eskimo women.

Fatty acids that have been altered by heat or during processing may also be a problem. One reason olive oil may not be as harmful as other vegetable oils is that olive oil, unlike the others, is not processed with heat. In addition, cooking methods that involve frying foods in fat at high temperatures for a long time, such as deep-fat frying, may cause harmful changes in fatty acids. And more of these altered fatty acids are likely to be absorbed into the food (even into foods that were originally low in fat) when such cooking methods are used.

The increase in breast cancer in the United States since World War II seems to closely parallel the greatly increased consumption of corn and soy oil, which contain linoleic acid. The consumption of large amounts of linoleic acid has been conclusively linked to cancer in animals. This postwar increase in breast cancer also parallels the increased consumption of *trans* fatty acids in this country. (When oils are processed to make hydrogenated fats, *trans* fatty acids are produced in those fats.) But the role of *trans* fatty acids in breast cancer, if any, is not known.

Finally, there is some concern about the amount of polycyclic aromatic hydrocarbons (PAHs) and other possible cancer-causing agents that are produced when fatty food is cooked using certain cooking methods. These agents are formed when fat drips onto flame, hot charcoal, lava rocks, or heating elements. The smoke produced picks up these agents and deposits them on the food. Some of these agents also form on the food when the flame touches the food itself.

Taking Action

Understanding the link between dietary fat and breast cancer is important. It gives women a way to help protect themselves from the disease. Many questions are still unanswered about the connection. However, it appears reducing the amount of fat in the diet may be beneficial.

Research seems to suggest cutting fat intake in half might help protect American women from breast cancer. This would mean decreasing the amount of total calories from fat to about 20 percent, which is substantially lower even than the 30 percent recommended for the general population. (See information on NCEP diets in Chapter 7.) While it is more difficult for many people to lower their fat intake to 20 percent, it is by no means an unsafe level. Lowering fat intake to this level may have added benefits in terms of lowering blood cholesterol and reducing the risk from heart disease as well.

The best way to lower fat intake to 20 percent is to reduce the amount of meat or poultry in the diet and replace it in most meals with fish or plant sources of protein, such as whole-grain breads and cereals and dried beans (particularly soybeans or tofu), peas, and lentils. Skim milk and nonfat yogurt should replace whole milk, ice cream, and cheese. Fresh fruits and vegetables along with starches such as pasta should be abundant in the diet. In addition, it would be desirable to replace oils and margarines with reduced-fat substitutes for cooking or in spreads, though even these substitutes would have to be avoided as much as possible.

A high-fat diet has the greatest potential for doing harm when it is eaten over a lifetime. Therefore, the earlier a woman adopts a low-fat diet, the better her chances of reaping its benefits. Real concerns exist about whether a diet that is very low in fat (20 percent of calories come from fat) is safe for children. However, steps can still be taken to reduce the current high level of fat consumed by children. A diet in which 30 percent of total calories come from fat appears to be safe for healthy adolescents and children over the age of two. (Fat should never be restricted in children under two years of age unless a doctor prescribes such restriction.) Such a diet plan would include lean cuts of meat, low-fat dairy products, and plenty of whole grains, starches, fruits, and vegetables.

PROSTATE CANCER

A Sketch of the Disease

The prostate is a small gland located near the testes in men. It is responsible for providing fluids to aid male sperm in uniting with a female ovum, or egg, so conception can take place. The prostate is a vitally active gland throughout a man's life.

Cells often change their appearance and behavior as we age. These changes are especially common in organs involved with reproduction, such as the prostate, and make the cells in these organs especially vulnerable to forming tumors. As a man ages, and more of these changes occur, the prostate becomes increasingly sensitive to substances like dietary fat that can promote the abnormal cell growth that leads to cancer.

Who Is at Risk?

Once a disease primarily affecting men over the age of 65, prostate cancer has been increasing in men of all ages, although it is still more common in men over 45 years of age. In the United States, prostate cancer is the second most fatal cancer among men after lung cancer. (While both of these cancers take a serious toll, however, coronary heart disease takes the lives of more American men than any form of cancer.)

Black men die from prostate cancer more frequently than white men. But prostate cancer is not as common in black men living in Africa as it is in black men living in the United States. In all likelihood, therefore, the environment, rather than genetics, plays a greater role in the higher rate of prostate cancer among black men in the United States.

Prostate cancer is more likely to occur in sons or brothers of men with the disease. But men in the same family share the same environment as well as the same genetics. While a family history of the disease probably points to a greater susceptibility for it, men without a history of prostate cancer can still tip the odds against themselves. Cigarette smoking and the consumption of a high-fat diet both increase risk. Becoming sexually active at an early age and having a history of venereal (sexually transmitted) disease may also increase the risk.

The Diet Connection

Dietary elements may influence the development of prostate cancer at more than one step along the way. Time after time, studies have pointed to a detrimental role for dietary fat. That role may include inflicting the original damage upon the DNA in the prostate cells as well as encouraging the growth of those cells. On the other hand, some research suggests that vitamin A may have a protective effect against this cancer, especially in men over the age of 70. The evidence is not as strong for this link, however. Interestingly, a diet that is high in fat is not likely to regularly include foods that are rich in vitamin A, such as yellowish-orange vegetables and fruits and dark-green leafy vegetables.

Prostate cancer, like breast cancer, also appears to be more common in countries where dietary fat intake is high. Typically, these countries are affluent and industrialized. Since exposure to chemicals increases with modernization, it's logical to suspect chemical exposure as a culprit in the higher incidence of prostate cancer in these countries. To determine whether diet or chemical exposure plays a greater role, researchers once again turned to Japan.

Although Japan is a modern, affluent, industrialized nation, the rate of prostate cancer in Japanese men is one of the lowest in the world. The Japanese diet is very low in fat compared to the diets in countries like the United States where prostate cancer is much more common. In addition, Japanese men living in the United States have a higher rate of prostate cancer than do Japanese men living in Japan.

Further evidence as to the role of diet may come from studying men in the United States who do not eat meat. For example, male Seventh Day Adventists, who are vegetarians, have a lower frequency of prostate cancer than do other men living in the United States. Seventh Day Adventists may also receive some cancer protection from their higher consumption of fruits and vegetables that are rich in vitamin A and also from their avoidance of alcohol, which is a powerful cancer promoter.

How Dietary Fat Is Involved

Little is understood about the exact way that prostate cancer develops, making it difficult to identify the precise role of dietary fat. Fat probably acts in the same general ways to promote prostate cancer as it does to promote the development of breast cancer (such as by providing a rich source of energy for cell growth). In addition, free radicals formed from the union of unsaturated fat and oxygen may play a part. Fat may also inhibit the work of the immune system in seeking out and destroying tumors in the prostate. And fat may upset the body's hormonal balance, which could affect the development of prostate cancer.

In the early stages of its development, prostate cancer may be dependent upon hormones. Testosterone, the hormone that directs sexual development in men, may be involved along with estrogen and prolactin (the hormone

responsible for production of breast milk). We don't usually think of finding estrogen or prolactin in men. But these hormones, along with testosterone, are also needed by men for normal growth and activity of the prostate gland. And just as dietary fat may affect the level of hormones in women, it may influence the level of testosterone, estrogen, and prolactin in men. When men change from a diet of meat and dairy products to a vegetarian diet, hormone levels decline. When they return to a meat-and-potatoes diet, hormone levels rise again.

In addition to influencing the level of prolactin, dietary fat may affect the number of prolactin receptors in prostate cells. Having a higher level of prolactin as well as a greater number of prolactin receptors in the prostate cells may make this hormone's effect on the growth of prostate cells even more powerful.

Younger men may not be as sensitive to dietary fat as older men appear to be. But since cancer may take more than 20 years to develop, the inception of the disease usually occurs at a young age. And the impact of fat is much more powerful when it is eaten in large amounts for a long period of time. Thus, young men, like young women, need to take steps now to protect themselves from the threat of cancer in the future.

COLON CANCER

The Origins of Colon Cancer

Colon cancer is one of several cancers affecting the digestive system. Digestive-system cancers can also occur in the mouth, throat, and stomach. By far the most common site, however, is the colon, which, together with the rectum, makes up the large intestine.

Cells in the colon and other parts of the digestive system are exposed to elements from the outside environment more directly than most other cells (cells in the skin and lungs are major exceptions to this general rule). This is because we take in a variety of substances besides nutrients when we eat and drink. The majority of these substances are harmless, but some may be dangerous.

As a part of the large intestine, the colon serves as a passageway. By the time food and liquids reach the colon, most of the nutrients have been taken into the body, leaving mainly waste and water. These remnants of digestion move much more slowly through the colon than they do through any other part of the digestive system. Thus, while it may take only 12 hours for these remnants to reach the colon, it can take up to a week for them to pass through it. This extended exposure makes colon cells more vulnerable to harmful substances present in the waste.

The harmful substances that may be found in foods and beverages are not limited to chemicals added as preservatives or to pesticides that are accidentally introduced into the foods through contamination. They can also be chemicals that are naturally produced by plants as protection from molds or other predators. They can even be harmless additives meant to improve the quality of food but that are altered in some way once they enter the large intestine.

The origin of these substances is probably not so important when you consider they probably have only a minor role in most cancers. And the amounts actually consumed are generally very small. Because of this, they can only have a weak cancer-causing impact. The promoters represent the real danger. When a promoter is present, even a weak cancer-causing effect can be amplified. Without the promoter, the cells would probably be able to handle the cancer-causing substances by themselves most of the time.

Who Is at Risk?

Colon cancer affects both men and women, and the chances of getting it become greater as we get older. Because cancer is a disease of exposure, the longer we are subjected to substances that cause cancer, the more likely we are to develop it. This tendency is even more pronounced for cancer promoters. The longer we allow a promoter to be present, the more likely it is that even a short-term exposure to a cancer-causing substance will do harm.

Cancer rarely develops in the colon before the age of 30. After that, however, the number of cases of colon cancer begins to increase sharply. The incidence of colon cancer at age 60 is double the incidence at age 50. Since colon cancer develops as a result of chronic, or long-term, exposure, this number would not increase so quickly unless the seeds of the cancer had already been sown a decade or two earlier.

The Big Picture

Once again, the rates of colon cancer are higher in the United States and other industrialized countries than they are in less-modernized or poorer countries. And again, the Japanese stand out from other wealthy, industrialized nations with their low frequency of this disease. The role a low-fat diet appears to play in protecting the Japanese from breast and prostate cancers is likely to be just as important in protecting them from colon cancer. And the Japanese experience illustrates chemical exposure cannot be the only cause of colon cancer, otherwise the Japanese would have as much colon cancer as do residents of the United States and other industrialized countries.

Within the United States, colon cancer is not common in vegetarians and other people who traditionally eat a low-fat diet. Colon cancer, therefore, may be more likely to develop in people who eat meat. The problem most likely lies not with the meat itself but with the fat in the meat and with the lack of other foods in the diet. People who eat a lot of meat do not usually eat many fresh fruits and vegetables or whole-grain breads and cereals. These foods may provide protection from colon cancer because of the dietary fiber and vitamins they contain. The Mormons in Utah eat meat, for example, but colon cancer is as uncommon among them as it is among the Seventh Day Adventists, who don't eat meat. The Mormons, however, also eat large amounts of whole-grain breads and cereals and therefore get more dietary fiber than the typical meat-eating American. Black people living in Africa, who get colon cancer less often than blacks living in the United States, also eat much more dietary fiber than their American counterparts.

How Dietary Fat Makes Its Impact

Colon cancer, like other cancers, begins with mutations in the DNA of colon cells. As waste passes through the large intestine, a number of harmful substances can be delivered to the colon's cells. But sometimes conditions within the colon facilitate the chemical reactions that turn harmless substances into harmful ones. Bile is one of the substances that can be changed.

In fact, bile—one of the compounds made in the body from cholesterol—plays a key role in colon cancer. Bile is normally released into the intestines to help the body absorb fat. Most of this bile is reabsorbed by the body, but some is left behind. Bile exists as an acid unless it combines with a mineral such as calcium, which makes it nonreactive. As an acid, if bile is present in large amounts, it can injure the cells of the colon. Since injured cells repair themselves by dividing to make new ones, the greater the injury sustained, the faster the cells divide. If these cells are also exposed to substances that cause cancer, then the rapidly dividing cells don't have time to repair the damaged DNA or any mistakes that might accidentally be made as the cells divide. A tumor can then begin to grow.

The extent of cell injury depends on the amount of bile acid delivered to the colon. Because bile is needed to digest and absorb fat, the quantity of fat in the diet dictates the amount of bile that is delivered to the colon. People who eat fat-rich foods need more bile to digest and absorb the fat. They therefore have more bile passing through their colon than do people who eat low-fat foods. More bile acids are found in the stools of people living in countries where colon cancer is common and fat intake is high.

While bile may be the most important link between dietary fat and colon cancer, there are other ways fat may be involved. For example, free radicals that are formed from the union of fat and oxygen are also capable of injuring colon cells. More of these free radicals would be present if fat intake were high, and even though any type of fat in the diet increases the production of bile, only unsaturated fats form free radicals.

Hidden Dangers of a High-Fat Diet

It may be not only the dietary fat that causes a problem for the colon but also other elements that may be present or lacking in a high-fat diet. When you choose foods rich in fat, you tend to select items such as meat, cheese, pizza, eggs, whole milk, ice cream, butter and margarine, fried foods, and baked goods. These foods do not leave much room for whole-grain breads and cereals; dried beans, peas, and lentils; and fresh fruits and vegetables. Because of this, a high-fat diet typically is high in energy and refined sugar but low in fiber, beta-carotene (a precursor of vitamin A), and vitamins A and C.

The beneficial effects of a diet high in fruits and vegetables appears stronger than the detrimental effects of a high-fat diet. Typically a diet that is high in fat is usually low in vegetables. Still, each of these factors may be important in its own way.

Along with whole grains, fruits and vegetables provide dietary fiber, which may be one of the most important protections the diet can offer against colon cancer. The primary benefit of fiber is that it can bind to bile acids and prevent them from injuring colon cells. Fiber also speeds up movement of waste through the colon so that harmful substances don't have as much contact with colon cells. Fatty foods, on the other hand, tend to be low in fiber and low in moisture, which can slow the movement of wastes through the colon. When the fat content of the diet is high and the fiber content is low, it may take up to seven days for waste to move through the colon. A low-fat, high-fiber diet, on the other hand, can shorten that travel time to almost 24 hours. Indeed, the higher amount of fiber from the whole grains eaten by the Utah Mormons is probably the reason that colon cancer is less common among them than among other meat-eaters in the United States. In fact, more than 30,000 years ago our early ancestors were eating considerable amounts of meat, but their fiber intake was about 46 grams—approximately four to eight times what most Americans eat today.

Fruits and vegetables provide rich sources of beta-carotene and vitamins A and C. Beta-carotene and vitamin C act as antioxidants. They protect cells from damage that could be done by free radicals produced in the cells or in the intestines. Vitamin A is believed to enhance the effectiveness of the cell systems that repair damage and mistakes in DNA. Plants also possess a variety of other protective substances called phytochemicals that we are just beginning to understand.

In addition, a high-fat diet is almost always high in energy, or calories, because fat provides more than twice the number of calories as protein or carbohydrate. Calorie-rich diets may also be involved in promoting the growth of colon tumors. Providing more energy to cells in any form, not only as fat, may encourage cells to grow faster. But the Seventh Day Adventists eat just as many calories as other Americans do, and colon cancer is still less common among them. The difference is that more of the calories they consume come from plant foods, which provide fewer calories from fat.

If any type of diet provides too much energy, body fat will be made to store the excess. Harmful cancer-causing substances that are able to get into the body find their way to fat reserves, where they can be stored indefinitely. Some cancers may be more common in people who are overweight, but whether the reason for this is related to the amount of cancer-causing substances they are able to store or to some other cause is as yet unknown.

Chapter 6: Body Fat and Health

Chances are, one of the reasons you picked up this book was concern over how to lose weight successfully. If you are interested in weight loss, you are not alone. A newsletter on obesity noted recently that 48 million American adults are dieting. This concern about overweight isn't without foundation. Being significantly overweight may trim your life expectancy, contribute to health problems, and lead to psychological distress.

Yet there's a good deal of confusion among the public as to what constitutes significant overweight and how best to correct it. While many of us check our weight on the bathroom scale daily, we may be unaware that the reading at our feet is not the best way to determine whether our weight increases our health risks. For example, that reading doesn't tell us how much of our weight consists of muscle and bone and how much consists of fat. Nor does it tell us where we are wearing excess fat—above the belt or below—or when we acquired it. The answers to questions such as these are important in determining whether any extra weight you may be carrying increases your susceptibility to a variety of health problems, including high blood pressure, diabetes, abnormal blood-fat levels, heart disease, and stroke. If the answers point to excess body fat—especially in the upper body—that was gained in early adulthood, then slimming down may help you decrease your risk of such health problems.

Eating a high-fat diet, especially if you don't exercise regularly, makes it easy to develop a fat body—with all the accompanying health risks. On the other hand, a low-fat diet and a program of regular exercise can play a key role in trimming excess fat from your body, lowering your risk of health problems, and improving the way you look and feel about yourself. To understand the relationships among dietary fat, body fat, and health risks, it's helpful to understand just what we mean when we refer to concepts such as overweight and body fat.

Overweight vs. "Overfat"

Being overweight is not the same as being overfat. The numbers on the bathroom scale may tell you if you are overweight, but they don't reveal how much body fat you have. Body weight includes the weight of the lean tissues—muscle, internal organs, and bone, and the water they contain—and body fat. So a muscular person might weigh more than a less-muscular person of the same gender, age, and height even though the more muscular person probably has less body fat.

Sometimes we may be heavier than usual because of water retention. Women are particularly sensitive to this "bloating" just before their menstrual period, though men may also experience this sensation after they eat a particularly salty meal. It doesn't take much water to add weight to the body: Two cups of water weigh slightly more than one pound. Weight gain from water retention is easy to recognize because, unlike weight gain from muscle or fat, it can appear almost overnight. It can also disappear just as quickly. But you need not be concerned about water retention unless it is excessive. For example, a weight gain of more than ten pounds of water usually reflects edema, which is a serious condition requiring immediate medical attention.

Muscle is also heavy; it contains water in addition to muscle cells. After you begin an exercise program, you may find you actually weigh a bit more than you used to. Muscles, especially the large ones in the legs, can increase in size with regular exercise, easily adding five pounds or more to your weight. But muscle takes up less space than fat, pound for pound, so you appear thinner even though you've gained weight. More important, you are likely to be healthier.

Fat, on the other hand, does not weigh as much as water or muscle. Ironically, you have to accumulate larger amounts of fat than of muscle (or water) to gain the same amount of weight. That's why you tend to appear slim when you gain weight from added muscle, but you tend to look larger when you gain weight from added fat.

Does it really make a difference whether this extra weight is from fat or from muscle or water? Absolutely. And this is why the numbers on the bathroom scale can be so deceptive.

In looking at the way weight relates to health, medical researchers use a measurement called the body mass index, or BMI, because it reflects the amount of body fat better than simply looking at weight alone. (BMI is discussed more thoroughly later in the chapter.) In fact, the BMI is almost as good at estimating how much fat you have as are actual measurements of body fat. Researchers have found that more deaths occur each year in the United States among people who have a high BMI compared with those who have an optimal BMI. When weight is considered instead of BMI, the differences in mortality for overweight compared with optimal weight are not as pronounced. In other words, the amount of body fat you have is a much better predictor of health status than is body weight. This means that excess body fat is the health risk, not excess muscle or moderate water retention. It is much more important to know how "fat" you are than how much you weigh.

Still, for people who are not particularly muscular or who are not going through a period of water retention, the weight that registers on the bathroom scale can provide useful information about body fat. In fact, most people fall into this category. That's why it may not be a bad idea to weigh yourself from time to time, as long as you remember that this measurement is only as important as the amount of body fat it reflects.

Estimating How Much Body Fat You Have

We all need some body fat in order to remain healthy, but too much body fat poses a health risk. Suprisingly, there is a fairly wide range of body fat a person can have and still be considered healthy.

One common way to get a general idea of whether you have an optimal amount of body fat is to compare your weight to a standard reference table. The weight standards most often used are the ones developed by the Metropolitan Life Insurance Company. These are the weights of applicants for life insurance who were found to have the longest life span. First published in 1942, these actuarial tables were revised in 1959 and again in 1983. The 1959 tables are preferred because the more recent tables include weights of cigarette smokers. Because smokers typically have low body weights but high death rates, the weights in the 1983 tables are higher than what might be truly desirable.

In the 1959 tables, "desirable" weight ranges are given for men and women at different heights and different body-frame sizes. A method of approximating whether you have a small, medium, or large frame is provided in the next section.

To Make an Approximation of Your Frame Size...

Extend your arm and bend the forearm upward at a 90-degree angle. Keep fingers straight and turn the inside of your wrist toward your body. Use calipers to measure the distance between the two prominent bones on either side of your elbow. Without calipers, place the thumb and index finger of your other hand on these two bones. Then measure the distance between your fingers, using a ruler or tape measure. Compare that number with the tables below, which list elbow measurements for men and women with medium frames. Measurements lower than those listed indicate that you have a small frame; higher measurements indicate a large frame.

Medium Frame Size	
Height in 1″ heels	Elbow Breadth
Men	
5′2″–5′3″	2½″–2⅞″
5′4″–5′7″	2⅝″–2⅞″
5′8″–5′11″	2¾″–3″
6′0″–6′3″	2¾″–3⅛″
6′4″	2⅞″–3¼″
Women	
4′10″–5′3″	2¼″–2½″
5′4″–5′11″	2⅜″–2⅝″
6′0″	2½″–2¾″

Courtesy of Metropolitan Life Insurance Company
Statistical Bulletin.

If your weight is above the range given in the tables for your gender, height, and body-frame size, you can use the following four-step formula to calculate what percent overweight you are. First, take the average of the weights in the range for your gender, height, and body-frame size. This is your reference weight. Second, subtract this reference weight from your actual weight. Third, divide the result by

1959 Metropolitan Life Height and Weight Table

MEN

Height (without shoes)	SMALL FRAME	MEDIUM FRAME	LARGE FRAME
Height (without shoes)	Weight (without clothes)		
Feet/Inches	Pounds	Pounds	Pounds
5'1"	105–113	111–122	119–134
5'2"	108–116	114–126	122–137
5'3"	111–119	117–129	125–141
5'4"	114–122	120–132	128–145
5'5"	117–126	123–136	131–149
5'6"	121–130	127–140	135–154
5'7"	125–134	131–145	140–159
5'8"	129–138	135–149	144–163
5'9"	133–143	139–153	148–167
5'10"	137–147	143–158	152–172
5'11"	141–151	147–163	157–177
6'0"	145–155	151–168	161–182
6'1"	149–160	155–173	166–187
6'2"	153–164	160–178	171–192
6'3"	157–168	165–183	175–197

1959 Metropolitan Life Height and Weight Table

WOMEN

Height (without shoes)	SMALL FRAME	MEDIUM FRAME	LARGE FRAME
Height (without shoes)	Weight (without clothes)		
Feet/Inches	Pounds	Pounds	Pounds
4'9"	90–97	94–106	102–118
4'10"	92–100	97–109	105–121
4'11"	95–103	100–112	108–124
5'0"	98–106	103–115	111–127
5'1"	101–109	106–118	114–130
5'2"	104–112	109–122	117–134
5'3"	107–115	112–126	121–138
5'4"	110–119	116–131	125–142
5'5"	114–123	120–135	129–146
5'6"	118–127	124–139	133–150
5'7"	122–131	128–143	137–154
5'8"	126–136	132–147	141–159
5'9"	130–140	136–151	145–164
5'10"	134–144	140–155	149–169

Courtesy of Metropolitan Life Insurance Company Statistical Bulletin.

your reference weight. Finally, multiply by 100 to determine the percentage by which you are overweight. For example, consider a man with a medium frame who is five feet eight inches tall and weighs 162 pounds. For him, the desirable weight range, as shown in the table, is from 135 to 149. To determine his reference weight, first add 135 to 149 and divide the result by 2, which gives you 142. Second, subtract 142 from 162, which is 20. Then divide 20 by 142, which gives you approximately 0.14. Finally, multiply 0.14 by 100, which is 14. Thus, the man is 14 percent overweight.

While comparing your weight to these height-weight tables can be helpful, there are some limitations to this method. For one, the desirable weights are based on people who take out life insurance and therefore are not necessarily representative of everyone in the United States. What may be true for this group of affluent, educated, and predominantly white individuals may not apply directly to other groups. In addition, the tables use the concept of "frame size," which is somewhat difficult to estimate accurately. They also tend to underestimate the desirable weight range for someone who has a high percentage of muscle to fat.

As mentioned previously, the body mass index, or BMI, can also give you an idea of whether you are lugging around too much body fat. Although this method does not actually measure the percentage of fat in your body, it does provide a better estimate than weight alone of how fat you are.

To calculate your BMI mathematically, you need to know your height (in inches) and your weight (in pounds). First, multiply your height times your height (square your height). Then divide your weight by that number. Finally, multiply the result by 703.1 to convert pounds and inches into metric numbers. As an example, if you are 64 inches tall and weigh 120 pounds, multiply 64 times 64, which gives you 4,096. Then divide 120 by 4,096, which gives you approximately .03. Finally, multiply .03 by 703.1, which gives you a BMI of approximately 21.

The optimal BMI is 20 to 25 for adult males under the age of 35. For adult females in the same age group, the optimal BMI is 19 to 24. The optimal BMI for both men and women 35 years of age and older is 21 to 27. This allowance for a small increase in weight levels for men and women after the age of 35 is in keeping with a proposal made in a volume called *Diet and Health,* published by the National Research Council in 1989, as well as with the weight tables in the dietary guidelines published in 1991 by the United States government.

As an option to performing the calculations consult the table entitled "Good Body Weights for Adults." This table lists weight ranges for adults that correspond to the optimal BMI for the two age groups.

While height-weight tables and BMI calculations can provide useful information, the best way to determine how fat you are is to have your body fat estimated. This can be done in your doctor's office, a weight-loss clinic, or a health club using an instrument called a skin-fold caliper. A skin-fold caliper estimates total fat in the body by measuring the amount of fat just underneath the skin at relatively lean places on the body, such as at the back of the upper arm, just under the shoulder blade, or at the hip. The caliper is used to measure the width of the fold of skin at one or all of these places; from this measurement, total body fat can be estimated. The amount of fat on the body of a lean person at the age of 25 is considered the optimal level of body fat. This value is between 16 and 18 percent of body weight for men and between 22 and 25 percent for women.

Other methods for measuring body fat are more sophisticated but not as widely available. One method, called bioelectric impedance, measures the degree of resistance to a weak electric current sent through the body. Since fat tends to resist the flow of electricity and lean tissue tends to conduct it, the degree of resistance can be used to estimate the percentage of body fat.

Underwater weighing is a more exact means of estimating body fat. It involves comparing your weight as measured underwater to your weight when measured on land. The difference in weights is related to your buoyancy in water, or how readily you float; buoyancy is determined by the amount of fat you have on your body, since fat is lighter than water and tends to float.

The newest technique for estimating body fat uses computed tomography, or CT scanning, to measure fat surrounding internal organs. But this technique is expensive and available only in specially equipped facilities.

How Much Fat Is Too Much?

What if, using one of these techniques, you discover you are above the desirable weight range or the desirable percentage of body fat? How great are the risks to your health? Studies examining the health risks associated with different BMIs have found you can be up to ten percent over a desirable reference weight without increasing the risks to your health. (The "good weight" ranges in the table take this allowance into account: The upper limits of the range are actually about ten percent or so over the "average," or reference, weights.)

Health risks increase only slightly from 10- to 20-percent overweight. But at 20 percent or more above reference weight, which is the general medical definition of obesity, overweight is considered a significant health hazard, according to a National Institutes of Health panel on obesity. At 30 percent or more above reference weight (a BMI greater than 30) the health risks increase dramatically.

It is important to note that even if overweight is in the 10- to 30-percent range, the risk for coronary heart disease may be increased if other risk factors, such as high blood pressure, diabetes, and abnormal blood-fat levels, are also present. And the location of excess body fat and the time in life when it was gained can also affect your risk of health problems from overweight.

You should also keep in mind that the reference weights and ranges are only a guide to approximating what you should weigh. Any such calculation should not be treated as exact. In addition, people can differ considerably in the weight they can handle before their health is

Good Body Weights for Adults				
	19 TO 34 YEARS		35 YEARS AND UP	
Height*	Average	Range	Average	Range
5'0"	112	97–128	123	108–138
5'1"	116	101–132	127	111–143
5'2"	120	104–137	131	115–148
5'3"	124	107–141	135	119–152
5'4"	128	111–146	140	122–157
5'5"	132	114–150	144	126–162
5'6"	136	118–155	148	130–167
5'7"	140	121–160	153	134–172
5'8"	144	125–164	158	138–178
5'9"	149	129–169	162	142–183
5'10"	153	132–174	167	146–188
5'11"	157	136–179	172	151–194
6'0"	162	140–184	177	155–199
6'1"	166	144–189	182	159–205
6'2"	171	148–195	187	164–210
6'3"	176	152–200	192	168–216
6'4"	180	156–205	197	173–222
6'5"	185	160–211	202	177–228
6'6"	190	164–216	208	182–234

*Height without shoes; weight without clothes.
Derived from National Research Council, 1989. Copyright 1991, George A. Bray, M.D.

compromised. Nevertheless, if you are between 10 and 20 percent over your desirable weight, you should begin to get serious about reducing body fat because, at this point, weight loss is still manageable. With a greater degree of over-weight, it becomes much more difficult to lose excess body fat. So if you find that you are over-weight now, you need to work to get your weight into the desirable range and keep it there.

Health Risks of Having Too Much Body Fat

Excess weight from excess body fat, especially when it exceeds 20-percent overweight, can seriously compromise your health. This is obesity, which can put a physical strain on your heart and blood vessels as well as on your joints. The burden of having to provide blood to nourish such a large mass of tissue can, over time, cause the blood pressure to rise and the heart to enlarge. High blood pressure and eventual heart failure can result. Even in the young, long-term obesity can eventually lead to heart failure.

The burden of carrying around massive weight takes an eventual toll on the weight-bearing joints, especially the knees. Osteoarthritis, the so-called "wear and tear" form of arthritis, is more frequently seen at younger ages in the obese than in individuals who are not obese. And gout, a painful disease involving the joints—particularly those of the big toes—may be seen more frequently in people who are obese.

Excess body fat can also result in abnormalities in the body's metabolism. Overweight people are four times more likely than lean people to develop type II, or non–insulin-dependent, diabetes, in which the level of sugar in the blood remains high despite the presence of high levels of insulin. Insulin is a hormone that normally helps the cells to take up sugar from the blood to use as fuel. In type II diabetes, insulin is produced in normal quantities, but the body's cells do not appear to respond well to the insulin. So the cells become starved for fuel even though the level of sugar in the blood is high. If blood-sugar levels remain high over time, high blood pressure, kidney damage, and even blindness can result.

Blood-lipid levels are often abnormal in overweight people. In some overweight individuals, the total blood-cholesterol level may be elevated. In most cases the overweight person has a low level of protective HDLs and a high level of blood triglycerides. Recent research has sparked renewed interest in high triglyceride levels as a key indicator of heart-disease risk

when they are associated with abnormal levels of other lipoproteins, such as HDLs or LDLs. These abnormal blood-fat levels, together with the possibility of developing high blood pressure and diabetes, put the overweight person at a very high risk for developing coronary heart disease. High blood pressure, diabetes, and high blood cholesterol are all considered to be primary risk factors for this disease (smoking is another major risk factor for heart disease). When these conditions are present, the risk of heart disease increases greatly even at lower levels of overweight.

A number of other health problems are also associated with significant overweight caused by excess body fat. Among them are gallstones (particularly in women) and respiratory (breathing) problems. In overweight men, less of the hormone testosterone is produced; in overweight females, more of the hormone estrogen is produced. The onset of menstruation occurs earlier in obese girls than in girls who are not obese. In obese women, however, periods are more irregular and menopause occurs earlier than in nonobese women. Obesity also increases complications during pregnancy, such as high blood pressure and toxemia, and is likely to cause difficulty with labor. Excess body weight also increases the usual risk of complications associated with surgery and can make it difficult for a doctor to perform accurate diagnostic tests.

The Age and Gender Gaps

Age and gender are important considerations in evaluating the seriousness of the health risks caused by excess weight. Generally, the younger you are when you gain excess weight, the more serious the impact on your health will be. But if you are a woman, you can generally tolerate the adverse effects of overweight on your health better than a man can. This is not to say that older people and women do not have to be concerned about their weight, but that younger people and men may have more to be concerned about.

The average weight in this country increases somewhat with each decade of adult life. It may come as no surprise to read that as you age, it may be more difficult to maintain your weight. But what is interesting is that the health risks for overweight people are not equal before and after the age of 45. For example, overweight people under the age of 45 are more likely to have high blood cholesterol than are older people who have a similar degree of overweight. This means that the risk for coronary heart disease is much greater in younger people who are overweight than in older people who are overweight. So the time in life when you gain excess weight may be just as important as how much weight you gain. And early weight gain may affect your ability to maintain optimal weight as you grow older.

A gender gap also exists in the health risks of overweight. Although more men than women are likely to be 10- to 20-percent overweight, more women are likely to be obese. Despite the greater degree of overweight seen in women compared with men, women do not seem to suffer from diseases related to their weight to the same extent that men do. The reason for this may be related to the difference in where fat tends to accumulate in men and women. In men, excess fat tends to accumulate around the stomach or abdomen. In women, excess fat tends to accumulate around the hips and buttocks. The overweight man, therefore, is generally shaped more like an apple while the overweight woman tends to be shaped more like a pear. These so-called apple and pear shapes are taken very seriously when considering health risks associated with overweight.

Overweight people who carry their excess body fat in the abdominal region ("apples") are more likely to have higher blood pressure, a higher triglyceride level, and a lower HDL-cholesterol level than are overweight people whose fat is deposited in the lower body ("pears"). Type II diabetes is also more common among overweight people with the apple shape than among those who are shaped like a pear. And, as mentioned previously, the presence of high blood pressure, abnormal blood-fat levels, and diabetes greatly increases the risk of coronary heart disease, even at lower levels of overweight. Indeed, in research on overweight individuals, those who carried their excess body fat like an inner tube around their waist had the highest risk for coronary heart disease, even though they were not always the most overweight.

Not all overweight men wear their excess body fat in the abdominal region, and not all overweight women carry theirs in the lower body. When overweight women have an apple shape, their health risks are similar to those of overweight men. Overweight men with a pear shape seem to have the same protection from these health risks as pear-shaped women.

The distribution of body fat may also explain some of the age gap in health risks associated with overweight. When weight is gained later in life, the excess fat is more likely to be deposited in the lower body. When it is gained at a younger age, excess body fat is more likely to be found in the abdominal area. It is not entirely clear why the location of fat deposits affects the health risks associated with excess body fat. One theory is that fat in the abdomen is more actively involved in the body's metabolism.

How Losing Body Fat Can Help

In Chapter 8, strategies for weight loss are discussed in detail. The important point to keep in mind about weight loss is if it is going to improve your health, the weight loss has to come from a decrease in body fat rather than a loss of water or muscle. After all, it is the excessive amount of fat that makes the weight a health hazard.

For extremely overweight people, weight loss can be lifesaving, especially if they have heart or respiratory problems. Loss of excess body fat can also make it easier to control blood-sugar levels and can cause high blood pressure to decrease dramatically. Symptoms of gout and arthritis may also lessen.

Certainly, the greatest benefits from weight loss are reaped by people who are severely overweight. However, benefits are also considerable for those who are only 20 percent overweight.

Thin Does Not Always Mean Lean

Losing weight is an important goal in promoting good health, but again the scale can be deceptive. When you weigh yourself and find that your weight falls in the desirable range of the Metropolitan Life tables, you are definitely thin. You may not, however, be lean. *Thin* applies to your appearance and reflects a desirable weight on the scale. *Lean* applies to the composition of that weight on the body.

To be lean, you have to have a low percentage of body fat. Most of the weight in a lean person comes from muscle. However, you can be thin without being lean. A thin person can have a high percentage of fat compared to muscle. As a result, although two people may both appear equally slim, the lean one will weigh more than the thin one but will probably have a lower level of health risks. An example of a person who may be thin but not lean is a cigarette smoker. Even though smoking may act indirectly to keep the individual thin, it does not improve the ratio of muscle to fat. It is also an extremely dangerous way to control weight.

The distinction between thin and lean is an important one for two reasons. The lean person is likely to have lower health risks because of a lower percentage of body fat. In addition, lean people are more likely to be successful at maintaining their weight in the long run than are those who are merely thin. That's because muscle, even when it is not engaged in exercise, requires more energy and burns more calories than does body fat.

Dietary Fat's Role in Overweight

It seems logical that fat in food should be linked to fat in the body. When you weigh more than you would like, it is usually because you have too much fat in your body. But body fat is really a reserve of the excess energy you've eaten, whether that energy came from fat or from carbohydrate, protein, or alcohol. Having too much body fat means you are consuming more energy, or calories, from foods and beverages than you need to perform your daily activities.

Fat has more than twice the energy value of carbohydrate or protein and slightly more than alcohol. Therefore, foods that contain large amounts of fat provide more calories than foods containing an equal amount of protein or carbohydrate.

Another reason fat-rich foods have more calories is they typically don't contain much water. Fat and water don't mix well, so nature usually doesn't put them together in foods. Recipes calling for fat also don't usually require much water to be added. Because they do not contain much water, fat-rich foods don't weigh as much or take up as much room on your plate as do low-fat foods that provide the same number of calories. This tempts us to eat larger servings of high-fat foods. Larger servings mean more calories, especially if the foods are already high in calorie-dense fat. So eating fat-rich foods may mean we end up eating more calories than we need.

The body may be more efficient in processing calories from fat than it is at processing calories from carbohydrate. When the body burns fat or carbohydrate to provide energy for the body's cells, part of the energy is harnessed to fuel the processes that sustain life. Breathing, the pumping action of the heart, and other essential activities of the body all require energy. The sum total of these energy needs is your metabolic rate. The

tension in your muscles that keeps you erect also uses some energy; movement requires even more.

Like all other machines, the body harnesses only a small fraction of the total energy available from its fuel to drive its activities. Most of this energy goes off as heat to keep our body temperature at 98.6 degrees Fahrenheit; we need to maintain this temperature so our metabolism runs smoothly. About 80 percent of the energy available from fuel is released as heat. Even so, our bodies are the most efficient machines around.

Less heat is produced when the body burns fat from foods than when it burns carbohydrate from foods. That means more energy is available to support metabolism and other activities. When these energy needs are met, any excess energy is stored as fat.

You have to eat more carbohydrate calories to get the same amount of useful energy that fat provides because more of the energy from carbohydrate goes off as heat. The result of this greater heat production is that fewer calories from carbohydrate are likely to be available for energy needs, so less will be left over to be stored as body fat. Therefore, you should be able to eat more calories from carbohydrate than you would from fat without gaining weight. Of course, it is possible to eat a low-fat diet that exceeds your calorie needs and therefore can cause weight gain, but weight gain is much less likely to occur on a low-fat diet than on a high-fat one.

Some studies have indeed found that people who eat a diet that is high in carbohydrates end up losing weight—even if they take in the same number of calories as people eating a high-fat diet. In one study, compared to one group of subjects whose calories came primarily from fat, a second group of subjects whose calories came primarily from carbohydrate actually had to consume more calories to prevent weight loss.

The participants who ate more carbohydrate in this study had less body fat than the participants who ate more fat, even after only six months. They also had more muscle than fat compared to people who ate the high-fat diets. This change was seen despite the fact that they did not increase their level of activity. A change in the proportion of muscle to fat of this kind is important for weight control because muscle tissue uses most of the energy needed by the body. Body fat, on the other hand, uses virtually none. The need for calories is always higher in people who have more muscle and less body fat. That's why highly muscled individuals can often get away with eating more calories without worrying about gaining weight. Although people who eat a carbohydrate-rich diet may have more muscle than people eating a low-carbohydrate, high-fat, diet, the muscle they gained is only a fraction of what can be gained with exercise. You have to use your muscles to have them substantially increase in size.

Recent diet trends have tried to capitalize on the lower body fat promoted by high-carbohydrate diets. The belief that you can eat all the calories you want as long as they come from carbohydrate has been widely put into practice, but without much success. The failure of this approach to control weight does not mean its scientific soundness should be questioned. The problems arise from oversimplifying the complex relationship between dietary carbohydrate, carbohydrate stores, and the use of carbohydrate for energy. In the clearest terms, the high-carbohydrate approach works only if combined with regular exercise.

High-carbohydrate diets are almost always low in fat because these two fuel sources are complementary in most foods. (There are exceptions, however: Baked goods are often high in both carbohydrate and fat.) As the proportion of energy contributed by fat rises, the proportion contributed by carbohydrate falls. Consider, for example, whole-grain cereals and breads; dried beans, peas, and lentils; and fruits and vegetables. These foods are low in fat and high in carbohydrate. Foods high in fat are almost always low in carbohydrate; they are usually good sources of protein as well.

Inactivity: Another Controllable Factor in Overweight

It is important to note a high-fat, high-calorie diet is not the only controllable factor contributing to overweight. An inactive lifestyle is also a key component in the development and maintenance of overweight. In terms of persistent overweight, lack of activity may play an even greater role than overeating.

As mentioned earlier, some of the energy from the calories you consume goes off as heat, some is used to drive basic body functions, and some is used to fuel movement. Whatever is left over is then stored as fat. By living an inactive lifestyle, you decrease the amount of energy used for movement, leaving more to be stored as fat.

Exercise is crucial for weight control because it burns calories and increases the proportion of muscle to fat. Muscles use most of the energy you need even while you are resting. So larger muscles mean more energy is needed and more calories can be eaten without adding excess fat. By decreasing body fat and increasing muscle, exercise can amplify the benefits of a low-fat diet.

The Fate of Being Fat

Although there has been quite a bit of research devoted to understanding why some people gain so much body fat that they become obese, there are still no certain answers. No single cause can be identified because there is probably an interplay between a number of different factors, including food intake, eating habits, activity level, emotional state, and genetics.

The simplest explanation for what causes obesity is that the energy balance is off. Either more food is eaten than is needed to support body functions and activity, or there is not enough activity to burn all the energy from the food that is eaten. One or both of these conditions usually have to be present before a person gains weight, but genetic makeup can exaggerate these effects.

Because of their genes, some people have a greater tendency to make body fat from the calories they eat, regardless of how active they are. These people may use food fuels so efficiently they do not need to burn as much of their body fat to sustain their activity level.

This tendency to efficiently store calories as body fat is present to some extent in all of us and can be shown when we restrict our intake of food. For example, if we eat our entire allotment of calories for the day in a single large meal, we are more likely to see these calories end up as body fat than if we ate the same number of calories in several smaller meals. People who gorge at one meal (usually in the evening) also tend to have higher levels of blood cholesterol and an inability to control their blood-sugar levels.

One way to analyze the impact of genetics on weight is to study identical twins raised in different households. Since identical twins share the same genetic endowment, this type of analysis allows genetic and environmental factors to be separated. In a Swedish study, body weights of one group of twins—who were raised together in the same households—were compared with body weights of a second group of twins who were split up and raised in different households. A striking similarity in weights was found within the pairs of twins, and this was true whether or not they had shared the same environment. This finding stresses that while the environment can influence dietary and exercise behavior, genetic factors have a greater impact on weight gain.

Another study with adult twins who were fed a high-calorie diet to promote weight gain showed that not only was weight gain more similar within twin pairs than between twin pairs, but the distribution of the fat—whether in the abdominal area or in the lower body—was also more similar within the twin pairs. Differences in weight gain and fat distribution between unrelated twins were noted even though the number of calories consumed was the same. Clearly, then, genetic makeup influences how efficiently energy is used and how excess energy is stored in the body.

A recent discovery has brought us closer to understanding the role of genetics in controlling weight. Scientists have identified a protein produced by mice from a specific gene called the ob gene, which is damaged in genetically obese mice. When normal protein, produced by an undamaged ob gene, was injected into the genetically obese mice, they reduced their food intake and became more active. They also lost 50 percent more weight than untreated mice eating the same diet. Even in mice with normal ob genes, an injection of the protein caused them to lose almost all of their body fat in four days. They were able to maintain this weight as long as they received the protein, which is believed to work by interacting with receptors in the brain that control appetite and metabolism. When protein reaches a certain level, appetite decreases, metabolism increases, and animals become more active. In other words, energy intake goes down and energy use goes up, promoting weight loss.

While this is exciting news, it does not give us an excuse to quit watching our diets to control our weight. Dietary fat in particular can decrease the amount of ob protein produced, even among mice with normal ob genes. When this happens, appetite is increased, but metabolism and activity levels are decreased. A low-fat diet has the opposite effect, making it easier to shed body fat. Although it is still uncertain if this discovery may have an influence on humans, it brings us closer to understanding the complex way our diet may interact with our genes to determine what we will weigh. It also helps explain why one person can eat the same diet and exercise at the same levels as another, yet have a very different body weight. At the same time, it also suggests that by simply lowering our fat intake, many of us have more control over our body weight than we may want to believe.

It is important to note, however, that while the genetic influence on weight gain may be strong, it does not imply that activity levels or eating habits are not important. A genetic predisposition may make some of us more likely to become obese, but it does not mean that obesity must develop. On the other hand, even with genetics in our favor, overeating and inactivity can make us gain weight. Either way, our eating and exercise habits make all the difference in terms of the impact genetics has on weight gain.

Other Causes of Overweight

As if overeating, inactivity, and genetics were not enough, other conditions can also contribute to weight gain. A common time when weight gain can occur is when a person stops smoking cigarettes. Cigarette smoking may slightly increase the amount of energy needed for metabolism. When cigarettes are withdrawn, former smokers find that they cannot eat as much as they did when they smoked and still maintain their weight. The weight gain that may develop after smoking cessation generally does not amount to much unless the person is using food to satisfy the craving for cigarettes. A smart approach to smoking cessation, therefore, would be to begin an exercise program as a distraction from thinking about smoking. By exercising, former smokers can prevent the usual post-cessation weight gain and obtain a lean physique instead of just a thin one.

Imbalances of some hormones can also contribute to the tendency toward overweight or obesity. Thyroid hormone imbalance is particularly noteworthy since this hormone regulates the rate at which energy is utilized to support the basic life functions (basal metabolism). A deficiency of this hormone causes the rate of metabolism to slow down, contributing to a tendency to gain a considerable amount of weight. For patients who have a deficiency of this hormone, or who have hyperthyroidism, replacement doses can help. However, most obese people have normal levels of thyroid hormone. Replacement doses of the hormones given to people who do not have hyperthyroidism can do more harm than good. The weight loss produced by unnecessary amounts of this hormone is usually only temporary and actually results more from a loss of muscle than from loss of excess body fat. Excess thyroid hormone can also lead to adverse cardiovascular symptoms, such as exaggerated heart rhythms, that may require hospitalization.

Some antidepressant drugs or mild tranquilizers can also lead to weight gain, as can some allergy medications. One way these drugs may act is through stimulating the appetite. Drugs like beta blockers (such as propranolol) that are commonly used for treating high blood pressure may promote weight gain as well. Ask your doctor or pharmacist if weight gain is a possible side effect of medication you are taking. By knowing this ahead of time, you may be able to take steps to control the amount of weight gained, either through a change in diet or an increase in activity level (consult your doctor before making such changes, however).

The Childhood Connection

Whatever the causes of overweight and obesity, the seeds are often planted early in life. When the pediatric records of a group of 20- to 30-year-old adults were examined, it was discovered that their weight during the first six months of life was strongly related to their adult weight. Among the heaviest infants, more than one-third were overweight as adults, while only 14 percent of infants who were of average or below-average weight became overweight adults. The heaviest infants were also more likely to have at least one parent who was overweight.

About 30 to 40 percent of heavy children grow up to be heavy adults. These same heavy children are also more likely to be the adults who are most obese. Children who are overweight when they enter their teenage years have four to one odds against ever attaining a normal weight as adults. If the children remain obese throughout their teenage years, then the odds increase to 28 to one. On the other hand, if an adult gains weight because of a severe life stress, such as divorce, loss of a job, or death of a close relative, there is usually a very good chance of correcting the weight gain once the cause of the stress has been dealt with successfully.

National health surveys have been measuring body fat in a population sample of children between the ages of six and 11 years of age who are considered representative of all children in the United States. These surveys found that between the early 1960s and the early 1980s the prevalence of obesity increased by 54 percent, and the number of children at the very highest level of body fat increased by a remarkable 98 percent. More recent surveys suggest that this trend is continuing due to the high fat intake and low level of physical activity among children. This dramatic increase in obesity among children over such a short time period is too rapid and too large to be explained by genetic changes.

Still, while genes may make a person more likely to be overweight, they do not make overweight unavoidable. Learning appropriate eating and exercise habits early in life can help ward off overweight, even in those who are genetically more likely to be heavy. Unfortunately, some parents may overfeed their young children in a sincere attempt to make them healthy and happy. In the process, however, parents unwittingly set the stage for weight problems in the future.

Children have an uncanny knack for regulating their food intake if left to their own devices. One study of two- to five-year olds found that although they might have seemed finicky about the foods they ate at any one meal, their overall diet over several days was surprisingly constant. In other words, these children tended to make up what they missed at one meal by eating it or something similar to it at another meal. Adults who try to force a child to eat certain foods could be setting the stage for difficulties with weight control in the future. Instead, offer children a variety of nutritious foods and encourage them to eat only as much as they need. Avoid putting too much emphasis on eating, and avoid using food as a reward or comfort.

Children need to learn to become involved in and enjoy physical activity at a very young age. This may help ward off future weight problems. Studies in which children have been observed at play have pointed to inactivity as critical to the development of overweight at young ages. Overweight children do not always eat more than lean children. In many cases they are simply less active than their leaner counterparts.

Recent studies have shown that there is some linkage between the amount of a child's body fat and the number of hours spent watching television. Long hours of television viewing means less time is available for more active pursuits. It may also encourage snacking, which only adds to the problem, especially if high-fat snacks are involved, such as potato chips or buttered popcorn. Although obesity is serious at any age, it has far more serious ramifications if it develops early in life.

Chapter 7:
The Dietary Approach

For years, researchers and doctors have been searching for a culprit behind the heart disease epidemic in the United States. More recently, attention has turned to tracking down the culprits in our environment that are responsible for most of the cancers in this country. The American diet has long been a prime suspect in both diseases.

As you learned in Part I of this book, scientific evidence continues to highlight the role of diet in elevated blood-cholesterol levels and in the development and progression of coronary heart disease. That evidence also shows that perhaps no other dietary substances have as great an effect on your blood-cholesterol level—and your risk of coronary heart disease—as saturated fat and cholesterol. You have also learned that diet is responsible for at least one-third of all cancers. It is no coincidence that cancers involving the breast, prostate, and colon are most common in countries around the world where coronary heart disease is also common. The common thread tying these diverse conditions together maybe a diet rich in fat, especially a diet that is also high in saturated fat. And you have also learned how a diet high in fat contributes to overweight and obesity and the health risks that go along with them. So it seems only reasonable to turn to a dietary approach designed to reduce fat in order to help fight off these health problems.

A Dietary Defense Against Heart Disease

Doctors consider dietary modifications to be the first line of defense against high blood-cholesterol levels. Indeed, even with the advent of more effective lipid-lowering drugs, diet modification continues to hold center stage. Drug therapy is considered only when dietary modifications has failed to achieve sufficient lowering of blood-cholesterol levels or when aggressive treatment is needed for existing coronary heart disease. Even when medication is prescribed, dietary modifications must be continued.

In light of the importance of diet in both the prevention and treatment of high blood cholesterol, goals and guidelines have been established over the years to improve the American diet. The earliest guidelines were established by the American Heart Association (AHA). Other organizations have since joined the fight for a heart-healthy diet. Their work has resulted in sound guidelines for control of cholesterol.

A Diet to Help Prevent Cancer

More recently, attention has turned to the importance of diet in the prevention of cancer. Unlike coronary heart disease, the dietary approach used in the treatment of cancer is very different from the preventive strategy. Dietary concerns of cancer patients are so highly individual that broad generalizations are impossible to make. Once cancer has developed, it is difficult to control by diet or any other means. This sober reality has created a strong interest in using diet to help prevent this disease and thus control its devastating consequences.

Several organizations have followed the early lead of the National Cancer Institute (NCI) in proposing dietary recommendations aimed at preventing cancer. The cornerstone of these recommendations is identical to that for coronary heart disease. Whether to prevent cancer or promote a healthy heart, a low-fat diet is the key.

Not a Passing Fancy

As early as 1957, a group of scientists presented to the AHA evidence that implicated an excess of calories, total fat, and saturated fat in the development of coronary heart disease. The AHA responded in 1961 by publishing its first set of dietary recommendations. These early recommendations encouraged Americans to modify their diet by decreasing calories, total fat, and cholesterol and by substituting polyunsaturated fats for saturated ones. Although details have since been added to indicate how much change is needed, the basic recommendations for lowering blood cholesterol have remained largely unchanged for over 25 years.

In response to the growing concern over the role of the American diet in a number of major diseases, the Senate Select Committee on Nutrition and Human Needs was convened in the mid-1970s. After hearing months of expert testimony, the committee issued recommendations called the Dietary Goals for the United States. These goals were broader in scope than those put forth by the AHA because they were intended to promote general health. The committee addressed concerns relating to starch, refined sugars, and sodium, as well as calories, fat, and cholesterol. The Senate committee's recommendations for lowering total fat, saturated fat, and cholesterol, however, were identical to those of the AHA.

A second edition of the Dietary Goals was published shortly after the first. The revised goals adjusted the recommendation for sodium (to about five grams per day) and added a recommendation for calories and weight. In 1978, the AHA also added a recommendation for sodium intake in response to the growing body of evidence that the sodium content of the American diet encourages high blood pressure (another risk factor for coronary heart disease) in certain individuals.

At about the same time, the Department of Agriculture and the Department of Health and Human Services released the Dietary Guidelines for Americans. These guidelines recommended changes in the consumption of dietary fat, saturated fat, and cholesterol that were consistent with those originally proposed by the AHA.

It wasn't until 1979 that the NCI first proposed dietary guidelines for reducing cancer risk. These recommendations were similar to those of the AHA, but they also advised increased consumption of certain food groups— namely whole grains, fruits, and vegetables. The NCI recommendations also differed from those of the AHA by not setting specific levels of fat or other nutrients. Instead, they made general recommendations concerning decreased intake of total fat and saturated fat along with increased consumption of foods that are high in complex carbohydrate, such as whole grains, fruits, and vegetables. It was more difficult for the NCI to set specific protective levels for nutrients; the NCI had information only about amounts of foods consumed in various countries where cancer was uncommon on which to base its recommen-

dations. The AHA, on the other hand, was able to use information from clinical studies in which specific amounts of nutrients were actually tested.

Since that time, two other agencies, the American Cancer Society (ACS) and the Committee on Diet, Nutrition, and Cancer of the National Research Council (NRC), have made dietary recommendations aimed at reducing cancer risk. Both groups specifically recommend that Americans get no more than 30 percent of their calories from fat. The NCI has also revised its guidelines. The most recent of these guidelines, announced in 1987, made a similar recommendation that no more than 30 percent of calories should come from fat. In addition, the NCI also recommended a fiber intake of 20 to 30 grams daily.

The point of this brief history is that the basic elements of the original AHA dietary recommendations have stood the test of time. Their endurance over the years, despite new scientific findings, is testimony to their credibility. They have also gathered momentum as other agencies, such as the NCI, the NRC, and the ACS, have built on them to develop dietary guidelines for cancer prevention. The *Surgeon General's Report on Nutrition and Health* in 1988 advocated a similar approach to promote general health and decrease premature death and disability among all Americans. In 1989, a special committee of experts, the National Research Council's Committee on Diet and Health, also endorsed this type of diet.

The push for a lower-fat diet for Americans is not a passing fancy; it is a serious attempt to stop the disability and premature loss of millions of lives caused by heart disease and cancer. The extent of the general consensus on this type of diet by a vast number of scientific experts is impressive. It emphasizes a comprehensive approach to cutting heart disease risk by controlling all risk factors for the disease, including high blood cholesterol. At the same time, a low-fat diet promotes a low-fat intake that should offer some protection from cancer and help prevent obesity.

The AHA Diet Plan
The original AHA dietary plan consisted of three phases. The Phase I diet recommended reducing the average dietary fat intake in the United States from the level current at the time of between 35 and 40 percent of total calories to

a moderate level of 30 percent of calories. In this phase, saturated fat, polyunsaturated fat, and monounsaturated fat would each provide a third of the fat calories (or 10 percent of the total calories) in the diet. Dietary cholesterol intake would be lowered from the level current at the time of about 500 milligrams (mg) a day to less than 300 mg. The Phase I diet was recommended as a first step for patients who needed to lower their blood cholesterol and as a safe, balanced plan for anyone who wanted to adopt healthier eating habits.

Phase II of the AHA diet was intended for people with high blood cholesterol who did not have success in lowering their blood cholesterol with the Phase I diet. Phase III was prescribed for those who could not lower their blood-cholesterol level enough using the first two phases. Phase II and Phase III would lower total fat intake in steps, first to 25 percent of total calories and then to 20 percent. Cholesterol intake would be reduced to between 200 and 250 mg in Phase II and to less than 100 mg in Phase III. The distribution of fat calories in both of these dietary plans would lower saturated fat intake to about six percent of total calories and polyunsaturated fat intake to between six and eight percent, leaving monounsaturated fat to make up the difference.

All three phases of the AHA dietary plan limited polyunsaturated fat intake to a maximum of 10 percent of calories because of questions about the possible harmful effects of high levels of this type of fat. All three phases also emphasized consumption of enough calories to maintain optimal weight.

The momentum for dietary change was accelerated further in 1984 with the Consensus Development Conference on Lowering Blood Cholesterol to Prevent Heart Disease. From this conference, the Expert Panel on Detection, Evaluation, and Treatment of High Blood Cholesterol in Adults was established. Based on its review of all the evidence at hand, the panel stressed the central role of diet in treating patients with high blood cholesterol—whether or not drugs were also being administered. As part of the National Cholesterol Education Program (NCEP), the panel also developed a set of dietary guidelines that simplified the original AHA approach by condensing the three-step AHA diet into two steps. In its latest recommendations, the AHA has abandoned its three-step approach in favor of the same Step One and Step Two diets of the NCEP.

Step-by-Step Reduction

Since excess calories and two nonessential dietary nutrients—namely saturated fat and dietary cholesterol—are the chief culprits in raising blood cholesterol, the Step One and Step Two diets focus on reducing these components of the American diet. The minimum goals of dietary therapy are to lower LDL-cholesterol levels to below 160 mg/dL (milligrams per deciLiter) for most people and to below 130 mg/dL for those who have either definite coronary heart disease or two or more risk factors for the disease.

The Step One diet is the initial dietary approach to lowering elevated blood-cholesterol levels. It is nutritionally adequate, yet it restricts the intake of saturated fat to 8 to 10 percent of total calories, total fat to less than 30 percent of total calories, and dietary cholesterol intake to less than 300 mg per day. Since the typical American diet contains 35 to 40 percent of calories from fat, this translates into a 14 to 25 percent reduction in total fat for large numbers of people. This dietary plan can be followed without the aid of a dietitian. Many people who have high cholesterol are already following a plan similar to the Step One diet. They should try to limit their intake of saturated fat even more and begin a Step Two diet.

In the Step Two diet, saturated fat is reduced to less than 7 percent of total calories, and dietary cholesterol is reduced to less than 200 mg per day. There is no further reduction in total fat intake in this diet because a diet that is much lower in fat would feel less filling and might, therefore, decrease the patient's willingness to adhere to the program in the long term. In addition, a recent study has shown that lower total fat intakes (that is, lower than the level prescribed in the Step One diet) are not necessary to adequately lower LDL cholesterol in the blood. The Step Two diet is more intensive than the Step One diet. So anyone following the Step Two diet should also seek the help of a registered dietitian. Some people have found it easy to add foods to their diet that are rich in soluble fiber or to switch to meat that is very lean. But it has been difficult for others to reduce their consumption of high-fat foods such as cheeses. The advice of a dietitian can be particularly helpful in finding alternatives and to simplify such adjustments.

Step One Diet

• Restrict saturated fat to less than 8 to 10 percent of total calories.

- Restrict total fat to less than 30 percent of total calories.
- Restrict dietary cholesterol to less than 300 mg per day.

Step Two Diet
- Restrict saturated fat to less than 7 percent of total calories.
- Restrict total fat to less than 30 percent of total calories.
- Restrict dietary cholesterol to less than 200 mg per day.

Keeping Tabs on Your Progress
Your doctor will periodically check your blood-cholesterol level. For simplicity, your doctor may use your total blood-cholesterol level for the majority of checks; your LDL level may only need to be checked periodically. The aim is to get total cholesterol levels under 240 mg/dL in most people and under 200 mg/dL in those who have definite coronary heart disease or at least two risk factors for it. By reducing total cholesterol in this way, the LDL level should also decrease. Once the goal for total cholesterol has been reached, the LDL level must be checked again to confirm the LDL goal has also been met.

During the first year of dietary therapy, your doctor may want to check your total blood-cholesterol level as frequently as every three months. After that, you'll probably be tested at six-month intervals. If your levels show that you're not meeting your goal through dietary therapy, you may be referred to a registered dietitian who can provide individualized dietary counseling.

If, despite this two-step diet and dietary counseling, your LDL goal is not met, your doctor may consider placing you on a drug to lower your cholesterol. For most patients, a minimum of six months of dietary therapy is required before drugs are prescribed to lower stubbornly high levels. There are some exceptions, however.

Some patients may require a year or more of dietary therapy and counseling before drugs are considered, while others may not be able to take the drugs at all. For example, some elderly patients are considered poor candidates for drug therapy and so must continue with intensive dietary therapy. On the other hand, in patients with severely elevated LDL levels (more than 225 mg/dL) indicating an underlying genetic disorder, or for those who have active coronary heart disease, shorter periods of dietary therapy may be tried before drug therapy is added.

It's important to note that even when a cholesterol-lowering drug is prescribed, the patient must still follow a cholesterol-lowering diet. The NCEP report emphasized that "drug therapy should be added to dietary therapy, and not substituted for it."

The Pyramids
Since the 1950s, many Americans have learned the principles of a balanced diet by choosing foods from an eating plan developed by the U.S. Department of Agriculture (USDA). In this plan, referred to as the Basic Four Food Groups, foods were divided into categories that were determined by their nutrient composition. Meat, fish, and poultry provided protein and iron; dairy products provided calcium and riboflavin; grains provided B vitamins, iron, and other minerals; and fruits and vegetables provided vitamins, with special emphasis on vitamins A and C. The Basic Four gave equal weight to each of the major food groups. The emphasis was placed on getting enough of the important nutrients, especially protein, iron, and the B vitamins.

In the 1990s, our nutritional problems have made the emphasis on nutrient deficiencies obsolete. It is not that we fail to eat enough of some nutrients, but that we eat too much—especially fat, cholesterol, sugar, and sodium. Because of these changing nutritional habits, the USDA developed the Food Guide Pyramid in 1992 to replace the Basic Four. Unlike the Basic Four, the Pyramid does not give each of the food groups the same weight. A sense of proportionality was established by the location and size of the pyramid section devoted to each group. The greatest emphasis is placed on grains, which constitute the foundation of the diet and are found at the base of the pyramid. Fruits and vegetables are divided into separate groups and placed on the next level. Meats and dairy products make up an even smaller part of the diet and appear in the smaller sections toward the top. At the tip of the pyramid, to emphasize that they should be consumed only in the smallest amounts, are the fats and sugars.

Does this Pyramid provide the best diet for protecting against heart disease and other diseases? Not everyone thinks so. A nutritionist from the Harvard School of Public Health recently proposed a modified version of the USDA Pyramid that has been endorsed by the European office of the World Health Organization as a guide to healthy eating for Europeans. This

Food Guide Pyramid

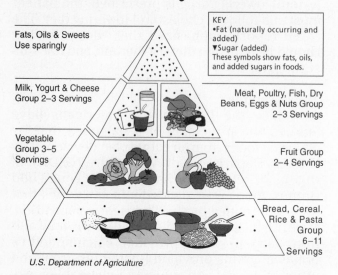

KEY
• Fat (naturally occurring and added)
▼ Sugar (added)
These symbols show fats, oils, and added sugars in foods.

Fats, Oils & Sweets
Use sparingly

Milk, Yogurt & Cheese
Group 2–3 Servings

Meat, Poultry, Fish, Dry Beans, Eggs & Nuts Group
2–3 Servings

Vegetable Group 3–5
Servings

Fruit Group
2–4 Servings

Bread, Cereal, Rice & Pasta Group
6–11 Servings

U.S. Department of Agriculture

dietary plan largely reflects the eating habits in the Mediterranean, particularly the island of Crete and southern Italy in the 1950s and 1960s, when heart disease rates there were among the lowest in the world. (Unfortunately, the dietary patterns of these countries are now changing to more closely resemble the American diet.) Additional pyramids are being formulated for Latin American and Asian countries, using the foods native to those areas. One reason for these proposals is to counteract a trend in those countries toward an American-type diet.

Some nutritionists believe the Mediterranean diet is more compatible with good health than the diet promoted by the USDA Pyramid. After all, if you want to develop dietary guidelines for optimal health, what better way to go about it than to copy the dietary patterns of people who live in parts of the world with the lowest rates of heart disease and cancer? Like the USDA Pyramid, grains serve as the foundation of the Mediterranean Diet, but bulgur, couscous, and polenta are emphasized in addition to rice and pasta for greater variety. The Mediterranean Pyramid devotes larger sections to fruits and vegetables than does the USDA Pyramid. Nevertheless, the USDA Pyramid has been endorsed by the U.S. Department of Health and Human Services, the American Heart Association, and the American Dietetic Association.

One notable difference between the two pyramids is olive oil has a separate place in the middle of the Mediterranean Pyramid. The message is that this particular fat should be included in significant amounts as a daily part of the diet and not com-

bined with other fats and oils, which are to be used "sparingly," as in the USDA Pyramid. Mono-unsaturated fat, which makes up 75 percent of the fat in olive oil, has a number of health benefits, including preserving HDL cholesterol, lowering triglycerides, and regulating insulin levels.

Dried peas and beans, or legumes, along with nuts, have their own section on the Mediterranean Pyramid at the same level as fruits and vegetables. In the USDA Pyramid, legumes and nuts are grouped with meats. Because food choices in the meat group are restricted, the important heart-healthy attributes of these foods could be overlooked on the USDA diet. Legumes are not only low-fat sources of protein that substitute for meat, they also provide soluble fiber, which meat does not provide.

Cheese and yogurt are the only dairy products recommended in the Mediterranean diet because lactose intolerance (the inability to digest milk-sugar lactose) is common in this region. Fish, poultry, and eggs occupy separate but increasingly smaller places higher up on the pyramid. At the tip, hovering above sweets in the smallest section on the pyramid, is red meat. The Mediterranean diet restricts red meat to a few servings per month, while the USDA pyramid, in sharp contrast, allows up to six ounces per day—depending on how many calories are needed. Red meat is limited in the Mediterranean diet because it has been implicated in the development of colon cancer in a few studies.

The restriction on meat is one of the most notable differences between these two diets. But

Mediterranean Pyramid

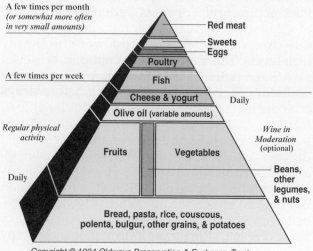

A few times per month
(or somewhat more often in very small amounts)

A few times per week

Regular physical activity

Daily

Red meat
Sweets
Eggs
Poultry
Fish
Cheese & yogurt
Olive oil (variable amounts)

Daily

Wine in Moderation (optional)

Fruits
Vegetables

Beans, other legumes, & nuts

Bread, pasta, rice, couscous, polenta, bulgur, other grains, & potatoes the Mediterranean diet addresses other aspects of lifestyle besides food choices. On either side of the Mediterranean Pyramid are reminders that draw attention to regular physical activity and suggest that wine be consumed in moderation. The USDA Pyramid does not address either exercise or alcohol. Perhaps most importantly, the two diets differ in the amount of fat they allow. The diet promoted by the Mediterranean Pyramid is higher in total fat than the diet depicted in the USDA Pyramid.

Following the Mediterranean diet pattern means you will receive 35 to 40 percent of your total calories from fat, while the USDA diet plan provides about 30 percent of calories from fat. Although the Mediterranean diet is significantly higher in total fat, the majority of fat calories are made up of monounsaturated fatty acids from olive oil. Unlike excess amounts of polyunsaturated fat, monounsaturated fat tends to reduce LDLs without lowering HDL cholesterol or interfering with the workings of the immune system.

Health professionals in this country believe Americans should be cautious when adopting the Mediterranean diet because of its higher fat content. One reason is Americans tend to eat larger portion sizes than Europeans: This can make the grams of fat add up more rapidly, even though both groups might make the same food choices. And even though fat grams from olive oil do not raise LDL cholesterol, they may contribute to weight gain. Europeans may get away with this diet because, on average, they tend to be more active than Americans.

Both the USDA and the Mediterranean diets are plant-based, and that is good for health. Based on a small study, people with diabetes constitute one group that may reap special benefits from a Mediterranean-type approach, with more monounsaturated fat in the form of olive oil or canola oil. The Mediterranean diet offers an alternative approach to planning a diet to promote heart health. Not everyone will benefit from the higher fat intake, however. In fact, health professionals caution that the Mediterranean diet has not been tested for its benefits to Americans.

The NCI Diet Plan

The dietary plan aimed at cancer prevention has some similarities to the AHA plan. Both stress the importance of controlling weight by eating only the calories needed to meet demands for energy. Both also recommend reducing total fat intake to no more than 30 percent of total calories. Although levels for specific types of fats have not been established by the NCI, the AHA's recommendation not to exceed 10 percent of calories for any type of fat is reasonable because there is some question about the dangers of high intakes of any type of fat in terms of cancer risk. For example, lipid peroxides from unsaturated fat and cholesterol–oxygen interactions may cause the damage to DNA that begins the tumor process.

The NCI dietary plan differs from the AHA plan in making a specific recommendation for fiber. A level of 25 to 30 grams of total dietary fiber is suggested. This dietary plan places its emphasis on the number of servings recommended from each food group as well as on specific foods within each group, rather than on levels of specific nutrients. Whole-grain breads and cereals, dried peas, beans, and lentils, and fresh fruits and vegetables are the primary focus (consumption of these foods is associated with low cancer risk in people around the world).

By recommending a specific number of servings from these food groups with emphasis on certain foods within each, the NCI's dietary plan guarantees that enough protective substances such as beta-carotene, vitamin C, vitamin E, and other plant-derived chemicals (phytochemicals) will be consumed. Beta-carotene and vitamins C and E are antioxidants that may offer protection against damage from free radicals. The phytochemicals may offer protection in ways not yet identified.

While the NCI plan does differ in some respects from the AHA plan, the two approaches are not mutually exclusive. It is possible and beneficial to follow both sets of guidelines to create a satisfying and nutritious dietary plan to reduce your risks of coronary heart disease and cancer.

Measuring Dietary Benefits for Cancer

Your blood-cholesterol level is the way to measure your progress toward protecting against heart disease risk. There is no such barometer to help assess your progress in preventing cancer, however. When you make dietary choices in line with the NCI plan, you are eating the way people in countries with low cancer risk do. Keeping your weight in check is one tangible measure of success toward improving your odds against getting both heart disease and cancer. Good overall health from the general nutritional benefits of a diet rich in whole grains, fruits, and vegetables is another.

Chapter 8:
Weight Control

Trim figures parade across the television screen, billboards, and magazine advertisements, encouraging us to hop onto the fitness bandwagon. But the importance of weight control goes beyond appearance...way beyond. As discussed in Chapter 6, if you are more than ten percent overweight, and especially if you are obese, your risk of developing a variety of health problems may be increased. Losing excess weight—particularly excess body fat—can help prevent or treat most of these problems.

Chances are, if you were to combine the low-fat diet outlined in Chapter 7 with a regular aerobic exercise program, you would lose weight. But what if you want a more structured approach to weight loss? Can any of the many weight-loss programs out there help?

You may be able to find a weight-loss program that can help you successfully lose excess weight and keep it off, but you have to choose wisely, especially if you also want the diet to promote good health and help reduce your risk of disease. So in this chapter, we give you general guidelines for assessing the value of popular types of diet programs. We give you advice on what to look for so you will be more likely to find a program that is good for your waistline and your health.

What's the Best Way to Lose Weight?

The weight-loss method you choose is important in determining how successful you will be, both at losing weight and keeping it off. As difficult as it is, losing the weight is really the easy part. The true challenge is maintaining the lighter weight over the long haul, since about 95 percent of all dieters gain their weight back within two years of losing it.

The reason most diets fail to remove weight permanently is that they do not get to the root of the problem. A successful long-term diet program has to replace poor eating habits with a healthy, balanced dietary plan that is flexible enough to be followed for life. The diet also has to target the excess body fat that caused the weight gain.

Many diet programs promise weight reductions of more than one or two pounds a week, but they are not being completely honest. Yes, the amount of weight that can be lost with some diets is considerable: 10 to 20 pounds in a couple of weeks or even days. But these weight reductions come mostly from the loss of water and the breakdown of muscle protein, not from the loss of fat. When you eventually replace these vital substances—as you will when you resume normal eating habits—you regain the weight. Diets that promote these transient weight losses are also the ones that do the most psychological harm. Few things are more discouraging than watching a 20-pound weight loss evaporate into a mere two-pound loss.

To begin with, a dietary plan to remove excess fat has to be low in fat. For most people, it should also be low in calories. A low-calorie diet creates an energy deficit in the body by supplying less energy than the body needs for daily functions. To meet its energy needs, the body then has to draw upon the energy stored in body fat. This is why moderate exercise—which increases the body's demand for energy—is such a useful addition to dietary therapy. By exercising and switching to a lower-calorie diet, you increase your body's energy needs and force your body to pull energy from body fat. Surprisingly, the best exercise for burning fat is not the best for burning calories. Moderate activity such as walking is actually a better fat-burner than running briskly. As shown in Chapter 9, exercise provides other benefits in terms of weight loss as well.

Many people are unsuccessful at losing weight because they get discouraged with the results. If you don't have realistic expectations, it is easy to become frustrated. Becoming overweight is not an overnight phenomenon; it takes months, even years, to accumulate that added weight. Reversing the process takes an equal amount of time. You have to be willing to invest the necessary effort if the weight you want to lose is body fat.

A good weight-loss program results in an average weight loss of one to three pounds a week. This is all the body fat it is possible to lose, on average, in that amount of time. Average is a key word here because the pattern of weight loss is not a steady one. In the beginning, as the body adjusts to a new diet, weight losses can be quite large. But in time this tapers off to a few pounds a week.

Many dieters experience plateaus during their attempts to lose weight. These are the people who swear they are following the diet, yet the weight loss appears to stop. These plateaus can often last for weeks, but if you are one of these people, don't be discouraged. They are temporary. Staying with the diet during these critical periods is essential if you want to continue to lose weight in the long run. The most effective way to overcome these plateaus is to increase the amount of exercise. Sooner or later, most people make it through this period and continue to lose weight.

If you are exercising to lose body fat, you may actually gain some weight, especially in the beginning, and particularly if your exercise program includes strength training with weights. This weight gain is not a sign that you are failing in your efforts to lose body fat. Because exercise increases the amount of muscle you have, and muscle weighs more than fat, some weight gain is to be expected. But muscle takes up less room than fat, so you'll find that you look slimmer even if you weigh slightly more. If it helps your morale, keep off the scale during this time. Remember that you need this extra muscle to help you burn more body fat. It's the fat that causes problems with overweight, not the muscle.

In addition to reducing body fat, a successful diet program has to provide your body with the essential nutrients it needs. And it must show you how to make wise food choices to meet those needs. If a diet doesn't provide your body with enough of the protein, carbohydrates, fat, vitamins, and minerals that it needs for healthfulness, the diet ends up doing more harm than good. And if a diet doesn't teach you how to change your eating habits, you're likely to fall back on the poor food choices that caused the weight gain in the first place. Before you know it, those lost pounds of body fat will be back to haunt you.

It's ironic how, when someone tells us we can't have a certain food item, we often end up wanting that food item even more. We feel deprived. And that feeling of deprivation has been the downfall of many a diet. To keep that feeling from sabotaging your weight-control efforts, the program you choose needs to encourage healthier eating habits that can be maintained in the long run. It should show you how to choose wisely from a wide variety of foods so you can control your weight, get the nutrients you need, and continue to enjoy food.

Losing body fat and keeping it off requires a change in your eating and exercise habits for life. Rather than simply going on a diet for a few weeks or months or "depriving" yourself of all those foods that you love, you need to adopt a dietary program that is flexible and realistic, one that can be adjusted to help you maintain your weight once you've lost that excess fat.

Finally, whether you want to lose weight to look better or to feel healthier, you should choose a weight-control program that encourages healthy eating and regular exercise. After all, a "thin" body is not necessarily a healthy one, but a lean, fit body is both attractive and healthy.

Losing Weight to Gain Health Benefits

There is more to weight loss than meets the eye. Perhaps no other single change you can make in your behavior—except to quit smoking—provides more health rewards than losing weight. For as long as they have been keeping records, insurance companies have known that overweight people tend to suffer more illnesses and die at an earlier age than people who maintain a desirable weight. So if you are overweight, and especially if you are obese, losing weight may actually help to lengthen your life.

The key to successful weight loss is the reduction of body fat. A low-fat, lower-calorie diet combined with regular exercise mobilizes body fat best. If you want to gain other health benefits, however, you need to pay attention to more than how much body fat you can lose. The composition of the diet is also very important. For example, to help hedge your bets against getting certain types of cancer, you want the diet to be low in fat and to provide enough cancer-fighting nutrients through fiber-rich whole grains, fruits, and vegetables. If you want to reduce your blood-cholesterol level, you also want to be sure that the low-calorie foods in your dietary plan are low in total fat, saturated fat, and cholesterol.

Sorting Through the Options

Deciding to lose weight is the first step toward improving your health. Choosing the diet that works best for you is the next step. Hundreds of different diets have been promoted for weight loss, but there are actually just a few general types of weight-loss diets. These diets are promoted in books, weight-loss centers, and health clubs. You can also have your doctor recommend a registered dietitian who can help you lose weight or you can contact your local chapter of the American Dietetic Association for a referral to a registered dietitian.

Whether you choose a book, a weight-loss center, or a health professional to help you with your weight loss depends on what you think would work best for you. Diet books can be helpful if you are self-motivated and do not need a lot of outside support. Weight-loss centers with their own lines of food products might work better if you need more structure and like the idea of group support. Anyone can benefit from the expertise of a registered dietitian. Going with a health professional also eliminates worry about whether the approach you have chosen is legitimate or whether it is a waste of your money and constitutes a risk to your health.

Most of the popular diets promoted in books fit into one of the general types of diets, yet only a few are really appropriate for controlling blood cholesterol or promoting general good health. And many diets offer such negative side effects that they cannot possibly help protect against cancer. To help you sort through the many diets currently available, the main features of the most common types of weight-reduction diets are described here. Once you become familiar with them, you will be able to recognize the latest diet trends for what they really are. You can also use these guidelines to help you decide about a weight-loss center or a line of weight-loss food products. Before you choose one to help you lose weight and promote general good health, examine the diet carefully and ask yourself these questions:

- Is it safe? It simply does not make good sense to trade the health problems caused by being overweight for a whole new set of problems caused by an ill-conceived weight-loss diet.
- Is it nutritionally sound? A diet has to be balanced, with enough foods from each of the major food groups, or it may not provide adequate fiber, vitamins, and minerals. The diet should include foods such as fish, poultry, lean meats, or legumes; skim (nonfat) milk and other low-fat dairy products; fruits; vegetables; and whole-grain breads and cereals.
- Does it promise too much too soon? Remember that weight is gained slowly and has to be lost slowly. Speedier weight losses do not greatly decrease body fat, and decreasing body fat is the key to long-term weight loss.
- Is the diet relatively low in calories? You cannot lose body fat over a reasonable time period unless your diet is low in calories. This is essential if you cannot exercise regularly. However, there is a limit to how low in calories the diet can be in order to remain safe and effective for weight loss (see the following section entitled "Low-Calorie Diets").
- Is the diet low in fat, saturated fat, and cholesterol? If it's not low in fat, chances are it's not low in calories, so it won't help you lose body fat, and it probably won't provide any benefits in terms of reducing cancer risk. If it's not low in saturated fat and cholesterol, your efforts may not pay off in lower levels of blood cholesterol.
- Does it teach you new eating behaviors that can be continued after you lose the weight? Without this change in perspective, the weight may be regained once you resume your old eating habits.

Low-Calorie Diets

A low-calorie diet is a low-energy diet. This is the weight-loss approach advocated by legitimate health professionals. The goal is to create an energy deficit by providing fewer calories than your body needs. In theory, a low-calorie diet has to provide 3,500 fewer calories than you need in order to lose one pound of body fat. (Most adults require about 1,900 to 3,000 calories each day to meet their energy needs.) Since most low-calorie diets provide 500 to 1,000 fewer calories than needed each day, one to two pounds of body fat will be used over the course of a week to compensate for the energy shortfall.

A low-calorie diet can be recognized by the types of foods recommended. Fresh fruits and vegetables; skim (nonfat) milk; and lean meats, poultry, or fish make up the bulk of the menu. Small servings are stressed. A low-calorie diet works best if it is also high in carbohydrate. In addition to fruits and vegetables, whole-grain breads and cereals, rice, and pasta are emphasized. Fried foods, sugary snacks, rich sauces, pies, cakes, and other sugary, fat-rich desserts should be restricted.

Foods should be prepared using low-calorie cooking methods. Meats, poultry, and fish should be roasted, baked, or broiled. Steaming or boiling is recommended for vegetables in order to keep them low in calories. Margarine and oils are to be used sparingly.

Margarine is still a better choice than butter in spite of the *trans* fatty acids in margarine. *Trans* fatty acids do not raise blood cholesterol to the same extent that saturated fat does. Butter is not only a rich source of saturated fat, but it also contains cholesterol, which exaggerates the effects of saturated fat on blood cholesterol. If margarine is used sparingly, only small amounts of *trans* fatty acids are consumed. Always choose the softest margarines, because they contain the lowest amounts of *trans* fatty acids.

Fiber is an especially important component of a low-calorie diet, particularly one that is also a low-fat diet. When calories are reduced, the body's natural response is to elicit the feeling of hunger in order to obtain more food. In fact, hunger is the number one enemy of a weight-loss diet. Foods rich in fat are effective at delaying feelings of hunger because fat-rich foods empty from the stomach more slowly than other foods. But fiber can provide the same service. Soluble fiber sources such as dried beans and peas, oats, and citrus fruits are effective at preventing hunger between meals. In fact, neglecting to include fiber-rich foods in a low-calorie, low-fat diet makes the diet more difficult to maintain over the long term.

Although the number of calories usually eaten has to be reduced before you can expect to lose weight, it is possible to lower your calorie intake too much. A real irony of dieting is that you actually lose more weight if you eat some food than if you eat nothing at all. The reason is that when too few calories are eaten, the body protects itself from the energy shortage by using available energy more economically. The body does this by slowing its metabolic rate, the rate at which it uses energy. This shift in the rate of metabolism when food is scarce has its roots early in human development. As hunter-gatherers, our ancestors could not always count on regular meals. They ate whenever they found food. As protection against the possible ill effects of an unreliable food supply, early humans developed this metabolic adjustment in order to conserve energy when food was not available.

As the body becomes more efficient at using the energy on hand, it actually needs less. A smaller energy deficit results, and less body fat is lost. To avoid this response, modern humans require at least 1,200 calories every day. Diets recommending less than this amount should be followed only under the supervision of a physician. Besides, such diets can do more than simply frustrate efforts to lose weight. If followed for an extended period of time, extremely low-calorie diets can lead to nutritional deficiencies. Eventually the body begins to break down muscle protein to provide energy. This loss of muscle also slows the metabolic rate, making weight loss even more difficult. And while a vitamin-mineral supplement added to a very-low-calorie diet may protect against nutritional deficiencies, supplements cannot ward off the loss of muscle protein.

A diet program that encourages regular exercise in addition to a low-calorie diet is the most beneficial. Most experts agree that regular exercise is an essential element of any successful weight-loss program, particularly to keep the weight off over the long run.

Low-Fat Diets

A low-calorie diet is usually low in fat and high in complex carbohydrate—starches and fiber. The high energy value of fat, which makes it so appropriate for storing energy, also makes its presence in food synonymous with a high caloric content. Fat has more than twice the energy potential (caloric content) of either protein or carbohydrate and slightly more than alcohol. So as a general rule, foods high in fat are also high in calories. Low-calorie diets take advantage of this fact and make lowering fat intake a priority. This allows a diet low in calories to also be low in fat, making it appropriate both for losing weight and perhaps helping to provide some protection from cancer. Since a low-fat diet tends to be low in saturated fats and cholesterol, it can help lower blood cholesterol as well.

The types of foods that make up a low-fat diet are nearly identical to those recommended in a low-calorie diet, making it almost impossible to distinguish between the two. But while a low-calorie diet is usually also a low-fat one, a low-fat diet is not necessarily low in calories. Once the desired amount of weight is lost, the low-fat nature of this diet can be preserved while raising the number of calories. This is achieved by adding more low-fat foods and increasing the size of servings. However, care must be taken to not replace fat calories with energy-dense sources of carbohydrate, such as candy and other sweets, which raise calorie levels but do not provide the nutritional value of starch and fiber foods.

Whether or not calories are restricted, a low-fat diet is made up primarily of foods that are rich in carbohydrate and fiber. In fact, because they are almost always low in fat, carbohydrate-rich foods are natural replacements for fat-rich foods. They are also the best foods for maintaining weight loss because they are not as likely to turn into body fat as are high-fat foods that carry the same number of calories.

Foods rich in complex carbohydrate are better choices than those rich in refined sugar. Complex carbohydrates include starch and fiber. Starchy vegetables such as lima beans and corn, pasta, and rice, along with whole grains, should make up the bulk of carbohydrate consumed. Even though they are rich in simple sugars, fruits should not be excluded from a weight-loss diet because they are important sources of fiber. In contrast, when refined sugars make up most of the carbohydrate you consume, you are not getting enough vitamins, minerals, or fiber. By increasing grains and vegetables rich in complex carbohydrate at the expense of animal foods that are rich in saturated fat, the amount of polyunsaturated and monounsaturated fat in the diet increases and the amount of saturated fat decreases. The protein in this diet is provided primarily by such low-fat sources as lean meats, chicken, fish, legumes, and skim (nonfat) milk or other low-fat dairy products.

A low-fat diet contains fewer foods from animal sources and more from plant sources. Plant sources provide almost all of the carbohydrate-rich foods in the diet, while skim milk is the only animal source of carbohydrate. Foods of plant origin do not contain cholesterol and are also usually lower in total fat and saturated fat than foods of animal origin. So when foods of animal origin are restricted in the diet, your intake of dietary cholesterol and saturated fat, as well as total fat, is lowered.

A low-fat diet also limits most commercially prepared snacks and baked goods. Most of these foods are not only high in saturated fat and cholesterol, they are also high in calories and cannot be included regularly in a weight-loss diet.

Weight control is only one of several uses for a low-fat diet. Blood cholesterol is reduced by a low-fat diet (regardless of whether weight is lost or not), making this type of diet important for preventing and treating heart disease. (People who suffer from diseases of the gallbladder also need a low-fat diet because they usually find fat-rich foods difficult to tolerate.) There is also limited but suggestive evidence that a low-fat diet may offer some protection against certain common forms of cancer, such as cancer of the breast and colon. In places around the world where these cancers rarely occur, low-fat diets are the norm. Although fat has not been identified as a cause of cancer, it is possible that eating large quantities of fat may promote its development.

Despite all the benefits a low-fat diet can bring, from a nutritional standpoint some dietary fat is essential. Dietary fat promotes the absorption of the fat-soluble vitamins A, D, E, and K. We get most of the vitamin A we need from low-fat plant sources such as carrots, squash, spinach, broccoli, and tomatoes, which contain a substance that the body converts into vitamin A. Without some fat present, we would probably not be getting enough vitamin A. One of the essential nutrients, linoleic acid, is also provided by dietary fat. Linoleic acid is a polyunsaturated fatty acid needed for growth and healthy skin. It is also vital for the production of a group of hormones called prostaglandins, which are responsible for regulating functions of the heart, blood vessels, kidneys, lungs, nerves, and reproductive organs.

Large amounts of dietary fat are not necessary to provide enough linoleic acid or to ensure adequate absorption of fat-soluble vitamins. Vegetable oils are the primary source of linoleic acid. Since there is no requirement for either saturated fat or cholesterol in the diet, the equivalent of about one tablespoon of vegetable oil, such as olive oil, can supply all the linoleic acid and fat needed each day. From a practical standpoint, experts previously thought that some fat in the diet was necessary in order to provide the feeling of being full. But if the diet is high in fiber, hunger can be prevented even when the intake of fat is very low. In fact, current research suggests that carbohydrate controls appetite more effectively than fat.

Low-Carbohydrate, High-Fat Diets

Popular forms of this type of diet include the Atkins Diet, the Mayo Diet, the Air Force Diet, the Calories Don't Count Diet, the Grapefruit Diet, and the Ski Team Diet, not to mention the

Stillman and Scarsdale diets. The appeal of these diets is and always has been the quick weight losses they promise. These diets also allow dieters the freedom to eat most foods that are normally restricted in weight-loss programs. Weight losses of as many as 10 to 20 pounds can occur within a few weeks after starting on these diets. While this amount of weight can actually be lost, at least temporarily, the drawback is that only a small part of the lost weight is body fat.

Any weight-reduction diet should be suspect if it allows you to consume all the calories you want, particularly when the calories come from high-fat foods. In doing this, the diet violates the basic rules of long-term weight loss: It does not achieve the energy deficit required for body fat to be removed, while it allows excessive amounts of dietary fat to be stored. Before ten pounds of body fat can be lost, a deficit of about 35,000 calories has to be created. For this to occur over a week, a daily deficit of about 5,000 calories is required. But it would be impossible for most people to manage a deficit this large, even if they ate nothing and performed heavy physical labor.

In practice, these low-carbohydrate diets may lower calorie intake because they simply do not offer much in the way of taste and, therefore, one is less tempted to eat. Lowering the amount of carbohydrate in the diet eliminates variety because it removes all the colorful foods and many of the flavorful ones. Fruits, vegetables, grains, and cereals are restricted. Meat, fish, poultry, eggs, cheese, milk, ice cream, and peanut butter are emphasized instead. Hard liquor is allowed, but wine and beer are prohibited.

Low-carbohydrate diets work by depriving the body of carbohydrate, the primary fuel source for the brain, nerves, and lungs. To compensate for this, the body produces acids called ketones that are made from body fat and can be used for energy in place of carbohydrate. Besides being used for energy, ketones are excreted in the urine. Proponents of low-carbohydrate diets claim that by excreting calories, weight loss is faster than if the calories are used only to provide energy. In reality, however, ketones can be excreted only in small quantities—at the rate of 100 calories a day. At that sluggish pace, it would take 35 days to build up the 3,500 calories needed to lose just one pound of fat.

In fact, large weight losses do occur rapidly on a low-carbohydrate diet but not because ketones are excreted. High levels of ketones in the blood interfere with appetite, so less food is eaten. The carbohydrate deficiency promoted by a low-carbohydrate diet also causes large amounts of salt and water to be lost from the body, and muscle protein is broken down to make fuel for use by the brain, nerves, and lungs. The loss of water and muscle responsible for most of the weight lost on a low-carbohydrate diet is only a temporary loss. As soon as normal eating patterns are resumed, the body replaces the water and muscle, and the weight is regained.

Low-carbohydrate diets are not recommended for lowering blood cholesterol because they do not promote the loss of body fat, which is key both for lowering cholesterol and for long-term weight loss. Such diets also encourage the consumption of foods that are high in fat, saturated fat, and cholesterol. By restricting carbohydrate-rich foods, these diets limit the only sources of dietary fiber, which play a role in lowering blood cholesterol and may offer protection against colon cancer (see page 37 for more information on the relationship between fiber intake and cancer risk). Indeed, blood-cholesterol levels are actually elevated in people who follow these diets. And colon cancer is more common in countries around the world where fiber intake is low.

The high level of blood ketones caused by a low-carbohydrate diet can in itself be dangerous. For pregnant women, damage to the fetus is an especially serious consequence, and blood sugar can fall to very low levels in people following low-carbohydrate diets. Hypoglycemia (another name for low blood sugar) causes dizziness, fatigue, weakness, irritability, and fainting spells. But the most serious threat from a low-carbohydrate, high-fat diet is a condition called ketoacidosis, which can lead to coma and even death. Followers of this type of diet are usually instructed to monitor their urine for ketones to prevent this condition from developing. Nevertheless, if ketone production is allowed to continue for a long time, ketoacidosis can result.

High-Protein Diets

Foods contain only three nutrients that contribute calories—protein, carbohydrate, and fat. When you change the amount of any one of these by your choice of foods, you automatically change the proportions of the other two. As a result, lowering your intake of carbohydrate automatically raises the proportion of fat or protein, or both.

A high-protein diet is usually one that is also high in fat, saturated fat, and cholesterol, because the foods that are richest in protein are those from animal sources. As such, it would not be appropriate for lowering blood cholesterol. Grains, nuts, and dried beans also contain plant protein, but only in small amounts relative to the quantities of protein found in meat, eggs, cheese, and milk. Thus, if a diet included nothing but plant foods, it would be difficult to make it high in protein without increasing calories considerably. In other words, you would have to eat enormous quantities of plant foods to get sufficient protein.

Since it is difficult to create a low-calorie, high-protein diet using normal foods, the high-protein diets that are promoted for weight loss are usually liquid or powdered-formula diets. Formula diets allow nutrients to be manipulated in proportions that would not be possible with ordinary food. The protein in these formula diets, however, is not the same structurally as the proteins found in foods. Instead, it has usually been predigested into mixtures of the individual units, called amino acids, that make up a protein.

To be considered a high-protein diet, a formula preparation has to contain enough protein to provide at least 50 percent of total calories. Usually, about 16 percent of the total calories we eat come from protein, while 35 to 40 percent come from fat and 45 to 50 percent come from carbohydrate. When protein makes up 50 percent of all the calories consumed, then the amount of both fat and carbohydrate is much lower than usual. Unlike a diet that is high in protein-rich foods, which would also be high in fat, a high-protein formula diet is manipulated to be low in both fat and carbohydrate.

The composition of high-protein formula preparations is also manipulated to be low in calories. The majority of these diets provide about 800 calories a day, but some preparations may contain as few as 300 to 600 calories. This low calorie level is supposed to create the energy deficit necessary to mobilize body fat. Such a highly restricted calorie intake, however, dips below the necessary minimum to prevent the body from slowing down its rate of metabolism. As a consequence, less body fat is lost on this type of diet than on a more moderately restrictive diet.

High-protein formula diets promote rapid and considerable weight losses because they are low in carbohydrate as well as calories. The carbohydrate deficiency accentuates the amount of weight lost by increasing loss of salt and water. The very-low-calorie intake should promote the breakdown of muscle protein to provide energy, but the large amount of protein supplied by the formula is supposed to prevent this from happening. By providing protein for the body to burn for energy, these diets should enable muscle protein to be preserved. For this reason, high-protein diets offering less than 800 calories a day are often referred to as very-low-calorie diets or protein-sparing modified fasts.

The experience with these high-protein formula diets indicates they may be a risky undertaking. Although the more modern versions have been improved over the earlier ones, the Food and Drug Administration requires that warning labels appear on all of such preparations. First introduced in 1977 as The Last Chance Diet, the high-protein diet was promoted in a formula preparation called Pro-Linn. One year after its introduction, 46 deaths had been linked to its use. Although the reasons for these deaths are still debated, the people who died were all consuming the 300- to 600-calorie preparations with amino-acid mixtures derived exclusively from collagen or gelatin proteins. Deficiencies in a number of minerals were believed to have played some role in the deaths.

High-protein formula diets are not appropriate for long-term weight loss, nor are they good candidates for lowering blood cholesterol. And even in the best of hands, there appears to be an increased risk of gallstone attacks. (In certain situations, when a very large amount of weight—50 pounds or more—needs to be lost and the more conventional weight-loss therapies have failed, a liquid-protein diet may be incorporated into an overall program of weight loss. But this is done only temporarily and only under a doctor's supervision.) Very obese people are able to conserve their muscle protein better than people who are merely overweight, so these diets are less dangerous to them. Some people believe that adopting a liquid-protein diet is a desirable way to start a weight-loss program. Studies show, however, that over time there is no advantage to this approach. Temporary elevations in blood cholesterol are so common in people who follow these diets that potential users are warned of the possibility. But temporary or not, without the needed long-term weight loss, blood cholesterol does not benefit from these diets. Cancer risk probably will not be affected much either.

Overweight is not a short-term problem but a lifelong one. A safe and long-term solution is the only reasonable approach. Any short-term toxic effects brought on by a weight-reduction program are simply not acceptable. They just do not make good sense if the whole point of losing weight is to improve your health.

Fasts

A fast is defined as a temporary abstinence from food and implies a severe restriction of calories. Completely abstaining from food over the long run is impossible, of course, so most fasts are really the same as very-low-calorie diets.

Although calorie intake is greatly reduced in these diets, the loss of body fat is slowed because the body decreases its metabolic rate. Indeed, fasting has been shown to lower the rate of metabolism by as much as 20 percent within just a few days. This lack of body-fat loss is camouflaged by the accelerated loss of salt and water. The breakdown of muscle protein brought about by a carbohydrate deficiency is another factor that plays a role in the failure to lose more body fat. Like the other diets that base their weight losses on limiting carbohydrate, fasting produces quick results. But these weight losses are accompanied by the possibility of developing hypoglycemia and ketoacidosis. Further, as with other carbohydrate-deficient diets, weight lost from fasting is only temporary. After all, the body works to maintain balance. Water and muscle protein are replaced once the fasting stops. Consequently, the amount of body fat lost is not be much different from what would be lost on a conventional low-calorie diet, but the price paid in discomfort is certainly much greater.

Elevations in blood-cholesterol levels often occur during fasting. As with high-protein diets, these elevations are transient. But because long-term weight loss is difficult to attain from fasting, blood cholesterol does not improve in the long run. And, because carbohydrates are limited during fasting, there is not likely to be much benefit in terms of reducing cancer risk.

Fad Diets

Beware of diets that promote gimmicks based on shaky scientific foundations. Two recent examples were The Good Calorie Diet and The Zone Diet. Both diets claim that carbohydrates with a high glycemic index should be avoided to lose weight. These carbohydrates presumably evoke a rapid increase in insulin when ingested. The excess insulin is then supposed to promote the storage of carbohydrate as body fat. The problem with this theory is that a food's glycemic index is modified when it is consumed with other foods in a meal. This theory also ignores the complexity of the way insulin regulates fat storage. Most importantly, this theory wrongly excludes some of our most nutritious foods, including carrots, rice, and pasta. (Pasta is not even a food with a high-glycemic index.) Diets such as these are not helpful; they really make weight loss a lot more difficult.

Sham diets can be recognized because they are usually touted as ways to lose fat quickly and effortlessly or they promote some gimmick about food for the body's metabolism. Beware of such gimmicks. There is nothing sensational about losing weight. Weight loss is a slow, methodical, and sometimes difficult process that takes a lot of discipline. Anything that promises otherwise is suspect. If you're fortunate, all you will lose from involvement with such a diet is the money you paid for the book.

Fad diets come and go because the field of nutrition is vulnerable to oversimplification and misplaced emphasis. Competent nutritional research expands our knowledge base daily, yet examples of famous people losing weight with diets that seem too good to be true continue to grab the headlines. Our advice is to look at these dietary programs carefully. Exercise the same critical judgment that you might use if you were to buy a new home. Would you jump right in without carefully checking it out? Are you purchasing for the short-term or the long-term? Whereas the motto for home buying is said to be "location, location, and location," the motto for choosing your next—and with luck your last—diet should be "nutritional balance, variety, and low fat." This approach should be combined with regular aerobic exercise.

Chapter 9: Exercise

Even if we control the amount of fat-rich foods in our diet, we may still have trouble controlling our weight if we are inactive. While a lack of exercise is generally not the sole cause of having excessive body fat, exercise is an important element in the weight-control equation as well as in a low-fat lifestyle. For example, lack of exercise may have more to do with persistent obesity in some people than does overeating. Many obese people are significantly less active than people who are not obese; this appears to be particularly true of obese women.

Although estimates vary widely as to how inactive Americans are, a recent report for the United States Preventive Services Task Force suggests that about 40 percent of adult Americans are completely sedentary (physically inactive). Another 40 percent do not exercise at the level required to benefit their heart and lungs, even though they may get other health advantages from their lower level of activity.

There are two major types of exercise—strength building and aerobic. Both types are important for controlling weight because they offer benefits that are similar, though there are differences. Either type of exercise can increase the body's energy expenditure. In other words, either one can burn calories, but they accomplish this feat in different ways.

Like a diet that is low in fat, regular strength-building exercise increases the proportion of muscle in the body and decreases the proportion of fat. Muscles use most of the energy you need even while you are resting, so larger muscles mean more energy will be needed and more calories can be eaten without adding excess body fat. Both types of exercise also tone muscles and make you look slimmer. And, if the exercise is aerobic (continuous, rhythmic activity involving large muscle groups that is performed at a pace intense enough to quicken your breathing and increase your heart rate) and performed on a regular basis, it can make your heart and lungs work more efficiently. Aerobic exercise burns calories

to supply the energy required for movement. (The number of calories burned is directly related to the intensity, which is measured by the heart rate.) In fact, while engaged in the activity, aerobic exercise burns more calories than strength training. But the burning of calories promoted by strength training is sustained over a longer duration because muscles demand energy even at rest. Whether the calories burned during exercise are from fat or carbohydrate also differs between these two types of exercise and depends on intensity. Finally, aerobic exercise can also improve your mood, making you less likely to eat in order to make yourself feel better.

The Case for Aerobic Exercise

A wealth of evidence supports the usefulness of aerobic exercise in increasing overall health and fitness and in preventing or treating overweight. For example, having a physically active lifestyle has been shown to increase longevity. Studies of Harvard alumni aged 35 to 74 showed that those who expended the least energy on such aerobic activities as walking, stair climbing, and sports had the highest death rates.

It is sometimes difficult to determine how much effect exercise has on health because exercise studies often rely on the subjects' own reports of activity level. To avoid this problem, researchers in two studies used fitness level (as measured by the length of time a person could exercise on a graded treadmill) to determine whether or not subjects were physically active.

Fitness level strikingly predicted survival in both studies. In one of the studies, researchers even took into account other potential health risks—such as age, smoking habits, blood-cholesterol levels, blood pressure, and fasting blood-sugar level—and still found those who were physically active tended to live longer. In the other study, inactivity was related to death from cardiovascular and coronary disease; the highest risk for death from cardiovascular disease was seen in those who were least physically fit.

In addition, the results from one of these studies indicated that the amount of physical activity needed to raise one's level of fitness above the level associated with decreased survival was just a brisk walk of 30 to 60 minutes each day. The Multiple Risk Factor Intervention Trial (referred to in Chapter 3) also confirmed the reduction in total deaths and risk from coronary disease with leisure-time physical activity. However, it did not find that participation in physical activity beyond an hour a day was associated with any further risk reduction. Thus, there are limitations as to the beneficial effects of exercise in decreasing risk of disease.

There is evidence that including some type of aerobic exercise in weight-loss programs can improve the abnormal blood-fat levels typically found in obese people. These abnormal levels increase the risk of coronary heart disease. Almost 40 years ago, Dr. George Mann and colleagues demonstrated that young men consuming high-fat diets were able to maintain constant body weight without raising their blood-fat levels simply by exercising vigorously. When they stopped exercising, they gained weight.

A review of the medical literature on exercise and obesity reveals that many overweight people are characterized more by lack of exercise than by overeating. In one study examining weight-reducing diets and vigorous exercise as methods of weight loss, the researchers compared the effects of a diet to the effects of a supervised exercise program. After one year, the dieters had lost significant amounts of total body weight, body fat, and muscle as compared to a control group of people who neither dieted nor exercised. The exercisers did not lose as much total weight as the dieters, but they also did not lose significant amounts of muscle.

Both the dieters and exercisers experienced an increase in "good" HDL cholesterol without significant changes in "bad" LDL cholesterol or total cholesterol. They also enjoyed lower triglyceride levels. (Recall that high triglyceride levels and low HDL levels tend to increase the risk of coronary heart disease.) These two conditions are more common in overweight people who carry their excess fat in the upper body, a condition that appears to increase the risk of heart disease.

Perhaps the most important study was one that compared the benefits of diet and exercise combined with the benefits of diet alone. There was a diet-and-exercise group, a diet-only group, and a control group of subjects who engaged in neither. The subjects ranged in age from 25 to 49 years of age.

The weight-reduction diet (which was designed in accordance with the National Cholesterol Education Program's guidelines) contained less than 300 mg of dietary cholesterol, limited total fat to 30 percent of total calories, and kept saturated fat to 10 percent or less of total calories. The subjects in the diet-and-exercise group were in a program of aerobic exercise (primarily walking and jogging) three days each week. The exercisers worked at 60 to 80 percent of their maximum heart rate (see page 65) for at least 25 minutes initially and then gradually increased their exercise period to 45 minutes by the fourth month of the study.

The subjects who underwent both diet and exercise lost significantly more weight, primarily from a decrease in body fat. Both the women and the men in the diet-and-exercise group improved their waist-to-hip ratio, while those in the diet-only group did not. (The waist-to-hip ratio is determined by measuring the circumference of the abdomen halfway between the lower rib cage and the hip area and comparing it to the circumference at the hips—including the buttocks.) The ratio is a simple way of getting an idea of how much fat is carried above the belt and how much below. (The higher the ratio, the more fat is carried above the belt.) This is important since, as discussed in Chapter 6, the more excess body fat located above the waist, the greater the risk of coronary heart disease and diabetes. In both the diet-and-exercise group and the diet-only group, there were also improvements in blood pressure.

Recent studies suggest that exercise may be an ideal way for preventing or improving the diabeteslike state seen in obese individuals who carry their weight above the belt. When diabetes appears in adulthood, it is associated with high concentrations of both glucose and insulin due to a state of insulin resistance. This is seen most commonly in those who are obese, those who have a family history of diabetes, or those who have high blood pressure. It is called non–insulin-dependent, or type II, diabetes mellitus. It affects approximately 10 to 12 million Americans. And it is a major health problem for the obese, whose overweight condition makes them more prone to developing diabetes in the first place. Overweight makes diabetes more difficult to control once it develops. Exercise, even in the absence of weight loss, can increase insulin sensitivity and improve glucose tolerance in people who have type II diabetes as well as in people who do not have diabetes.

Physically inactive persons also have a 35 to 52 percent greater risk of developing high blood pressure than those who exercise. Exercise appears to be more beneficial in lowering high blood pressure in significantly overweight individuals than it is in normal-weight individuals who have high blood pressure. More research into the effects of exercise on high blood pressure needs to be done, however.

Weight-bearing exercise, in which the bones are "loaded," or forced to carry weight, may help in an overall program to reduce the bone loss that tends to occur in postmenopausal women. A recent study of 120 postmenopausal women who had low bone density (and were thus considered to be at increased risk of developing osteoporosis) looked at the effects of exercise, exercise plus dietary calcium, and exercise plus estrogen-progesterone replacement therapy. There was significant bone loss over the two-year study period in the control group (subjects who had normal bone density to begin with) and the exercise-only group. Bone loss was slowed significantly in the exercise-calcium group. And bone density actually increased in the exercise-estrogen group, although these women experienced more side effects such as breast tenderness and vaginal bleeding.

There may also be substantial psychological benefits to a regular exercise program. The psychological lift that can come from engaging in regular exercise may be especially helpful since dieting tends to have just the opposite effect. Many doctors feel exercise is associated with an improved sense of well-being; they point to studies that have shown reductions in signs of anxiety, depression, and hostility in people who engage in regular exercise. Regular exercise may also be critical to restful sleep patterns. Those who derive the greatest psychological benefit from exercise are usually those who are the least physically fit to begin with.

Still, the evidence regarding the psychological benefits of exercise is not conclusive. Exercise is not a cure-all. Including it in your weight-loss program does not mean you can neglect your eating habits. But considering the possible psychological benefits and the proven physical benefits of regular exercise, it is certainly a desirable addition to a healthy, low-fat lifestyle.

The Case for Strength Training

If you think of body building when you think of strength training, you may be surprised to find out that this type of exercise offers much more than a muscular physique. Strength training complements the benefits offered by aerobic exercise while adding some of its own. You do not have to build bulky muscles with strength training. You can simply tone your muscles and make them stronger and more flexible. It all depends on the type of program you set for yourself.

Muscles must be used or they decrease in size over time. The purpose of strength training is to work specific muscle groups (arms, legs, abdomen, back, and shoulders, for example) so you will not lose them. If muscle is lost, energy requirements decline because muscle uses most of the energy the body needs. This is true not only during activity, but during times of rest as well. Unless you regularly participate in a strength-training program, your muscle mass could decline by 35 percent by the time you reach age 65. Therefore you will gain weight over time unless you also decrease the calories you eat to compensate for the loss of muscle.

Muscle is also used during aerobic exercise. But exercising at high intensity may actually break down some of the muscle protein. This protein is used to help with the special needs of metabolism during activity. Building muscle through strength training offsets that loss. Strength training can also help increase endurance. After all, muscle is the energy-producing factory during exercise. The more muscle you have, the more energy you have. If you can exercise for longer periods, you burn more calories and fat.

As with aerobic exercise, strength training makes insulin more effective in controlling blood sugar. It also helps to keep blood lipids and blood pressure at normal levels. Strengthening the muscles in the abdomen can offer relief for those who frequently suffer from lower back pain. For women concerned about bone loss, strengthening the muscles in the back may help slow down bone loss from the spine.

Strength training helps older adults maintain their ability to move around freely. Muscle strength can decline by more than 20 percent by age 65. Studies done at the Human Nutrition Research Center on Aging at Tufts University found that resistance exercise helped adults who had previously been unable to walk without assistance. By simply strengthening the muscles in their legs, they were able to walk unaided. Unlike aerobic exercise, where age may limit participation, it is never too late to start a strength-training program. The Tufts studies determined that strength training could increase the amount of muscle in subjects as old as 90 years of age.

The Exercise Prescription

According to the guidelines of the American College of Sports Medicine, an exercise program should include both aerobic and strength-building components.

An exercise is aerobic when it forces your heart and lungs to work harder to meet your muscles' demand for oxygen. Aerobic exercise is any activity involving continuous, rhythmic movements of major muscle groups (such as the muscles in the legs) performed at a pace intense enough to quicken breathing and make the heart pump faster than normal. The activity should not be so intense you cannot keep it up for more than a few minutes at a time. Examples of aerobic activities include jogging, bicycling, swimming, brisk walking, and cross-country skiing. Some sports, such as basketball, and some leisure-time activities, such as dancing, can also be aerobic as long as you engage in them continuously and for a sufficient period of time.

Early studies suggested that to do the most good for the cardiovascular system, aerobic exercise had to be performed for at least 20 minutes a day, at least three times a week, at a heart rate (pulse) between 60 and 85 percent of maximum. More recent studies have challenged this contention. Any type of activity, even when performed at lower intensities, can benefit the heart and lungs and may be more effective at promoting loss of body fat than the higher intensity, more vigorous exercises recommended in the past. You can assess your intensity by gauging the quickness of your breathing. That is, you should be breathing more rapidly than you would be when resting, yet you should not be breathing so rapidly that you are unable to talk while continuing to perform the activity.

Another way to assess the intensity of your activity is by measuring heart rate. This is especially useful when performing more vigorous types of aerobic activity. The intensities of these activities are typically rated by the percentage of maximum heart rate achieved when they are performed.

To get an estimate of your maximum heart rate, subtract your age from 220. If you are 35 years old, for example, your maximum heart rate is 220 minus 35, or 185 beats per minute. (This is an estimate. To get a more precise reading, contact your physician.) Sixty percent of your maximum heart rate would be 185 multiplied by .60, or 111 beats per minute; 85 percent of your maximum heart rate would be 185 multiplied by .85, or about 157 beats per minute. Therefore, if you are 35 years old, you would need to exercise hard enough to increase your heart rate to between 111 and 157 beats per minute in order to obtain the greatest aerobic benefits.

To check your heart rate, you need to take your pulse. The safest place to take your pulse is at the radial artery in your wrist. (Taking your pulse at the carotid artery in the neck during intense exercise can be dangerous, especially if you have heart or blood-pressure problems.) Gently place the index and middle fingers of one hand on the inner side of the opposite wrist, below the heel of the hand, to feel the pulse. Count the number of beats for 10 seconds, then multiply by six to get the number of beats per minute. You should take your pulse several times during your workout to be sure you are operating in your target range. Take your pulse quickly, so your heart rate does not drop below its exercise level before you get an accurate reading.

The Resistance (Strength-Building) Exercise Prescription

To keep from losing muscle as you age, a regular program of strength-building or resistance exercise should be added to your exercise routine. If you do not belong to a health club, visit a local community center that offers exercise programs and seek individual guidance on how to get started. If using an instructional manual is more to your liking, you should expect to find a wide selection at any good bookstore.

Be sure that you work all your muscle groups. The legs contain the largest muscles in the body, so strengthening them can have the greatest impact on your caloric needs. But your arm muscles can make the most noticeable difference in feelings of strength. Strong abdominal muscles take pressure off your back and help to relieve lower-back pain. Strong shoulder and back muscles help your posture. Working the muscles in your back may also help slow down bone loss from the spine.

To prevent injury from strength training, always stretch prior to working with weights. You should also take care not to work the same muscles every day. Muscles need to rest for at least 24 hours after they have been exercised.

Getting started requires a disciplined schedule. Most people need to perform strength-building exercises for at least 30 minutes, three times a week. Once you have achieved your desired strength level, you can maintain your muscles on only two 20-minute sessions each week.

Surprisingly, lower-intensity exercise burns more fat than higher-intensity exercise. This is because the body burns fat most efficiently when heart rates are slower. When you are resting or sleeping, body fat provides the fuel. (Unfortunately, rest and sleep do not require many calories, so you don't lose much body fat while snoozing.)

When oxygen is in short supply, carbohydrate yields energy more quickly and more efficiently than fat. When engaged in high-intensity exercise, you cannot breathe fast enough to get the amount of oxygen needed to rely on fat for energy. The body then has to draw upon carbohydrate stored in the muscles (glycogen) instead. You burn some fat during high-intensity exercise, but it is proportionately less than the amount you burn during low-intensity exercise. (If you are among the select group that is very fit, you can burn more fat at high intensity than most people.)

Another reason low-intensity exercise burns more body fat is that you can engage in lower-intensity exercise for a longer time before tiring. High-intensity activity may use more calories in thirty minutes, but it is difficult for most of us to keep such a pace for much longer than that. For all but the most fit among us, the body does not start to use any significant amount of fat for energy until about 20 minutes into the activity. Thus, you can see why being able to exercise for longer periods should result in a greater loss of body fat.

Starting Out and Staying With It
The vast majority of healthy adults can start an exercise program in a sensible manner without elaborate medical testing. But it is a good idea to have a medical evaluation that includes a supervised treadmill test before beginning an exercise program if you have cardiovascular disease or if you have symptoms such as chest pain or shortness of breath when you exert yourself. A supervised treadmill test is recommended if you are 35 years of age or older and one or more of the following traits applies to you:

- Cigarette smoking
- Family history of heart disease
- Type II diabetes mellitus
- High blood pressure
- More than 30 percent overweight
- HDL-cholesterol level under 35
- High total cholesterol
- High LDL-cholesterol level

For those who have heart disease or have recently experienced a heart attack, unless the patient's physician directs otherwise, it is a good idea to exercise only in a supervised environment.

If you have been inactive, have never exercised regularly before, or are obese, start out slowly. For example, begin with no more than three workouts per week. If you are sedentary and do not have heart disease, aim first for a heart rate of 60 to 65 percent of your maximum heart rate while exercising. As your fitness level improves, you can gradually increase your exercise intensity up to about 80 to 85 percent of your maximum heart rate.

Start out with 20- to 30-minute exercise sessions. If necessary, you can even break this up into two or three sessions per day. If you have a particularly busy schedule, you might try taking a 10- to 15-minute walk in the morning, at lunch, and then again before dinner. The United States Preventive Services Task Force stresses that "Beginners should emphasize regular rather than vigorous exercise." As your fitness level improves, you can gradually increase the length of your workouts by adding five minutes each week until you are exercising continuously for 45 to 60 minutes, four to five times each week.

There are some general warnings and precautions that apply to all exercisers. For instance, before beginning every exercise session (including strength-building activity), you need to warm up. If you are going to be walking, for example, you should spend five to 10 minutes walking at a slower intensity before you actually begin your workout. At the end of your workout, you should again slow your pace for five to 10 minutes to give your body a chance to cool down and to allow your heart rate to gradually return to normal. Your warm-up period should also consist of stretching exercises, which are essential to minimize the risk of muscle injury.

If you are engaging in a weight-bearing exercise, such as walking or jogging, you should wear sturdy, comfortable, well-fitting shoes that support and cushion your feet. Since knee problems are common among obese people, swimming might be a better choice of activity than walking or jogging.

You should also dress comfortably in clothing and footwear appropriate for weather conditions. This is particularly important for heart patients, since cold weather (and especially cold air that is inhaled) can cause the heart rate to go higher than it normally would for the intensity of the exercise performed. This can result in a workout that is more strenuous than planned or desired.

If while exercising you experience any unusual symptoms, such as chest discomfort, dizziness, or extreme shortness of breath, stop exercising immediately and contact your doctor. Avoid exercising on days when you do not feel good.

Planning an exercise program that you can stick with is very important, because exercise is not a "quick fix." It must become a regular part of your lifestyle, just as a low-fat diet needs to become part of your life. And, just as moderation, variety, and balance are the essence of a sound nutritional program, they are also necessary for a long-term exercise program.

You want to choose an activity that burns a relatively high number of calories. If the exercise does not expend energy at a very high rate, it may take prohibitively long to see results. Brisk walking, jogging, swimming, stair climbing, and cycling are but a few of the exercises that burn a relatively high number of calories.

You also want the chosen activity to be one that you enjoy doing, that is safe, and that fits into your lifestyle. Otherwise, your chances of continuing decrease. If you have been sedentary, for example, you might want to try brisk walking at first rather than jumping into a more strenuous or jarring activity, such as jogging, in which the risk of injury is higher. If you have orthopedic problems, you might want to opt for swimming, which is easier on the knees and other joints than jogging.

When you choose your activity, take your lifestyle into account. If you're a very busy person, you might want to choose an activity that can be done at almost any time, anywhere, with little equipment, and without a partner. Activities such as walking, jogging, and stair climbing fit the bill perfectly for many people. Most people can manage a walk during their lunch hour.

If you think you might have trouble sticking with an exercise program, you might want to select an activity that can be done with a partner who can help get you moving on those days when you'd rather not exercise. Walking, jogging, dancing, and working out with weights, for example, can be done with a partner; there are even walking clubs that meet and walk at local shopping malls. Sharing an activity with a partner or a group creates social benefits that encourage long-term participation. Another idea for keeping yourself motivated might be to keep a diary of your workouts; writing down the duration, location, and kind of exercise can help you keep track of your progress and keep you interested in the program.

You can build variety into your exercise plan by cross-training, or alternating between different aerobic activities. For example, you might want to alternate days of walking with days of cycling or swimming. If you jog three days during the week, you could substitute a tennis match on the weekend. You might also want to try alternating days of aerobic exercise with days of weight training. And when training with weights, you can split up your regimen by doing an upper-body workout on one day and a lower-body workout on another.

You can even spice up your exercise routine and increase benefits simply by building extra activity into your everyday routine. For example, you can try parking farther away from the stores in the shopping mall parking lot and then taking a longer walk. This not only helps to burn extra calories, it relieves the frustration of searching for that "desirable" spot next to the mall entrance. If you usually take the elevator up two or three floors to your office, you might try taking the stairs instead. Keep in mind that any activity burns calories. And while your ultimate objective is to establish a regular exercise routine, adding any amount of activity to your lifestyle can help, especially when you're just starting to get active.

Exercise and a Low-Fat Diet

Regular high-intensity exercise may also help you stay with your low-fat diet. People who regularly participate in vigorous aerobic activity tend to have a greater preference for carbohydrates than for fats. One explanation is that the carbohydrate stored in the muscle used during exercise must be replaced, so the appetite for carbohydrate is increased by exercise.

Chapter 10:
How to Change Your Diet

Now that you know how diet affects your heart, your cancer risk, and your waistline, it's time to take a look at your diet. By comparing your eating habits with what the experts advise, you'll have a better idea of how to make changes that benefit your heart and your figure and help protect you from cancer.

Look at What You Eat

The American Heart Association (AHA) and the National Cholesterol Education Program (NCEP) have developed dietary guidelines for adults that are designed to reduce fat intake as well as to lower high blood-cholesterol levels and keep them in a desirable range. These guidelines are similar to those developed by the National Cancer Institute (NCI) and other health agencies concerned about cancer.

According to these guidelines, less than 30 percent of your total calorie intake should come from fat. Less than 10 percent of your total calories (or less than one-third of your total fat calories) should come from saturated fat, and no more than 10 percent of your total calories should come from polyunsaturated fat. The remaining fat calories (10 to 15 percent of your total calorie intake) should come from monounsaturated fat. You should consume 50 to 60 percent of your total calories as carbohydrate with at least 80 percent of that coming from moderate- to high-fiber sources. Most experts recommend 25 to 30 grams of dietary fiber daily, and consumption of cholesterol should be less than 300 milligrams (mg) each day.

In the typical diet actually consumed by the average American, however, 35 to 40 percent of calories come from fat, about 47 percent come from carbohydrate (with most coming from refined or highly processed starches and sugars), and about 16 percent come from protein. The average adult diet also provides less than half of the recommended amount of fiber and anywhere from 400 to 500 mg of cholesterol each day. In other words, the average American adult gets too many calories from fat, not enough calories from carbohydrate, not enough fiber, and too much cholesterol. Fruits and vegetables are the least popular of all the food groups. Many Americans almost never eat fruit, and almost as many never eat vegetables. Even people who eat these foods usually do not get the recommended number of servings each day.

A Word of Caution

When you make the food choices necessary to reduce the amount of fat you eat, you will be eating more carbohydrate along with about the same amount of protein (or slightly less). These choices should mean you are also getting more fiber. But this may not be so unless you are careful to choose low-fat foods that are also low in refined sugars and flour. You already know the benefits a high-carbohydrate diet can bring. Your total and LDL cholesterol are likely to be lower because you have replaced saturated-fat calories with carbohydrate calories. And depending on how low your fat intake actually gets, you might even find you have lost some weight without a great deal of effort.

But while many people respond well when they change to a high-carbohydrate diet, some do not. Instead of reducing total cholesterol, a high-carbohydrate diet (60 percent of calories) or a low-fat diet (20 to 25 percent of total calories) may have the undesirable effect of raising triglycerides and lowering HDL. LDL may either stay the same or decline. Both diets may also cause blood sugar and insulin to remain elevated for an extended time after a meal. People who respond to a high-carbohydrate diet like this are considered to be "carbohydrate-sensitive." This response frequently occurs among adults who have the type of diabetes (type II) that does not usually require insulin. People with high-fasting triglyceride or insulin levels in their blood are likely candidates for this type of response, even if they have not been diagnosed with diabetes. What do you do then if, after switching to a low-fat diet to lower your total and LDL cholesterol, you find you have higher triglycerides and lower HDL? This result is especially discouraging if you have diabetes, because your risk of heart disease is already high even without high blood cholesterol. If your response to a low-fat diet suggests you are carbohydrate-sensitive, you can still benefit from changing the fat in your diet. Continue to limit your intake of saturated fat to less than 10 percent of your total calories. However, you should try to keep your total fat intake from dipping below 30 percent. You may find you need to keep your total fat at a level even higher than 30 percent to prevent HDL cholesterol from falling. But first you should see how you respond at the 30-percent level.

If you find you need to raise your fat intake to more than 30 percent of total calories, you should add monounsaturated fat and omega-3 polyunsaturated fatty acids. These two fats have benefits that are especially important for carbohydrate-sensitive people. Monounsaturated fat lowers total and LDL cholesterol for such individuals as effectively as a low-fat diet does for others. But it also offers the advantage of preventing the increase in blood sugar and insulin that these people experience after eating a high-carbohydrate meal. Omega-3 fatty acids can add to the benefits of monounsaturated fat by lowering triglycerides considerably. They may also offer the advantages of lowering blood pressure and preventing the formation of clots that clog the arteries.

To get more monounsaturated fat into your diet, use olive oil and canola oil in place of other vegetable oils. Add avocado or nuts to a salad or main dish. Avocado can make an interesting flavor substitute for cheese, sour cream, or yogurt in some recipes, while nuts are good sources of protein and fiber. Your intake of omega-3 polyunsaturated fat can be increased by eating more fish. Even though you may have a slight fat windfall if you are carbohydrate-sensitive, it would not be sensible to consume more vegetable oils or meat and dairy products. Eating more polyunsaturated fats would not give you a better blood sugar and insulin response, and eating more saturated fat raises your LDL cholesterol.

If your fasting-triglyceride and insulin levels suggest you might respond to a low-fat diet the way a carbohydrate-sensitive person does, you may want to pay particular attention to the sugar fructose. The few studies conducted to date have found total and LDL cholesterol were presumably higher than the norm in some people who consumed fructose in amounts common in the American diet. Most people had to consume three to five times the normal amount of fructose before this happened. And some people never showed any adverse effects. The more carbohydrate-sensitive you are, the more likely you are to respond negatively to fructose. In addition, the amount of fat in your diet could influence the way your blood lipids respond to fructose: It may be more detrimental when consumed in large amounts in a high-fat diet.

Fructose is found naturally in honey and in most fruits. However, the single most important source of this sugar in your diet is likely to be a sweetening ingredient called high-fructose corn syrup (HFCS), which is widely used in food processing. For economic reasons, this sweetener is replacing sucrose, the more expensive table sugar used in most commercially sweetened foods and beverages. HFCS is produced from cornstarch treated with an enzyme. To limit your consumption of this sweetener, watch your intake of baked goods, desserts, presweetened breakfast cereals, candy, and soft drinks. Be especially wary of low-fat baked goods and desserts, which are frequently loaded with sugar in the form of fructose.

Conquering the Fat Craving

Cutting back on the fat you eat may be one of the most difficult tasks you will ever attempt. Face it—high-fat foods just taste good. The preference for fatty foods is so strong that sometimes you may feel as if you actually crave them. Yet many people are able to not only conquer their strong desire for fatty foods, they begin to favor foods with little or no fat. These people continue to enjoy the experience of eating, even preferring the taste of low-fat foods. Moreover, besides quitting smoking, reducing your fat intake could be the single most important thing you can do for your health. It may help you to not only lower your cholesterol, but also to control your weight. Cutting back on the fat in your diet may even improve your odds some of our most common cancers, such as colon or breast cancer.

It might help you to lower your fat intake if you have a better understanding of what may be driving your preference for fat and what you can expect to happen as you try to change it. Most people go through an adjustment period of about 8 to 12 weeks when they begin to adapt to a low-fat way of eating. After this time has passed, high-fat foods do not have the same appeal as before, so there is much less desire for them. The whole process is made easier if you also incorporate regular exercise into your life, for active people find that they prefer high-carbohydrate foods. Even so, you can afford to indulge in a favorite fatty food every once in a while without setting yourself back. Just remember that it is possible to wipe out your progress completely if you allow yourself to slip back into eating high-fat foods on a regular basis.

The Fat Appetite

The popularity of high-fat foods makes it hard to believe we have no innate need or "appetite" for fat. A few theories support the idea that there may be a desire for fat late in the day or during times of the year when it gets cold, and that this desire may be motivated by a physical need. Proponents of these theories believe the craving for fat is a physiological remnant left over from the days when our ancestors needed energy-dense foods to store as body fat in preparation for times when access to food was limited. This is certainly not the case in the United States today: The supply is abundant, and for most of us food is available at any time.

As far as our nutritional needs for fat are concerned, they are satisfied by only a small amount of polyunsaturated fat—about one tablespoonful per day. That is just enough to provide the needed amount of linoleic acid, which is an essential fatty acid. As for cholesterol, infants and young children may have a modest requirement for this substance, but adults do not. And neither children nor adults have any need for saturated fat. Indeed, it is almost impossible for healthy people in this country to develop a nutritional deficiency because of insufficient fat. Therefore, an innate fat appetite cannot be the force behind our preference for fatty foods.

On the contrary, our appetite for fat is a learned one. Sweetness is the only taste recognized by very young infants, who smile when they are given sugar but do not register any positive facial responses to fat. On a sensory level, we do not actually taste fat, we experience it. In other words, fat is detected in foods by its sensory appeal or "mouth feel." Fat can impart a variety of sensory experiences to different foods—mayonnaise, meat, cheese, chocolate, ice cream, and cake have little about their flavors in common. This variety of flavors contributed by fat is part of what makes the adjustment to low-fat foods so difficult.

Our appetite for fat may be learned through a process psychologists call associative conditioning. Simply put, if you associate an experience with pleasure, you want to repeat it. Fatty foods are among the most flavorful in our diets. Most of the chemicals responsible for flavor in foods are delivered in fat, so when you eat a food rich in fat, it almost always tastes good. This experience can be so pleasurable that you want to taste the food again. Understanding the power behind this drive may help you to exert a higher level of control over your eating patterns.

Making the Adjustment

Learning to enjoy food without depending on the flavors of fat is a key element to successfully lowering your fat intake. When you decrease the number of fatty foods you eat, you can begin to lessen their impact on your desire for them. This process is enhanced if you experiment with new ways to prepare low-fat foods in more flavorful ways. Using low-fat ingredients or substituting reduced-fat or low-fat foods for the high-fat versions is a better approach than simply eliminating the fatty foods altogether.

It is important to restrict foods that contain the most fat. For example, butter, margarine, mayonnaise, salad dressings, sour cream, and whole-fat dairy creams are some of the more obvious sources of fat. Studies have shown that the most critical step for lowering fat intake over the long term may be reducing fat from these sources. Because these fat sources are used as flavorings for many foods, they provide the most powerful of the pleasurable sensory experiences you need to overcome. Fortunately, a number of good quality reduced-fat or low-fat substitutions for these foods are now widely available.

When the fat content of a high-fat food is less obvious—as is the case with meat or cheese—overcoming the preference for such foods becomes more difficult. In addition, the low-fat substitutes available for these foods are generally not as good in quality as the low-fat margarines and salad dressings. But technology is advancing in these areas, so you can expect the situation to improve soon for reduced-fat or low-fat meats and cheeses. In the meantime, eating less of these foods and experimenting with meatless meals that emphasize dried beans and cereal grains can help with the transition away from high-fat foods. A number of cookbooks are currently available to help make this way of eating more of a sensory delight.

Perhaps the most difficult of the fatty foods to give up are the baked goods and desserts. In addition to being the foods people crave the most, these foods have the most insidious effects because their fat content is hardest to recognize and the sweet taste provided by the presence of sugar makes the fat flavor more difficult to detect. The sugar-fat blend is considered one of the most compelling of all flavor combinations.

Consuming sugar with fat may also encourage more of the calories to end up in body fat, because sugar stimulates the hormone insulin. One of the activities of insulin is to round up fatty acids and deposit them into body fat. So fat eaten along with sugar may be more likely to end up in body fat because insulin makes it easier for this to occur. Happily, a number of reduced-fat or low-fat baked goods and desserts can be readily found in food stores.

Staying on Course

The prospect of never again being able to enjoy some of your favorite high-fat foods may be enough to sabotage your efforts towards a healthier way of eating. But there is also some good news: You don't have to give up these foods forever. A low-fat eating style can still accommodate some high-fat indulgences. The trick is to keep to a minimum the number of times you indulge in these foods.

Research shows that once you adjust to a low-fat diet, you can eat an occasional high-fat food without necessarily undoing everything you have accomplished. For it is not the total amount of fat in a particular food that does the damage but the number of times you consume that food. An occasional indulgence—even if it is very high in fat—does not set you back noticeably unless you eat it or something comparable to it frequently or nearly every day. Foods lower in fat, such as cookies, can also sabotage your efforts to adjust to a low-fat diet if you eat them three or four times a day. According to what we know about making adjustments to a low-fat diet, it is how often you indulge that makes the difference, not how much you eat when you do indulge.

A Word about Fat Substitutes

The first low-fat products introduced on the market were not nearly as acceptable as those available today. Consumers are demanding more low-fat alternatives, and food manufacturers have invested in new technologies to develop a variety of ways to deliver the flavor that high-fat foods offer. Between 1989 and 1990 alone there was an increase of 127 percent in the number of new low-fat foods introduced.

These new technologies have enabled food processors to reduce the fat content of some foods like margarine and salad dressings. Sometimes the reduced-fat product loses some of the characteristics of its higher-fat version. For example, some of the reduced-fat cheeses may not melt as well as regular cheeses. Other new technologies use ingredients that actually provide the mouth feel of fat. These ingredients give the same sensory experience of fat, so they taste just like fat, but they do not provide any real fat at all. These so-called fat substitutes may be a real breakthrough for people who need to lower their fat intake but cannot bring themselves to give up their favorite foods on a regular basis.

If you are considering including foods containing fat substitutes in your diet to help lower your fat intake, you should be aware that there is a drawback: These foods may not be helpful in easing your adjustment to a low-fat diet. In a recent study, one group consumed a conventional low-fat diet which included naturally low-fat foods or reduced-fat foods. A second group consumed foods containing fat substitutes, while a third group (the control group) continued to consume their usual high-fat diet. After 12 weeks, only the group on the conventional low-fat diet showed less preference for fat. The group receiving the fat substitutes had the same preference for fat as the third group. The lesson learned from this study is that fat substitutes may not help you lower your fat intake over the long term. Because they give the same sensory experience of fat, they do not allow your palate to adjust to the absence of fat and learn to appreciate the sensory experience of low-fat foods.

Still, foods containing fat substitutes can be useful in a low-fat diet because they help you lower your fat intake by substitution. As a result, you get all the health benefits of a low-fat diet. If you want to include some foods containing fat substitutes in your diet, that's fine; just make sure you also include lots of reduced-fat and naturally low-fat foods as well. Also keep in mind that when you rely only on fat substitutes to lower your fat intake, your adjustment to a low-fat diet may not be as easy to make.

Your Plan of Action

To adopt a healthier diet that is low in total fat, saturated fat, and cholesterol, you need a plan of action. In other words, you should set goals for yourself and then decide on the changes you can make in order to meet those goals. As mentioned previously, the AHA and NCEP have developed guidelines to help you create a heart-healthy diet, and the NCI has made recommendations for cancer prevention. So before going any further, you need to take a look at what those guidelines mean in terms of your diet and your eating habits.

The guidelines recommend that you receive less than 30 percent of your total daily calorie intake from fat. What does that mean? Well, first of all, you need to know what your average daily calorie intake is (or should be). How many calories your body needs each day largely depends on your gender and your level of activity. For the most part, because they have more muscle, men require more calories than women to maintain their weight. And the more active you are, the more energy, or calories, your body needs to fuel your activity. Fewer calories are needed as people grow older, but this change is due primarily to the lower level of activity typically found among older people who do not work to maintain muscle.

To help you determine what your average daily calorie intake should be, we've set up a simple table for adults. The calorie information is taken from the Recommended Dietary Allowances (RDAs) of the Food and Nutrition Board of the National Academy of Sciences. These estimates are based on the calorie needs of men and women of average height and desirable weight who engage in moderate activity. (The intake of total fat and saturated fat is also listed.)

Once you have an idea of what your daily calorie intake should be, you want to know how many of those calories should come from fat. According to the guidelines (see the table in Chapter 7), less than 30 percent of your total calorie intake should come from fat. To find out the maximum number of calories that should come from fat, multiply your total calorie intake by .3 (30 percent). For example, if your daily calorie intake is 2,300, multiply 2,300 by .3, which is 690. Therefore, no more than 690 of the calories you consume each day should come from fat.

This figure is helpful, but you can go further to determine the maximum number of grams of fat you can consume each day. The new nutrition labels on food products now prominently list calories from fat as well as grams of fat (see the following section); the old labels provided only grams of fat. Similarly, many recipes list their fat content in terms of grams, rather than calories. Since 1 gram of fat yields 9 calories, (regardless of whether it is saturated or unsaturated) you simply divide 690 calories by 9 to determine the maximum number of grams of fat you are allowed. In this case, you should consume less than 77 grams of fat each day (that is, 690 divided by 9). The accompanying table lists total fat intake in grams for a diet that gets a maximum of 30 percent of its calories from fat.

The guidelines also specify how that daily fat intake should be divided between the three types of fat—saturated, polyunsaturated, and monounsaturated. They recommend that less than 10 percent of your total daily calorie intake should come from saturated fat. Now you already know that the 30 percent of your total calories that comes from fat amounts to 690 calories or 77 grams. To figure the maximum amount of fat (in grams) allowed from saturated fat (10 percent), simply calculate one-third of 77, which is 26 grams. The same method holds true for figuring maximum amounts of polyunsaturated and monounsaturated fats.

To review, no more than 30 percent of an individual's total calories should come from fats of all kinds. Most important, no more than 10 percent should come from saturated fat. No more than 10 percent should come from polyunsaturated fat, and the balance should come from monounsaturated fat. But this doesn't mean that you should increase your fat intake to reach these amounts. These are the maximums or upper limits; it is desirable to consume less. Remember that you are not trying to reach a level of 26 grams; on the contrary, you are trying to make sure you don't exceed that number.

In order not to exceed these limits for fat intake, you need to eat fewer foods high in fat, especially foods high in saturated fat. Since the high-fat foods typically consumed in the American diet are usually also high in saturated fat, you automatically decrease your saturated fat intake when you decrease your total fat intake.

Much of the saturated fat in the typical American diet comes from animal products. Dairy products made from whole milk, for example, contain large amounts of saturated fat: Butter, cheese, and ice cream all add hefty doses of saturated fat to the diet. The marbling and visible fat in meat are also high in saturated fat. Poultry and fish generally contain smaller amounts of saturated fat than meat.

While vegetable fats are generally low in saturated fats, there are a few exceptions: Coconut oil, palm oil, palm kernel oil, and cocoa butter are high in saturated fat. In the past, vegetable oils were used in a variety of prepared baked goods, snack foods, nondairy creamers, cake mixes, and frozen dinners. Today, vegetable oils have largely been replaced by hydrogenated or partially hydrogenated vegetable oils. Although these hydrogenated vegetable oils are more saturated than their unhydrogenated forms and are sources of *trans* fatty acids, they are still far preferable to the animal fats they replace because they don't contain cholesterol and are much lower in saturated fat.

When you do choose foods that contain fat, you should select those that contain mostly monounsaturated fats more often than those that contain mostly polyunsaturated fats, and you should choose either of these over foods high in saturated fats. Oils rich in monounsaturated fatty acids include olive oil and canola (rapeseed) oil. Monounsaturated fat and the polyunsaturated fat from fish should be the most abundant of the fats in your diet. Other sources of polyunsaturated fats are cooking oils made from corn, sunflower, safflower, soybean, sesame, and cottonseed. (The process of hydrogenation increases the saturated fat content of these oils, so you'll need to limit products—margarines, shortenings, and others—made from hydrogenated oils.) Fish oils also contain polyunsaturated fats known as omega-3 fatty acids. Consuming large amounts of the omega-6 polyunsaturated fatty acids found in vegetable oils, on the other hand, may adversely affect the functioning of the immune system. For this reason, it is wise to limit your polyunsaturated fat intake to no more than 10 percent of your total calories.

Since you decrease the number of calories in your diet that come from fatty foods, if you wish to maintain your current weight, you need to increase the number of calories that come from other types of food. According to the guidelines, you should increase your intake of complex carbohydrates (starch and fiber) to make up for the lost calories. Fiber is especially important for controlling hunger on a low-fat diet. Foods rich in complex carbohydrates include whole-grain breads and cereals, pasta, rice, dried beans, vegetables, and fruits.

On the other hand, if you prefer to lose weight, you can decrease both your total calorie intake and your total fat intake by eliminating fatty foods and not replacing the lost calories. For example, if you cut out 500 calories' worth of fat from your diet each day and didn't replace them with calories from other sources, like carbohydrates, you could lose about a pound of fat a week, on average.

You also need to limit your dietary cholesterol intake. If you eat a typical American diet, chances are you're getting between 400 and 500 mg of cholesterol each day. The guidelines recommend that you decrease the amount of cholesterol in your diet to less than 300 mg each day. Cholesterol is found exclusively in animal products, including dairy products, meat, eggs, poultry, fish, and shellfish. Foods from plant sources, on the other hand, contain no cholesterol (unless they are served with animal products like cheese or sauces that contain butter or cream). These plant sources can also be rich in fiber, especially if you emphasize whole-grain breads and cereals and fresh fruits and vegetables. Since many of the foods high in saturated fat also contain cholesterol, your cholesterol intake is likely to decrease as you decrease the amount of saturated fat in your diet. And because much of the cholesterol in the American diet comes from egg yolks (a single egg yolk contains about 213 mg of cholesterol), you can make a determined effort to decrease the number of eggs yolks you consume each week to no more than three. That should include all eggs used in the preparation or processing of other foods.

Read the Label

Nutrition information has been available on packaged foods for a number of years now. But in December 1992, sweeping food labeling reform was jointly approved by the Food and Drug Administration (FDA) and the U.S. Department of Agriculture (USDA). The new law requires that all processed food must carry a new label, in a new format, that clearly shows nutrition facts. Foods are also required to meet specific standards before food manufacturers can make claims about the nutritional value of their products. Terms such as fat free, low fat, and cholesterol free have specific definitions that must be met before the terms can be used on the label to describe the food. (The standards vary slightly for single foods, entrees, and meal-type products.) Fat free means that a food contains less than 0.5 gram of fat per serving; low fat means 3 grams or less of fat per serving; and cholesterol free means less than 2 mg of cholesterol and 2 grams or less of saturated fat per serving. The implementation of these new regulations means that for the first time, claims about a food's health benefits are allowed on the label.

On the new labels (see sample), manufacturers are required to express nutrient amounts in a reasonable, standardized serving size defined for each type of food and based on a quantity that is typically consumed. This should make it easier to compare similar foods and decide which ones best fit into your dietary plan. And it is more difficult for a manufacturer to make a food appear low in fat or cholesterol by using an unrealistically small serving size.

In addition to using standardized serving sizes, the new labels include valuable information not required on the old labels. For example, at the very top, the new labels now list the number of calories from fat as well as the number of calories

Nutrition Facts

Serving Size ½ cup (114g)
Servings per Container 4

Amount Per Serving	
Calories 90	Calories from Fat 30
	% Daily Value*
Total Fat 3g	5%
Saturated Fat 0g	0%
Cholesterol 0mg	0%
Sodium 300mg	13%
Total Carbohydrate 13g	4%
Dietary Fiber 3g	12%
Sugars 3g	
Protein 3g	
Vitamin A 80% •	Vitamin C 60%
Calcium 4% •	Iron 4%

*Percent Daily Values are based on a 2,000-calorie diet. Your daily values may be higher or lower depending on your calorie needs.

	Calories:	2,000	2,500
Total Fat	Less than	65g	80g
Sat Fat	Less than	20g	25g
Cholesterol	Less than	300mg	300mg
Sodium	Less than	2,400mg	2,400mg
Total Carbohydrate		300g	375g
Fiber		25g	30g

Calories per gram:
Fat 9 • Carbohydrate 4 • Protein 4

in a standard serving size of the food. The number of grams of total fat, saturated fat, cholesterol, sodium, carbohydrate, fiber, sugar, and protein in one serving are also listed.

Despite this improved format, consumers should continue to be wary of the failure of some food processors to provide information in a clear and unambiguous way. For example, some mixes require the addition of ingredients such as margarine, milk, and eggs. But the information on the label may pertain only to the dry mix. Since no one eats the mix this way, such information is of little help and may even mislead buyers. A tiny asterisk may refer consumers to a note in very small type that explains the calories, fat, saturated fat, and cholesterol added to the food "as prepared" and finally consumed.

The number of calories contained in a gram of fat, a gram of carbohydrate, and a gram of protein are shown at the very bottom of the label. These values do not change.

For total fat, saturated fat, cholesterol, sodium, carbohydrate, and fiber, the new labels list a "% Daily Value" at the upper right corner. These values indicate how a particular food item fits into a day's total dietary pattern of nutrients. The "Daily Value" assumes a diet of 2,000 calories per day, a standard weighted toward women and older people, and is a compromise among a number of alternatives. Nevertheless, this number can be a helpful guide, even if you consume somewhat more or less than 2,000 calories each day.

The Daily Value refers to the amount of a nutrient recommended by the various health policy groups. For example, in a 2,000-calorie diet, the Daily Value for total fat is less than 65 grams, which is equal to about 30 percent of calories; while the Daily Value for saturated fat is less than 20 grams, equal to about 10 percent of calories.

The % Daily Value column for each nutrient—found in the upper part of the label—indicates how much of that Daily Value is supplied by the food. Thus, to consider a new example, if a food provides three grams of fat per serving, then it contributes only about five percent of the Daily Value of 65 grams for total fat. If you choose one food that provides so little total fat, then you have considerable flexibility in choosing other foods for the remainder of the day and staying within the recommended maximum level of 30 percent of calories from fat. If, on the other hand, you choose one food that provides 13 grams of fat in a single serving (as shown in our sample label), that food provides a significant 20 percent of the Daily Value for total fat, and your choices for the rest of the day become more limited.

To make it easier to find foods that fit into dietary plans to cope with heart disease, you can also look for health claims on the food label beyond the nutritional facts. Not all foods carry such claims, even if they meet the standards, because a manufacturer may choose not to do so. Still, you want to check labels to make sure you are not overlooking foods that could fit into a low-fat diet. If a food carries a claim about heart disease, for example, it has to be low in total fat, low in saturated fat, and low in cholesterol. In some cases, it is also a good source of soluble fiber. Only if a food claims to have benefits for high blood pressure does it have to meet the standard for low sodium. And limits have been established to prevent excessive amounts of sodium in foods making heart-disease claims.

The Cholesterol & Fat Counter in this book adds percentages of calories for total and saturated fat to the information on the new labels. These percentages provide a useful perspective on choosing healthful foods because the percentage of fat in a given item doesn't change, regardless of the portion size. In addition, our counter helps in selecting foods for which labels are voluntary, such as fresh produce and raw meat products (chicken breasts, beef roasts, and seafood, for example).

USDA Labeling

The new food labels, which can be identified by the black box displaying Nutrition Facts in bold letters (see example on page 74), appeared on packaged foods in May of 1994. Now the same information is available for processed meat and poultry products. Food labels on these products were developed by the USDA, the government agency that regulates the safety and quality of meat and poultry. Since the FDA regulates the safety and quality of all other foods, the USDA worked with the FDA to make meat and poultry labels virtually identical to the labels developed for all other foods.

But not all packaged meat and poultry products actually carry the new labels. Packaged meats and poultry sold in a fresh or uncooked condition to use as meal entrees, such as chicken breasts, ground beef, and unbasted turkeys, are not required to be labeled. Instead, you should be able to find the relevant nutrition information posted somewhere close to the meat counter where these items are displayed. For the time being, posting the nutrition facts is purely voluntary. But if not enough stores offer this information on a voluntary basis, the USDA has warned it will become mandatory in the future. Items manufactured by small businesses are not required to carry the new labels, nor are items purchased in small packages, at deli counters, or in restaurants.

Labels for meat and poultry have the same nutrition information as the labels on other foods, and they use exactly the same format. There are some differences, however. One is that the "% Daily Value" column for a serving of meat or a poultry product may be expressed "as packaged" or "as consumed" or both. Because these foods can lose 25 percent or more of their raw-fat content during preparation, the "as consumed" values provide a better indication of the amount of fat actually consumed. A serving of bacon, for example, would contain a considerably smaller amount of fat after it is cooked, or "as consumed," compared to the amount in its raw form, or "as packaged." Food processors are required to calculate the "as consumed" values from foods prepared by common cooking methods and without added ingredients.

Another difference is that amounts of a new nutrient appear on the USDA labels for processed meat and poultry that never before appeared on a food label and is not allowed on packaged foods regulated by the FDA. This nutrient is a saturated fatty acid called stearic acid. Stearic acid is included in the total amount of saturated fat, but this particular fatty acid does not appear to raise blood-cholesterol levels the way other saturated fatty acids do. To get a better idea of how a particular meat might fit into a heart-healthy eating pattern, you can make a simple calculation: Subtract the amount of stearic acid from the total amount of saturated fat provided in a serving. You may find that some meats, particularly lean cuts of beef, do not have the same potential for raising cholesterol as it might seem from looking only at the total amount of saturated fat. This does not mean that the total amount of fat in these meats has changed: On the contrary, meats high in fat still contribute to weight gain, whether they are rich in stearic acid or contain only small amounts.

The USDA has also defined how the terms lean and extra lean may be used. Meat or poultry products labeled lean contain less than 10 grams of fat, less than four grams of saturated fat, and less than 95 mg of cholesterol in a three-ounce serving (the serving size is one cup for meat or poultry-based sauces). Extra-lean meat and poultry products must have half the fat and saturated fat per serving as lean products, but they can have the same amount of cholesterol.

Check the Ingredients

Regardless of what else is on the label, there is much valuable information to be learned about a food by studying its list of ingredients. All food labels list the ingredients in order of weight: The ingredient contained in the greatest amount is listed first; contained in the least amount is listed last. Therefore, if a product lists a fat (or oil) as the first ingredient, it contains more fat than any other ingredient.

Also pay special attention to the specific types of fats and oils the product contains. For example, some products simply list vegetable oil as an ingredient. While that may imply a healthful oil, remember two vegetable oils are highly saturated—coconut oil and palm oil. Remember, too, hydrogenated or partially hydrogenated vegetable oil products such as margarine and shortening are preferable to butter and lard for use as spreads or in cooking because they do not contain cholesterol. But since hydrogenation increases the saturated-fat content in the oils to make them solid, these hydrogenated products do not have the same effect on lowering cholesterol as the oils themselves. Hydrogenation also changes the structure of some of the polyunsaturated fatty acids into *trans* fatty acids. *Trans* fatty acids may actually raise blood cholesterol, though not as much as saturated fatty acids. The solution? Look for products that list a specific polyunsaturated vegetable oil like safflower, sunflower, corn, sesame, soybean, or cottonseed.

Choosing and Preparing Foods

It's important to keep in mind that both the foods you choose to eat and the way you choose to prepare them affect the amount of total fat, saturated fat, and cholesterol they provide. So we've included practical suggestions not only for choosing foods that are lower in total fat, saturated fat, and cholesterol, but for preparing those foods without adding fat, particularly saturated fat and cholesterol.

Meats

- Choose the leanest cuts of meat and decrease your usual portion size. Limit your daily meat intake to no more than six ounces, and use low-fat foods such as vegetables, pasta, and rice to fill in the meal. Substitute vegetable protein such as beans, tofu, and whole grains for meat when possible.
- Well-marbled meat (meat with streaks of fat running through it) is higher in total fat and saturated fat than meat with less marbling. While marbling tends to make the meat tastier, meats from the "round" cuts, which have less marbling, can be tasty if suitably prepared.
- The grade of beef, veal, and lamb reflects the fat content. Prime has the most fat, choice has less fat, and good has the least fat.
- Under the new regulations, terms such as lean and extra lean have specific meanings based on portions of 100 grams (about 3½ ounces). Lean means fewer than 10 grams of fat, four grams of saturated fat, and 95 milligrams of cholesterol. Extra lean means fewer than five grams of fat, fewer than two grams of saturated fat, and fewer than 95 milligrams of cholesterol per 100-gram portion. These descriptions also apply to poultry.
- Avoid or decrease your consumption of luncheon meats and other high-fat processed meats, including hot dogs, bacon, bologna, and sausages. Processed meats are also usually high in sodium.
- Organ meats such as liver, sweetbreads, and kidneys are high in cholesterol.
- Trim visible fat from meat.
- Instead of frying, try baking, broiling, or roasting. When roasting, place the meat on a rack so fat can drip away. When basting, use wine, lemon juice, or tomato juice rather than fatty drippings from the meat itself. Stir-frying can be a lower-fat alternative to other methods of frying because it does not require much fat; in addition, because cooking time is shorter, less fat is absorbed by the food.

Poultry

- Compared to meat, poultry is generally lower in saturated fat, so replace some of the meat dishes in your weekly menu plan with poultry dishes.
- Limit goose and duck, since they are very high in saturated fat.
- Remove the skin and visible fat before eating.
- Instead of frying, try baking, broiling, or roasting. When basting, use wine, lemon juice, or tomato juice instead of fatty drippings. When roasting, place the poultry on a rack so fat can drip away.

Fish

- Most fish is lower in saturated fat than poultry or meat, so choose fish more often.
- Although some varieties of shellfish, such as shrimp, are relatively high in cholesterol, shell-

fish generally has less saturated fat than meat, poultry, and most other varieties of fish.
- Instead of frying fish, try baking, broiling, or poaching.
- Choose tuna and other canned fish that comes packed in water; if that is impossible and only fish packed in oil is available, be sure to rinse it thoroughly in a strainer before preparing it.

Dairy Products
- Choose dairy products that come in low-fat varieties.
- Skim milk and one-percent milk provide the same nutrients as whole milk and two-percent milk—in fact, they have more protein and calcium—but they are much lower in saturated fat and cholesterol.
- Cream, half-and-half, whipped cream, and most nondairy creamers and whipped toppings are high in saturated fat (check the label) and should be avoided. Nondairy creamers sometimes contain vegetable oils that have been hydrogenated or partially hydrogenated, a process that increases their saturated-fat content and adds *trans* fatty acids.
- Most cheeses are high in saturated fat and cholesterol because they are made from whole milk. Natural and processed hard cheeses contain the most saturated fat. Imitation cheeses made with vegetable oil along with cheeses made partly with skim milk may contain less saturated fat, but they may still be higher in saturated fat than meat. Soft cheeses such as cottage, farmer, and pot cheese are your best choices because they are typically lower in fat than the others. Since cottage cheese can be sold with different levels of fat, make sure you read the label carefully and then choose only those varieties that contain one-percent milk fat or less.
- Cream cheese is high in saturated fat and should be avoided. Cream cheeses advertised as light may be lower in saturated fat, but you should still go easy on them because of the number of calories they contain.
- Grated Parmesan cheese can contribute less fat per serving than other cheeses because less is consumed in grated form.
- Ice cream, which is made from whole milk and cream and thus contains a good deal of saturated fat and cholesterol, should be limited. Try substituting frozen ice milk, frozen yogurt, or sherbets, all of which are low in saturated fat. Nonfat varieties, of course, contain no fat.

- Low-fat or nonfat yogurt is a heart-healthy food that can also be used as a substitute for high-fat foods. For example, drained, plain, nonfat yogurt can be substituted for sour cream as a topping for baked potatoes or for mayonnaise in salad dressings.

Eggs
- Egg yolks, which contain about 213 mg of cholesterol each, are too high in cholesterol to be regular items on your menu. Draw the line at three egg yolks a week, including those used in baked goods and processed foods (read the labels for ingredients).
- Egg whites, in contrast, contain no cholesterol, so for omelets and other recipes that call for eggs, substitute two egg whites for each egg.
- Try egg substitutes.

Fruits and Vegetables
- Because they come from plants, fruits and vegetables contain no cholesterol. With the exception of olives and avocados, fruits and vegetables are also low in fat. They make excellent side dishes and are nutritious substitutes for high-fat snacks and desserts.
- Avoid preparing vegetables with sauces made from butter, cream, or cheese.
- Use herbs and spices, onion, garlic, ginger, lemon and lime juice, and mustard instead of butter, fats, oil, cheese, or cream sauce to add flavor to vegetables.
- Cook vegetables as quickly as possible and use as little liquid as you can to help preserve their flavor and nutrient value.
- Leave the skins on potatoes, fruits, and vegetables, since this outer layer is high in fiber. Be sure to clean the skins well.

Cereals, Breads, Pasta, Rice, and Dried Peas and Beans
- These types of foods are all high in complex carbohydrates (starch and fiber). They are also low in saturated fat and therefore should be included frequently in your meals.
- Use pasta, rice, and dried peas and beans frequently as main dishes in place of meat, poultry, and fish.
- Try high-fiber grains such as buckwheat (kasha), brown rice, and cracked wheat (bulgur). Use them in place of white rice or white flour, as a side dish, and in soups and stews.
- Check labels to be sure the commercially prepared bread and cereal products you choose

are made with unsaturated fats—or you can make your own bread using polyunsaturated oils. Sometimes breakfast cereals can have added fat. Be careful of granola and other rich cereal mixes.

- Choose bread (and bagels, which are low-fat breads), English muffins, sandwich buns, and dinner rolls more often. Limit your consumption of croissants, butter rolls, sweet rolls, Danishes, bakery muffins, and doughnuts.
- Choose low-fat crackers, such as saltines and matzo, instead of snack crackers, (usually made with butter, cheese, or saturated oils).

Fats and Oils

- In cooking, instead of using butter, lard, fat-back, or solid shortening, use vegetable cooking spray, unsaturated vegetable oils, or soft margarine made from polyunsaturated vegetable oils. The softer the margarine, the less hydrogenated it is, and the fewer saturated fatty acids and *trans* fatty acids it contains. Tub margarines are better than stick margarines; squeeze-bottle margarines are better still.
- Use soft margarine made from polyunsaturated vegetable oils as a spread, instead of butter. The softer the margarine, the less hydrogenated it is, and the fewer saturated fatty acids it will contain.
- Choose commercially prepared products made with unsaturated, unhydrogenated vegetable oils. Limit those made with palm oil, palm kernel oil, or coconut oil.
- When making gravy or sauces, add flour or cornstarch to cold liquid slowly and blend well instead of adding fat.
- If you make soup or stew that contains meat or poultry, refrigerate it until the fat hardens on the surface. Remove the congealed fat before heating or serving.
- Instead of adding fats or fatty sauces and gravies for seasoning, use fresh herbs and spices.

Sweets and Snacks

- Many commercially prepared baked goods and snacks, such as cakes, cookies, pies, and some types of chips, are high in total fat, saturated fat, and cholesterol. They may also be sources of hydrogenated vegetable oils. Check the Cholesterol & Fat Counter at the back of this publication or compare package labels.
- Whenever possible, substitute baked goods made at home (using soft margarine instead of butter, skim milk instead of whole milk, and egg whites instead of whole eggs) for commercially prepared baked goods, which are often high in both saturated fat and cholesterol.
- Even home-prepared baked goods can be high in fat. Instead, choose fresh or dried fruits, vegetables, flavored ices, angel food cake, and breadsticks as snacks or desserts.
- Popcorn makes an excellent low-calorie, high-fiber snack as long as it is made using a low-fat method. Use an air popper rather than a standard popper or pan to prepare it. To make the air-popped variety more tasteful, spritz it lightly with water and season with herbs or low-fat grated cheese such as Parmesan. The water helps the seasoning stick to the popcorn. Microwave varieties can be very high in fat and, like some of the prepackaged stove-top varieties, can be sources of hydrogenated vegetable oils or saturated fats. There are now some lower-fat varieties available, but you need to read labels carefully.

A Word about Sodium

- While you limit your intake of cholesterol and saturated fat, you should also pay attention to dietary sodium. It is recommended that the average adult not consume more than 2,400 mg of sodium daily. To keep your sodium intake in a healthy range, check food labels, try to choose foods that have the lowest sodium values, and limit the use of sodium, both in cooking and at the table.

Recipes for a Low-Fat Lifestyle

In this section, you will find recipes designed to help you decrease your intake of total fat, saturated fat, and cholesterol. Every recipe is accompanied by a chart that lists the calories, grams (g) of total fat and saturated fat, and milligrams (mg) of sodium. This information can help you create healthy, varied meal plans.

While most of the recipes in this section get less than 30 percent of calories from fat and less than 10 percent from saturated fat, some are slightly above these levels. That does not mean that you need to avoid these recipes. They, too, can be part of a healthy diet plan. The key point is that you want your overall intake of total fat to be less than 30 percent of calories and your saturated fat intake to be less than 10 percent of total calories.

As you plan dishes for a meal and plan meals for the week, you should try to balance your food choices so that your overall intake of nutrients falls within the recommended guidelines. You do not need to cut out *every* food that is above the limits in terms of saturated fat and total fat. However, you should choose these higher-fat foods less frequently, eat smaller portions of them, and try to complement them with foods that are below the recommended limits, so that your overall diet is a healthy one. For example, if the entrée you choose for an evening meal gets slightly more than 30 percent of its calories from total fat, choose a low-fat vegetable side dish and a salad with a small amount of low-fat dressing to go along with it. By doing so, the total fat for the meal is likely to fit the guidelines nicely.

Remember, healthy eating does not mean depriving yourself of all the foods you enjoy. You don't have to buy food at specialty or health-food stores. Indeed, most of the recipes in this section use brand-name items available at your local grocery or supermarket. Healthy eating simply means making wiser food choices and adjusting your eating habits so that your diet works *for* you rather than *against* you.

The recipe and nutritional information in this section was submitted, in part, by participating companies and associations. Every effort has been made to check the accuracy of these numbers. However, because numerous variables account for a wide range of values for certain foods, all nutritive analyses in this section should be considered approximate. *The recipes in this book are NOT intended as a medically therapeutic program, nor as a substitute for medically approved diet plans for individuals on fat-, cholesterol-, or sodium-restricted diets. You should consult your physician before beginning any diet plan.*

The nutrient analysis for each of the recipes in this book includes all the ingredients that are listed for that recipe, except ingredients labeled "optional" or "for garnish." If a range is given in the yield of a recipe ("Makes 6 to 8 servings," for example), the *higher* yield was used to calculate the "per serving" information. If a range is offered for an ingredient ("¼ to ⅛ teaspoon," for example), the *first* amount given was used to calculate the nutritional information. If an ingredient is presented with an option ("2 tablespoons margarine or butter"), the *first* item listed was used to calculate the nutritional information. Foods offered as "serve with" suggestions at the end of a recipe are *not* included in the recipe analysis unless this is stated in the "per serving" line. When a recipe calls for "vegetable oil," canola oil was used to determine the nutritional information. Some nutrient values are listed as "tr." The "tr" means that only trace amounts of the substance are found in one serving of the recipe.

The technical review of this book by the American Dietetic Association does not imply an endorsement or recommendation of any brand-name product mentioned in the recipe section of this book.

Appetizers & Beverages

Spicy Chicken Bites

Makes 4 appetizer servings

½ cup lemon juice
¼ cup water
1 tablespoon dried rosemary, crushed
2 cloves garlic, minced
1 teaspoon hot pepper sauce
1 teaspoon Worcestershire sauce
2 boneless, skinless chicken breast halves, cut into small cubes
1 slice mixed grain bread, toasted
¼ cup BLUE DIAMOND® Chopped Natural Almonds, toasted
2 egg whites, lightly beaten

Combine lemon juice, water, rosemary, garlic, hot pepper sauce and Worcestershire sauce in small bowl. Stir in chicken cubes; cover and chill 24 hours. In blender or food processor, grind toast to coarse crumbs. Remove to a small bowl; stir in almonds. Lift chicken from marinade. Roll in egg whites, then in crumb mixture to coat evenly. Place on nonstick baking sheet. Bake at 400°F for 10 to 12 minutes. Serve hot or cold.

Nutrients per serving:

Calories	150	Cholesterol (mg)	34
Total Fat (g)	5	Sodium (mg)	100
Saturated Fat (g)	1		

Italian Bread Pizza

Makes 12 appetizer servings

1 large loaf Italian bread
1½ cups (6 ounces) shredded lower salt Monterey Jack cheese, divided
1 (16-ounce) jar prepared no-salt-added, no-sugar, no-fat pasta sauce
1½ tablespoons dried Italian seasoning
12 ounces ARMOUR® Lower Salt Ham, thinly sliced
1 (20-ounce) can pineapple rings, well drained
8 thin green pepper rings
8 thin red pepper rings

Slice bread lengthwise in half. Toast cut sides under broiler until lightly browned. Sprinkle ¼ cup of the cheese on each half; broil again about 1 to 2 minutes, or until cheese is melted. Combine pasta sauce and seasoning in small saucepan; cook over medium heat until hot. Spoon sauce evenly over bread halves; top evenly with ham and pineapple rings. Place green and red pepper rings alternately on top. Sprinkle each half with ½ cup of remaining cheese; place on baking sheet. Broil 4 to 5 inches from heat source about 4 to 6 minutes, or until cheese is melted. Cut each half into 6 pieces. Garnish with parsley, if desired.

Nutrients per serving:

Calories	253	Cholesterol (mg)	29
Total Fat (g)	6	Sodium (mg)	482
Saturated Fat (g)	3		

Guacamole

Makes 12 appetizer servings

1 package (4-serving size)
    JELL-O® Brand Lemon
    Flavor Sugar Free Gelatin
1 cup boiling water
1 container (16 ounces)
    1% lowfat cottage cheese
1 cup chopped ripe avocado
¾ cup chopped green onions,
    divided
¼ cup drained pickled jalapeño
    pepper slices
¼ cup lemon juice
2 garlic cloves
1 to 2 teaspoons chili powder
¼ cup diced tomato
4 chopped ripe olives
    Fresh vegetables (optional)
    Chili Tortilla Chips (recipe
    follows)

In small bowl, completely dissolve gelatin in boiling water. Pour into blender container. Add cottage cheese, avocado, ½ cup green onions, jalapeños, lemon juice, garlic cloves and chili powder. Blend on low speed, scraping down sides occasionally, about 2 minutes or until mixture is completely smooth. Pour into shallow 5-cup serving dish; smooth top. Chill until set, about 4 hours.

Just before serving, garnish with remaining ¼ cup chopped green onion, tomato and ripe olives. Serve as a dip with fresh vegetables or Chili Tortilla Chips.

Nutrients per serving:

Calories	60	Cholesterol (mg)	0
Total Fat (g)	3	Sodium (mg)	230
Saturated Fat (g)	tr		

Chili Tortilla Chips

6 (7-inch diameter) flour
    tortillas
    Non-stick cooking spray
    Chili powder

Heat oven to 350°F.

Lightly spray tortillas with non-stick cooking spray; sprinkle with chili powder. Turn tortillas over; repeat process. Cut into 8 pie-shaped wedges. Place on cookie sheet; bake 8 to 10 minutes until crisp and lightly browned. Makes 12 servings.

Nutrients per serving:

Calories	60	Cholesterol (mg)	0
Total Fat (g)	1	Sodium (mg)	90
Saturated Fat (g)	tr		

Black Bean Dip

Makes 2 ¼ cups

1 can (15 ounces) black beans,
    rinsed, drained
½ cup MIRACLE WHIP® FREE®
    Nonfat Dressing
½ cup reduced calorie sour cream
1 can (4 ounces) chopped green
    chilies, drained
2 tablespoons chopped cilantro
1 teaspoon chili powder
½ teaspoon garlic powder
    Few drops hot pepper sauce

Mash beans with fork. Stir in remaining ingredients until well blended; refrigerate. Serve with tortilla chips.

Prep time: 10 minutes plus refrigerating

Nutrients per serving (2 tablespoons):

Calories	70	Cholesterol (mg)	5
Total Fat (g)	1	Sodium (mg)	100
Saturated Fat (g)	1		

Mountain Cherry Smoothie

Makes 4 servings

2 ripe, medium DOLE®
    Bananas, peeled
1½ cups DOLE® Pure & Light
    Mountain Cherry Juice,
    chilled
1 cup peach sorbet or
    frozen peach yogurt,
    softened
1 cup sliced DOLE® Peaches

Place all ingredients in blender.
Process until smooth.

Nutrients per serving:

Calories	174	Cholesterol (mg)	0
Total Fat (g)	tr	Sodium (mg)	10
Saturated Fat (g)	tr		

Easy Chocolate Pudding Milk Shake

Makes 5 servings

3 cups cold skim milk
1 package (4-serving size)
    JELL-O® Chocolate Flavor
    Sugar Free Instant Pudding
    and Pie Filling
1½ cups vanilla ice milk

Pour milk into blender container.
Add remaining ingredients; cover.
Blend at high speed for 15 seconds
or until smooth. Serve at once.
(Mixture thickens as it stands.) Thin
with additional milk, if desired.

Nutrients per serving:

Calories	150	Cholesterol (mg)	10
Total Fat (g)	2	Sodium (mg)	370
Saturated Fat (g)	1		

Hot Orchard Peach Cup

Makes 6 servings

1 bottle (40 ounces) DOLE®
    Pure & Light Orchard Peach
    Juice
¼ cup brown sugar, packed
2 cinnamon sticks
2 tablespoons margarine
½ cup peach schnapps, optional
    Additional cinnamon sticks
    for garnish, optional

Combine juice, brown sugar,
cinnamon and margarine in Dutch
oven. Heat to a boil.

Remove from heat; discard
cinnamon sticks. Add schnapps, if
desired. Garnish with cinnamon
sticks, if desired.

Nutrients per serving:

Calories	181	Cholesterol (mg)	0
Total Fat (g)	4	Sodium (mg)	70
Saturated Fat (g)	1		

Orange Milk Shake

Makes 4 servings

2 cups skim milk
1 package (4-serving size)
    JELL-O® Brand Orange
    Flavor Sugar Free Gelatin
1 cup vanilla ice milk

Pour milk into blender container.
Add remaining ingredients; cover.
Blend at high speed 30 seconds or
until smooth. Serve at once.

Note: For a thicker shake, pour over
crushed ice or add 1 cup crushed ice
to ingredients in blender.

Nutrients per serving:

Calories	100	Cholesterol (mg)	10
Total Fat (g)	2	Sodium (mg)	150
Saturated Fat (g)	1		

Breakfast & Brunch

Gingerbread Pancakes

Makes 12 pancakes

1½ cups all-purpose flour
½ cup **SPOON SIZE®** Shredded Wheat, finely rolled (about ⅓ cup crumbs)
1 tablespoon **DAVIS®** Baking Powder
1 teaspoon pumpkin pie spice
1¼ cups skim milk
½ cup **EGG BEATERS®** 99% Real Egg Product
3 tablespoons **BRER RABBIT®** Light Molasses
2 tablespoons **FLEISCHMANN'S®** Margarine, melted

In large bowl, mix flour, cereal, baking powder and pumpkin pie spice. In small bowl, blend milk, egg product, molasses and margarine; stir into dry ingredients just until moistened.

On lightly greased preheated griddle or skillet, pour ¼ cup batter for each pancake. Cook over medium heat until surface is bubbly and bottom is lightly browned. Turn carefully and cook until done. Remove and keep warm. Repeat to make a total of 12 pancakes.

Nutrients per serving (1 pancake):

Calories	110	Cholesterol (mg)	1
Total Fat (g)	2	Sodium (mg)	128
Saturated Fat (g)	0		

Rice Bran Buttermilk Pancakes

Makes about 10 pancakes

1 cup rice flour or all-purpose flour
¾ cup rice bran
1 tablespoon sugar
1 teaspoon baking powder
½ teaspoon baking soda
1¼ cups low-fat buttermilk
3 egg whites, beaten
Vegetable cooking spray
Fresh fruit or reduced-calorie syrup (optional)

Sift together flour, bran, sugar, baking powder, and baking soda in large bowl. Combine buttermilk and egg whites in small bowl; add to flour mixture. Stir until smooth. Pour ¼ cup batter onto hot griddle coated with vegetable cooking spray. Cook over medium heat until bubbles form on top and underside is lightly browned. Turn to brown other side. Serve with fresh fruit or syrup.

Variation: For Cinnamon Pancakes, add 1 teaspoon ground cinnamon to dry ingredients.

Nutrients per serving (1 pancake):

Calories	99	Cholesterol (mg)	1
Total Fat (g)	2	Sodium (mg)	119
Saturated Fat (g)	1		

Favorite recipe from **USA Rice Council**

Double Oat Muffins

Makes 12 muffins

2 cups QUAKER® Oat Bran Hot
    Cereal, uncooked
⅓ cup firmly packed brown sugar
¼ cup all-purpose flour
2 teaspoons baking powder
¼ teaspoon salt (optional)
¼ teaspoon ground nutmeg
    (optional)
1 cup skim milk
2 egg whites, slightly beaten
3 tablespoons vegetable oil
1½ teaspoons vanilla
¼ cup QUAKER OATS® (quick or
    old fashioned, uncooked)
1 tablespoon firmly packed
    brown sugar

Heat oven to 400°F. Line 12 medium muffin cups with paper baking cups. Combine oat bran, ⅓ cup brown sugar, flour, baking powder, salt and nutmeg. Add combined milk, egg whites, oil and vanilla, mixing just until moistened. Fill muffin cups almost full. Combine oats and remaining 1 tablespoon brown sugar; sprinkle evenly over batter. Bake 20 to 22 minutes or until golden brown.

Microwave Directions: Line 6 microwaveable muffin cups with double paper baking cups. Combine oat bran, ⅓ cup brown sugar, flour, baking powder, salt and nutmeg. Add combined milk, egg whites, oil and vanilla, mixing just until moistened. Fill muffin cups almost full. Combine oats and remaining 1 tablespoon brown sugar; sprinkle evenly over batter. Microwave at HIGH (100% power) 2 minutes 30 seconds to 3 minutes or until wooden toothpick inserted in center comes out clean. Remove from pan; cool 5 minutes before serving. Line muffin cups with additional double paper baking cups. Repeat procedure with remaining batter.

Tips: To freeze muffins, wrap securely in foil or place in freezer bag. Seal, label and freeze.

To reheat frozen muffins, unwrap muffins. Microwave at HIGH about 30 seconds per muffin.

Nutrients per serving (1 muffin):

Calories	140	Cholesterol (mg)	0
Total Fat (g)	5	Sodium (mg)	90
Saturated Fat (g)	1		

Ham Breakfast Sandwich

Makes 3 sandwiches

1 ounce Neufchatel or light
    cream cheese, softened
2 teaspoons apricot
    spreadable fruit
2 teaspoons plain nonfat
    yogurt
6 slices raisin bread
    Lettuce leaves
1 package (6 ounces)
    ECKRICH® Lite Lower Salt
    Ham
3 Granny Smith apple rings

Combine cheese, spreadable fruit and yogurt in small bowl. Spread on bread.

To make each sandwich: Place lettuce on 1 slice bread. Top with 2 slices ham, 1 apple ring and another slice of bread.

Nutrients per serving (1 sandwich):

Calories	223	Cholesterol (mg)	37
Total Fat (g)	5	Sodium (mg)	963
Saturated Fat (g)	2		

Belgian Waffle Dessert

Makes 10 servings

1 package (4-serving size)
   JELL-O® Vanilla Flavor
   Sugar Free Instant Pudding
   and Pie Filling
2¼ cups cold 2% lowfat milk
2 tablespoons lemon juice
1 teaspoon grated lemon peel
1 cup thawed COOL WHIP®
   LITE® Whipped Topping
1 pint (about 2 cups)
   strawberries, quartered
½ pint (about 1 cup) raspberries
½ pint (about 1 cup) blueberries
   or blackberries
10 small frozen Belgian or
   regular waffles, toasted

Combine pudding mix, milk, lemon juice and peel in large mixing bowl. Beat with wire whisk until well blended, 1 to 2 minutes. Gently stir in whipped topping. Refrigerate.

In separate bowl, combine fruits; refrigerate.

Assemble desserts as needed for each serving. Spoon about 3 tablespoons pudding mixture on a dessert plate. Top with a waffle, an additional 2 tablespoons pudding mixture and a scant ½ cup fruit. Store leftover pudding mixture and fruit in refrigerator.

Nutrients per serving:

Calories	170	Cholesterol (mg)	5
Total Fat (g)	5	Sodium (mg)	310
Saturated Fat (g)	2		

Bran Sticky Buns

Makes 9 servings

1 cup NABISCO® 100% Bran,
   divided
⅓ cup firmly packed light brown
   sugar
¼ cup FLEISCHMANN'S®
   Margarine, melted
1 apple, cored and sliced
2 cups buttermilk baking mix
½ cup water
¼ cup EGG BEATERS® 99%
   Real Egg Product*

In small bowl, combine ¼ cup bran, brown sugar and margarine; spread in 8×8×2-inch pan. Top with apple slices; set aside.

In medium bowl, mix baking mix, remaining ¾ cup bran, water and egg product until soft dough forms. Drop dough by ¼ cupfuls over apple slices, forming 3 rows with 3 buns in each row.

Bake at 450°F for 13 to 15 minutes or until lightly browned. Invert onto heat-proof plate, leaving pan over buns for 2 to 3 minutes. Remove from pan; cool slightly. Serve warm.

*2 egg whites can be substituted

Nutrients per serving:

Calories	225	Cholesterol (mg)	0
Total Fat (g)	9	Sodium (mg)	490
Saturated Fat (g)	2		

Soups & Breads

Cuban Black Bean & Ham Soup

Makes 4 servings

1 cup uncooked black beans, soaked overnight and drained
1 slice (2 ounces) ARMOUR® Lower Salt Ham
½ cup chopped green bell pepper
1 medium onion, finely chopped
2 teaspoons MRS. DASH®, original blend
1 teaspoon garlic powder
1 teaspoon ground cumin
¼ teaspoon black pepper
1½ cups (6 ounces) ARMOUR® Lower Salt Ham, cut into ¾-inch cubes

Combine beans, ham slice, green pepper, onion and seasonings in medium saucepan; add enough water to just cover beans. Bring to boil; reduce heat, cover and simmer about 1½ to 2 hours, or until beans are tender and most of liquid is absorbed. Add ham cubes. Cook 10 minutes, or until ham is heated through. Remove ham slice before serving. Serve over rice, if desired.

Nutrients per serving:

Calories	244	Cholesterol (mg)	28
Total Fat (g)	4	Sodium (mg)	489
Saturated Fat (g)	1		

Chicken Lemon Soup Oriental

Makes 6 servings

1 can (16 ounces) California cling peach halves in juice or extra light syrup
8 cups water
2 chicken flavored bouillon cubes
2 cloves garlic, minced
1 pound skinless, boneless chicken breasts
¼ cup long grain white rice
2 cups fresh mushroom caps, cut in half
⅓ cup *each* sliced green onions and chopped cilantro
¼ cup lemon juice
1 tablespoon grated fresh ginger
¼ teaspoon red pepper flakes (optional)

Drain peaches, reserving all liquid. Dice peaches and set aside. Combine peach liquid with water, bouillon cubes and garlic. Bring to a boil; stir in chicken and rice. Simmer 15 minutes, or until chicken is cooked through. Remove chicken and chop into bite-size pieces. Stir chicken, reserved diced peaches and remaining ingredients into soup. Simmer 5 minutes.

Nutrients per serving:

Calories	160	Cholesterol (mg)	44
Total Fat (g)	1	Sodium (mg)	318
Saturated Fat (g)	1		

Favorite recipe from **California Cling Peach Advisory Board**

Beef Noodle Soup

Makes 6 servings

1 tablespoon CRISCO®
   PURITAN® Oil
½ pound boneless beef sirloin, cut
   into thin, bite-size pieces
½ cup coarsely shredded carrot
   (1 medium)
⅓ cup diced celery
1 clove garlic, minced
1 tablespoon all-purpose flour
7 cups water
3 tablespoons very low sodium
   beef flavor bouillon granules
1 tablespoon Worcestershire
   sauce
1 bay leaf
¼ teaspoon salt
¼ teaspoon dried basil leaves
1 cup ¼-inch-wide uncooked egg
   noodles
⅓ cup chopped green onions and
   tops
¼ cup chopped parsley

1. Heat CRISCO® PURITAN® Oil in
large saucepan on medium-high
heat. Add beef; sauté until browned.
Add carrot, celery and garlic. Sauté
until crisp-tender.

2. Stir in flour. Add water and next 5
ingredients. Simmer 20 minutes,
uncovered.

3. Add uncooked noodles, green
onions and parsley. Follow package
directions for cooking noodles.

4. Remove bay leaf before serving.

Nutrients per serving:

Calories	140	Cholesterol (mg)	15
Total Fat (g)	5	Sodium (mg)	150
Saturated Fat (g)	2		

Asparagus and Surimi Seafood Soup

Makes 4 servings

3 cans (10½ ounces *each*) low-
   sodium chicken broth (about
   4 cups)
2 thin slices fresh ginger
2 cups (about ¾ pound)
   diagonally sliced asparagus
   (½ inch long)
¼ cup sliced green onions,
   including part of green tops
3 tablespoons rice vinegar or
   white wine vinegar
¼ teaspoon crushed red pepper
8 to 12 ounces Surimi Seafood,
   crab flavored, chunk style or
   leg style, cut diagonally

Bring chicken broth and ginger to
a boil in a large saucepan. Add
asparagus, green onions, vinegar
and crushed pepper. Simmer 5
minutes or until the asparagus is
crisp-tender. Add Surimi Seafood
and simmer 5 minutes longer or
until seafood is hot. Remove and
discard ginger. Serve hot.

Nutrients per serving:

Calories	136	Cholesterol (mg)	18
Total Fat (g)	3	Sodium (mg)	784
Saturated Fat (g)	1		

Favorite recipe from **National Fisheries
Institute**

Wild Rice Soup

Makes about 4 cups; 4 servings

⅓ cup chopped carrot
⅓ cup chopped celery
⅓ cup chopped onion
2 teaspoons margarine or butter
1⅓ cups cooked wild rice
1 jar (12 ounces) HEINZ®
    HomeStyle Turkey Gravy
1½ cups skim milk
2 tablespoons dry sherry

In 2-quart saucepan over medium heat, sauté vegetables in margarine until tender. Stir in rice, gravy and milk. Simmer 5 minutes. Stir in sherry. Serve immediately.

Nutrients per serving:

Calories	164	Cholesterol (mg)	7
Total Fat (g)	4	Sodium (mg)	645
Saturated Fat (g)	1		

Broccoli Tarragon Soup

Makes 2 servings

2 cups DOLE® Broccoli florettes
1 can (14½ ounces) chicken broth
½ cup chopped onion
¼ teaspoon dried tarragon,
    crumbled

Combine all ingredients in saucepan. Cook, covered, until broccoli is tender but still bright green. Purée in blender. Chill before serving.

Nutrients per serving:

Calories	68	Cholesterol (mg)	0
Total Fat (g)	2	Sodium (mg)	925
Saturated Fat (g)	tr		

Hearty Minestrone Gratiné

Makes 4 servings

1 cup diced celery
1 cup diced zucchini
1 can (28 ounces) tomatoes with
    liquid, undrained, tomatoes
    chopped
2 cups water
2 teaspoons sugar
1 teaspoon dried Italian herb
    seasoning
1 can (15 ounces) garbanzo beans,
    drained
4 slices toasted French bread
    (each 3×½ inch)
1 cup (4 ounces) SARGENTO®
    Preferred Light Fancy
    Shredded Mozzarella Cheese
2 tablespoons SARGENTO®
    Grated Parmesan Cheese
Fresh parsley, chopped

Spray a large saucepan or Dutch oven with nonstick vegetable spray. Over medium heat, sauté celery and zucchini until tender. Add tomatoes, water, sugar and herb seasoning. Simmer, uncovered, 15 to 20 minutes. Add the garbanzo beans and heat an additional 10 minutes. Meanwhile, heat broiler. Place toasted French bread on broiler pan. Sprinkle mozzarella evenly over bread slices. Broil until cheese melts. Ladle soup into bowls and top with mozzarella French bread. Sprinkle Parmesan cheese evenly over each bowl and garnish with parsley. Serve immediately.

Nutrients per serving:

Calories	273	Cholesterol (mg)	15
Total Fat (g)	5	Sodium (mg)	999
Saturated Fat (g)	3		

Seafood Corn Chowder

Makes 6 servings

1 tablespoon margarine
1 cup chopped onions
½ cup chopped green bell pepper
½ cup chopped red bell pepper
⅓ cup chopped celery
1 tablespoon all-purpose flour
1 can (10½ ounces) low-sodium chicken broth
2 cups skim milk
1 can (12 ounces) evaporated skim milk
8 to 12 ounces Surimi Seafood, crab flavored, chunk style
2 cups fresh or frozen whole kernel corn
½ teaspoon black pepper
½ teaspoon paprika

Melt margarine in large saucepan over medium heat. Add onions, peppers and celery. Cook, uncovered, over medium heat for 4 to 5 minutes or until vegetables are soft. Add flour to vegetable mixture; cook and stir constantly for 2 minutes. Gradually add chicken broth and bring to a boil. Add milk, evaporated milk, Surimi Seafood, corn, black pepper and paprika. Heat, stirring occasionally, 5 minutes or until chowder is hot. Serve.

Nutrients per serving:

Calories	217	Cholesterol (mg)	17
Total Fat (g)	3	Sodium (mg)	630
Saturated Fat (g)	1		

Favorite recipe from **National Fisheries Institute**

Golden Tomato Soup

Makes 8 servings

4 teaspoons reduced-calorie margarine
1 cup chopped onion
2 cloves garlic, coarsely chopped
½ cup chopped carrots
¼ cup chopped celery
8 medium-size tomatoes, blanched, peeled, seeded and chopped
6 cups chicken broth
1 ounce uncooked rice
2 tablespoons tomato paste
1 tablespoon Worcestershire sauce
¼ to ½ teaspoon black pepper
½ teaspoon dried thyme
5 drops hot pepper sauce

Melt margarine in large Dutch oven over medium-high heat. Add onion and garlic; cook and stir 1 to 2 minutes or until tender. Add carrots and celery; cook 7 to 9 minutes or until tender, stirring frequently. Stir in tomatoes, broth, rice, tomato paste, Worcestershire sauce, pepper, thyme and hot pepper sauce. Reduce heat to low; cook about 30 minutes, stirring frequently.

Remove from heat and let cool about 10 minutes. In food processor or blender, process soup in small batches until smooth. Return soup to Dutch oven; simmer 3 to 5 minutes or until heated through. Garnish as desired.

Nutrients per serving:

Calories	91	Cholesterol (mg)	1
Total Fat (g)	2	Sodium (mg)	641
Saturated Fat (g)	1		

Favorite recipe from **Florida Tomato Committee**

Vegetable Dinner Rolls

Makes 12 rolls

2 cups all purpose flour
1 cup whole-wheat flour
2 cups KELLOGG'S®
     BRAN FLAKES cereal
2 tablespoons sugar
½ teaspoon salt
1 teaspoon herb-spice seasoning
1 package active dry yeast
1 cup water
2 tablespoons margarine
2 egg whites
1 cup shredded zucchini
½ cup shredded carrots
¼ cup sliced green onions
2 teaspoons sesame seeds
     (optional)

In small bowl, stir together flours. In large electric mixer bowl, combine KELLOGG'S BRAN FLAKES cereal, 1 cup of the flour mixture, the sugar, salt, seasoning and yeast. Set aside.

Heat water and margarine until warm (115° to 120°F). Add to cereal mixture with egg whites. Beat on low speed with electric mixer 30 seconds or until thoroughly combined. Increase speed to high and beat 3 minutes longer, scraping bowl frequently. Mix in vegetables.

By hand, stir in enough remaining flour mixture to make sticky dough. Cover loosely. Let rise in warm place (80° to 85°F) until double in volume. Stir down dough. Portion evenly into 12 (2½-inch) muffin-pan cups coated with nonstick cooking spray. Sprinkle with sesame seeds, if desired. Let rise in warm place until double in volume.

Bake at 400°F about 17 minutes or until golden brown. Serve warm.

Nutrients per serving (1 roll):

Calories	170	Cholesterol (mg)	0
Total Fat (g)	2	Sodium (mg)	156
Saturated Fat (g)	tr		

Whole Wheat Herb Muffins

Makes 12 muffins

1 cup all-purpose flour
1 cup whole wheat flour
⅓ cup sugar
2 teaspoons baking powder
½ teaspoon baking soda
½ teaspoon salt
½ teaspoon dried basil leaves
¼ teaspoon dried marjoram leaves
¼ teaspoon dried oregano leaves
⅛ teaspoon dried thyme leaves
¾ cup raisins
1 cup buttermilk
2 tablespoons margarine or
     butter, melted
1 egg, beaten
2 tablespoons wheat germ

Preheat oven to 400°F. Grease 12 (2½-inch) muffin cups. In large bowl, combine flours, sugar, baking powder, baking soda, salt, herbs and raisins. In small bowl, combine buttermilk, margarine and egg. Stir into flour mixture just until dry ingredients are moistened. Spoon into muffin cups. Sprinkle wheat germ on tops. Bake 15 to 20 minutes or until lightly browned and wooden toothpick inserted in center comes out clean. Remove from pan.

Nutrients per serving (1 muffin):

Calories	152	Cholesterol (mg)	19
Total Fat (g)	3	Sodium (mg)	230
Saturated Fat (g)	1		

Entrées

Orange Roughy with Cucumber Relish

Makes 4 servings

1 can (11 ounces) mandarin oranges, drained
1 small cucumber, peeled, seeded, finely chopped
⅓ cup HEINZ® Distilled White Vinegar
1 green onion, minced
1 tablespoon snipped fresh dill *or* 1 teaspoon dried dill weed
Nonstick cooking spray
4 orange roughy fillets (about 5 ounces *each*)
Dill sprigs

Reserve 8 orange sections for garnish; coarsely chop remaining sections and combine with cucumber, vinegar, onion and dill. Spray broiler pan with cooking spray; place fish on pan. Spoon 1 tablespoon liquid from cucumber mixture over each fillet. Broil, 3 to 4 inches from heat source, 8 to 10 minutes or until fish just flakes when tested with fork. To serve, spoon cucumber relish on top of fish. Garnish with reserved orange sections and dill sprigs.

Nutrients per serving:

Calories	178	Cholesterol (mg)	34
Total Fat (g)	6	Sodium (mg)	115
Saturated Fat (g)	tr		

Pepper-Chicken Fettuccini Toss

Makes 12 servings

1 (1-pound) package CREAMETTE® Fettuccini, uncooked
¼ cup olive or vegetable oil
3 whole boneless skinless chicken breasts, cut into strips (about 18 ounces)
2 large red bell peppers, cut into strips
2 large yellow bell peppers, cut into strips
1 medium green bell pepper, cut into strips
1 medium onion, cut into chunks
2 cups sliced fresh mushrooms
1 teaspoon salt-free herb seasoning
2 tablespoons grated Parmesan cheese

Prepare CREAMETTE® Fettuccini according to package directions; drain. In large skillet, heat oil; add chicken, bell peppers, onion, mushrooms and seasoning. Cook and stir over medium heat until chicken is cooked through, 8 to 10 minutes. Add hot cooked fettuccini and Parmesan cheese; toss to coat. Serve immediately. Refrigerate leftovers.

Nutrients per serving:

Calories	264	Cholesterol (mg)	36
Total Fat (g)	7	Sodium (mg)	33
Saturated Fat (g)	1		

Garden Style Pizza

Makes 8 servings

Crust
  1 cup QUAKER OATS® (quick or
    old fashioned, uncooked)
1¼ cups all-purpose flour
  1 teaspoon baking powder
  ½ teaspoon salt (optional)
  ¾ cup skim milk
  2 tablespoons vegetable oil

Topping
  2 cups sliced mushrooms
1½ cups shredded carrots
  1 cup thinly sliced zucchini
  ½ cup chopped onion
  1 teaspoon vegetable oil
  1 can (8 ounces) pizza sauce
1½ cups (6 ounces) shredded part-
    skim mozzarella cheese
  ½ teaspoon Italian seasoning
    (optional)

For Crust, heat oven to 425°F. Spray 12-inch round pizza pan with no-stick cooking spray or oil lightly. Place oats in blender container or food processor bowl; cover. Blend about 1 minute, stopping occasionally to stir. Combine ground oats, flour, baking powder and salt. Add milk and oil; stir with fork until mixture forms a ball. Knead dough on lightly floured surface about 10 times. With greased fingers, press dough into prepared pan; shape edge to form rim. Bake 20 minutes or until light golden brown.

For Topping, sauté mushrooms, carrots, zucchini and onion in oil over medium heat about 3 minutes. Spoon pizza sauce over partially baked crust, spreading evenly to edge; top with sautéed vegetables. Sprinkle with cheese and Italian

seasoning; continue baking about 15 minutes or until cheese is melted.

Nutrients per serving:

Calories	244	Cholesterol (mg)	13
Total Fat (g)	9	Sodium (mg)	300
Saturated Fat (g)	3		

Tuna-Lettuce Bundles

Makes 1 serving

  2 large leaves leaf lettuce
  1 can (3¼ ounces) STARKIST®
    Tuna, drained and broken
    into small chunks
  ½ cup shredded red cabbage
  ¼ cup shredded zucchini
  ¼ cup alfalfa sprouts
  1 tablespoon reduced-calorie
    Thousand Island or blue
    cheese dressing
    Pepper to taste
  2 red or green bell pepper rings

Trim stalks from lettuce leaves. In a small bowl toss together tuna, cabbage, zucchini and sprouts. Stir in dressing; season to taste with pepper. Spoon ½ of the salad mixture in center of each leaf. Roll up leaves, enclosing filling. Secure lettuce bundles by slipping a bell pepper ring over each. Place bundles seamside down on plate.

Nutrients per serving:

Calories	190	Cholesterol (mg)	43
Total Fat (g)	2	Sodium (mg)	570
Saturated Fat (g)	tr		

Microwave Oriental Swordfish Steaks

Makes 4 servings

1 pound swordfish steaks
2 tablespoons orange juice
1 tablespoon low-sodium soy sauce
1 tablespoon catsup
1 tablespoon chopped parsley
2 teaspoons sesame oil
1 teaspoon lemon juice
1/4 teaspoon dried oregano
1/8 teaspoon pepper
1 small clove garlic, minced
1 (8-ounce) can sliced water chestnuts, drained
1 large orange, peeled, seeded and sectioned

Place steaks in large, shallow microwave-safe dish, with thickest areas to outside edges of dish. Combine remaining ingredients, except water chestnuts and orange sections, and pour over steaks. Cover with plastic wrap and refrigerate 30 minutes, turning once. Top steaks with water chestnuts. Re-cover dish with plastic wrap, turning back one corner to vent. Microwave on High power (100%) 2 minutes. Rotate dish 1/4 turn and top steaks with orange sections. Re-cover, vent, and microwave on High power (100%) an additional 2 to 3 minutes, or until fish flakes with fork. Let stand, covered, 2 to 3 minutes.

Nutrients per serving:

Calories	209	Cholesterol (mg)	41
Total Fat (g)	5	Sodium (mg)	304
Saturated Fat (g)	1		

Favorite recipe from **National Fisheries Institute**

Spinach Lasagna

Makes 8 servings

2 cups lowfat cottage cheese (1% milkfat)
2 (10-ounce) packages frozen chopped spinach, thawed
1/2 cup EGG BEATERS® 99% Real Egg Product
1 teaspoon Italian seasoning
2 cups no-salt-added spaghetti sauce
9 cooked lasagna noodles, prepared without added salt
1 cup shredded part-skim mozzarella cheese (about 4 ounces)
3 tablespoons grated Parmesan cheese

In medium bowl, combine cottage cheese, spinach, egg product and Italian seasoning; set aside.

Spread 1/2 cup spaghetti sauce in bottom of greased 13×9×2-inch baking dish. Layer 1/3 each of cooked noodles, spinach filling and remaining sauce; repeat twice. Sprinkle top with mozzarella cheese and Parmesan cheese; cover. Bake at 375°F for 20 minutes. Uncover; bake an additional 25 minutes. Let stand 10 minutes before serving.

Nutrients per serving:

Calories	260	Cholesterol (mg)	12
Total Fat (g)	7	Sodium (mg)	196
Saturated Fat (g)	2		

Greek Lamb Sauté with Mostaccioli

Makes 8 servings

½ of a (1-pound) package CREAMETTE® Mostaccioli, uncooked
1 tablespoon olive or vegetable oil
1 medium green bell pepper, chopped
1 medium onion, chopped
1 medium eggplant, peeled, seeded and cut into 1-inch cubes
2 cloves garlic, minced
¼ pound lean boneless lamb, cut into ¾-inch cubes
2 fresh tomatoes, peeled, seeded and chopped
¼ teaspoon ground nutmeg
¼ cup grated Parmesan cheese

Prepare CREAMETTE® Mostaccioli according to package directions; drain. In large skillet, heat oil; add green pepper, onion, eggplant and garlic. Cook and stir until tender-crisp. Add lamb; cook until tender. Stir in tomatoes and nutmeg; heat through. Toss mixture with hot cooked mostaccioli and Parmesan cheese. Serve immediately. Refrigerate leftovers.

Nutrients per serving:

Calories	205	Cholesterol (mg)	29
Total Fat (g)	5	Sodium (mg)	82
Saturated Fat (g)	2		

Rotini Stir-Fry

Makes 8 servings

½ of a (1-pound) package CREAMETTE® Rotini, uncooked
2 tablespoons olive or vegetable oil
2 whole boneless skinless chicken breasts, cut into strips (about 12 ounces)
1 cup fresh broccoli flowerets
1 cup carrot curls
½ cup sliced red onion
¼ cup water
½ teaspoon WYLER'S® Chicken-Flavor Instant Bouillon
½ teaspoon dried tarragon leaves
2 tablespoons grated Parmesan cheese

Prepare CREAMETTE® Rotini according to package directions; drain. In large skillet, heat oil; add chicken, broccoli, carrots and onion. Cook and stir over medium heat until broccoli is tender-crisp. Add water, bouillon and tarragon; cook and stir until chicken is cooked through. Add hot cooked rotini and Parmesan cheese; toss to coat. Serve immediately. Refrigerate leftovers.

Note: To reduce sodium, substitute low-sodium bouillon.

Nutrients per serving:

Calories	225	Cholesterol (mg)	37
Total Fat (g)	6	Sodium (mg)	123
Saturated Fat (g)	1		

Chef Paul's Macaroni and Cheese

Makes 10 servings

1½ cups chopped onions
¾ cup chopped celery
2 tablespoons plus 1 teaspoon Chef Paul Prudhomme's PORK & VEAL MAGIC®
½ cup defatted chicken stock, divided
5 egg whites
1 container (12 ounces) lowfat cottage cheese
1 can (12 ounces) evaporated skim milk
1 to 2 teaspoons salt (optional)
10 cups cooked small elbow macaroni (from 5 cups uncooked)
6 ounces (1½ cups) lowfat cheddar cheese (7 grams fat per ounce), shredded

Preheat oven to 375°F.

Heat 10-inch skillet over high heat. Add chopped onions, celery and Pork & Veal Magic. Cook 2 minutes, then stir to blend in seasoning. When vegetables begin to stick hard to the pan (about 2 to 3 minutes), add ¼ cup stock; scrape up the brown on the pan bottom, stir well and cook 1 to 2 minutes. Turn heat down to medium and stir. Cook until vegetables begin to stick hard again, about 4 to 5 minutes, and add the remaining ¼ cup stock. Scrape pan bottom, stir well and continue cooking another 4 to 5 minutes. Remove from heat and let cool slightly.

Place egg whites in food processor. Process 30 to 45 seconds, or until the egg whites are frothy (but *not* until they form peaks). Add the cottage cheese and milk and process. Don't let the mixture get too smooth; a bit of lumpiness in the cottage cheese will give the dish more texture. Add the cooled mixture from the skillet and process again, about 20 seconds. Add salt to taste, if desired. Place the cooked, drained macaroni into a bowl, pour the sauce over and mix well. Pour into an *un*buttered casserole dish, sprinkle the cheddar cheese on top and bake at 375°F for 35 to 40 minutes or until brown and bubbly.

Nutrients per serving:

Calories	235	Cholesterol (mg)	14
Total Fat (g)	4	Sodium (mg)	679
Saturated Fat (g)	2		

Turkey Bacon Club Sandwich

Makes 2 sandwiches

4 slices LOUIS RICH® Turkey Bacon
4 teaspoons reduced-calorie mayonnaise
4 slices whole wheat bread, toasted
2 lettuce leaves
4 thin slices tomato
4 slices LOUIS RICH® Oven Roasted Deli-Thin Turkey Breast

Heat Turkey Bacon in nonstick skillet over medium heat for 8 to 10 minutes or until lightly browned; cut slices in half. For each sandwich, spread 2 teaspoons mayonnaise on one toast slice; top with half the Turkey Bacon, lettuce, tomato, Turkey Breast and another toast slice.

Nutrients per serving (1 sandwich):

Calories	255	Cholesterol (mg)	30
Total Fat (g)	10	Sodium (mg)	845
Saturated Fat (g)	2		

Linguine Primavera

Makes 8 servings

2 tablespoons olive or vegetable oil
2 tablespoons lemon juice
1 medium red bell pepper, cut into strips
1 large onion, chopped
1 package (8 ounces) fresh mushrooms, sliced
½ pound lean fully cooked ham, cut into julienne strips
1 package (10 ounces) frozen green peas, thawed
1 package (6 ounces) frozen snow peas, thawed
1 can (5 ounces) evaporated skimmed milk
½ cup shredded Provolone cheese, divided
½ of a (1-pound) package CREAMETTE® Linguine
Fresh ground pepper

In large skillet, heat oil and lemon juice over medium-high heat. Add red pepper, onion and mushrooms; cook until tender-crisp. Add ham, green peas, snow peas, milk and ¼ cup cheese; heat through, stirring frequently. Keep warm. Prepare CREAMETTE® Linguine according to package directions; drain. Combine hot cooked linguine and vegetable mixture; toss to coat. Top with remaining ¼ cup cheese. Serve immediately with fresh ground pepper. Refrigerate leftovers.

Note: To reduce sodium, substitute ½ pound fully cooked turkey breast for the ham.

Nutrients per serving:

Calories	273	Cholesterol (mg)	22
Total Fat (g)	8	Sodium (mg)	493
Saturated Fat (g)	3		

Scallop Kabobs

Makes 8 kabobs

¼ cup REALEMON® Lemon Juice from Concentrate
2 tablespoons vegetable oil
1 teaspoon dried oregano leaves
½ teaspoon dried basil leaves
1 clove garlic, finely chopped
⅛ teaspoon salt
1 pound sea scallops
8 ounces fresh mushrooms
2 small zucchini, cut into chunks
2 small onions, cut into wedges
½ red, yellow or green bell pepper, cut into bite-size pieces
Additional REALEMON® brand

In shallow dish, combine ReaLemon® brand, oil and seasonings; add scallops. Cover; marinate in refrigerator 2 hours, stirring occasionally. Remove scallops from marinade; discard marinade. Divide scallops and vegetables equally among 8 skewers. Grill or broil as desired until scallops are opaque, basting frequently with additional ReaLemon® brand. Refrigerate leftovers.

Nutrients per serving (2 kabobs):

Calories	213	Cholesterol (mg)	37
Total Fat (g)	8	Sodium (mg)	255
Saturated Fat (g)	1		

Salads

Chef's Salad

Makes 3 ½ cups or 3 servings

1 package (4-serving size)
  JELL-O® Brand Lemon Flavor
  Sugar Free Gelatin
¼ teaspoon salt
¾ cup boiling water
½ cup cold water
  Ice cubes
1 tablespoon vinegar
2 teaspoons reduced-calorie
  French dressing
¼ teaspoon Worcestershire sauce
⅛ teaspoon white pepper
¾ cup chopped tomato
½ cup finely shredded lettuce
½ cup slivered cooked turkey
  breast
½ cup slivered Swiss cheese
2 tablespoons chopped scallions
2 tablespoons chopped radishes

Completely dissolve gelatin and salt in boiling water. Combine cold water and ice cubes to make 1¼ cups. Add to gelatin mixture, stirring until slightly thickened. Remove any unmelted ice. Stir in vinegar, dressing, Worcestershire sauce and pepper. Chill until slightly thickened.

Stir remaining ingredients into gelatin mixture. Spoon into 3 individual plastic containers or dishes. Chill until firm, about 2 hours.

Nutrients per serving:

Calories	100	Cholesterol (mg)	30
Total Fat (g)	4	Sodium (mg)	330
Saturated Fat (g)	2		

Chinese Chicken Salad

Makes 6 servings

3 cups cooked rice
1 cup cooked chicken breast
  cubes
1 cup sliced celery
1 can (8 ounces) sliced water
  chestnuts, drained
1 cup fresh bean sprouts*
½ cup (about 2 ounces) sliced
  fresh mushrooms
¼ cup sliced green onions
¼ cup diced red pepper
3 tablespoons lemon juice
2 tablespoons reduced-sodium
  soy sauce
2 tablespoons sesame oil
2 teaspoons grated fresh ginger
  root
¼ to ½ teaspoon ground white
  pepper
  Lettuce leaves

In large bowl, combine rice, chicken, celery, water chestnuts, bean sprouts, mushrooms, onions and red pepper. Combine lemon juice, soy sauce, oil, ginger root and white pepper in small jar with lid. Pour over rice mixture; toss lightly. Serve on lettuce leaves.

*Substitute canned bean sprouts, rinsed and drained, for fresh bean sprouts, if desired.

Nutrients per serving:

Calories	248	Cholesterol (mg)	20
Total Fat (g)	6	Sodium (mg)	593
Saturated Fat (g)	1		

Favorite recipe from **USA Rice Council**

Lemony Apple-Bran Salad

Makes 6 servings

½ cup plain low-fat yogurt
1 tablespoon chopped parsley
1 teaspoon sugar
1 teaspoon lemon juice
½ teaspoon salt
2 cups chopped, cored red apples
½ cup thinly sliced celery
½ cup halved green grapes *or*
    ¼ cup raisins
½ cup KELLOGG'S®
    ALL-BRAN® cereal

1. In medium-size bowl, combine yogurt, parsley, sugar, lemon juice and salt. Stir in apples, celery and grapes or raisins. Cover and refrigerate until ready to serve.

2. Just before serving, stir in KELLOGG'S ALL-BRAN cereal. Serve on lettuce, if desired.

Nutrients per serving:

Calories	60	Cholesterol (mg)	1
Total Fat (g)	1	Sodium (mg)	260
Saturated Fat (g)	tr		

Yogurt Dressing

Makes 2 cups

2 cups plain lowfat yogurt
4 teaspoons chopped fresh mint
    or ¼ teaspoon dried dill weed
¼ teaspoon TABASCO® pepper
    sauce

In small bowl combine yogurt, mint and TABASCO® pepper sauce; mix well. Cover; refrigerate.

Nutrients per serving (1 tablespoon):

Calories	10	Cholesterol (mg)	0
Total Fat (g)	0	Sodium (mg)	10
Saturated Fat (g)	0		

Tuna & Fresh Fruit Salad

Makes 4 servings

Lettuce leaves (optional)
1 can (12½ ounces) STARKIST®
    Tuna, drained and broken into
    chunks
4 cups slices or wedges fresh
    fruit*
¼ cup slivered almonds (optional)
Fruit Dressing
  1 container (8 ounces) lemon,
      mandarin orange or vanilla
      low-fat yogurt
  2 tablespoons orange juice
  ¼ teaspoon ground cinnamon

Line a large platter or 4 individual plates with lettuce leaves, if desired. Arrange tuna and desired fruit in a decorative design over lettuce. Sprinkle almonds over salad if desired.

For Fruit Dressing: In a small bowl stir together yogurt, orange juice and cinnamon until well blended. Serve dressing with salad.

Suggested fresh fruit: Apples, bananas, berries, citrus fruit, kiwifruit, melon, papaya, peaches or pears.

Nutrients per serving (including ¼ cup dressing):

Calories	233	Cholesterol (mg)	39
Total Fat (g)	1	Sodium (mg)	434
Saturated Fat (g)	tr		

Confetti Rice Salad

Makes 6 servings

2 chicken flavored bouillon
   cubes
1 cup long grain white rice
1 can (16 ounces) California cling
   peach slices in juice or extra
   light syrup
3 tablespoons tarragon-flavored
   white wine vinegar
1 tablespoon Dijon-style mustard
1 tablespoon olive oil
¼ teaspoon dried tarragon
1 cup chopped red bell peppers
½ cup frozen peas, thawed
⅓ cup raisins
¼ cup sliced green onions

In medium saucepan, combine
chicken bouillon cubes and 2 cups
water; bring mixture to a boil. Stir in
rice. Cover and simmer 20 minutes,
until liquid is absorbed and rice is
tender. Remove from heat; cool 5
minutes. Drain peaches, reserving
¼ cup liquid. Save remainder for
other uses. Cut peach slices in half
and set aside. Mix reserved peach
liquid with vinegar, mustard, olive
oil and tarragon. Stir into cooled
rice; add remaining ingredients
except reserved peaches. Cool
completely, tossing occasionally. Stir
in reserved peaches and chill before
serving.

Nutrients per serving:

Calories	210	Cholesterol (mg)	tr
Total Fat (g)	3	Sodium (mg)	317
Saturated Fat (g)	tr		

Favorite recipe from **California Cling Peach
Advisory Board**

Light Pasta Salad

Makes 6 servings

½ cup MIRACLE WHIP® LIGHT
   Reduced Calorie Salad
   Dressing with no cholesterol
½ cup KRAFT® "Zesty" Italian
   Reduced Calorie Dressing
2 cups (6 ounces) corkscrew
   noodles, cooked, drained
1 cup broccoli flowerets, partially
   cooked
⅓ cup chopped green bell pepper
½ cup chopped tomato
¼ cup green onion slices

In large bowl, mix salad dressings
until well blended. Add remaining
ingredients; mix lightly. Refrigerate.
Serve with freshly ground black
pepper if desired.

Prep time: 15 minutes

Nutrients per serving:

Calories	180	Cholesterol (mg)	0
Total Fat (g)	6	Sodium (mg)	460
Saturated Fat (g)	1		

Cucumbers and Onions

Makes 6 servings

1 medium cucumber, thinly
   sliced
1 small onion, thinly sliced
1 can (5 fluid ounces) PET® Light
   Evaporated Skimmed Milk
¼ cup vinegar
1 teaspoon salt
1 teaspoon dried dill weed

In medium bowl, combine
cucumber and onion. In small bowl,
combine remaining ingredients and
pour over cucumber and onion; toss
well. Chill before serving.

Nutrients per serving:

Calories	33	Cholesterol (mg)	1
Total Fat (g)	0	Sodium (mg)	389
Saturated Fat (g)	0		

Creamy Fruit Mold

Makes 7 servings

1 package (0.3 ounces) sugar free
    lime flavor gelatin
1 cup boiling water
1 cup PET® Light Evaporated
    Skimmed Milk
2 cups fresh fruit, cut up*

Dissolve gelatin in boiling water.
Cool slightly to prevent milk from
curdling. Stir in evaporated
skimmed milk. Chill until mixture is
the consistency of unbeaten egg
whites. Stir in fruit. Pour into an
8-inch square pan or a 5-cup mold.
Chill until firm. Garnish with
additional fruit.

Suggested fresh fruit: Apples, bing
cherries, oranges, peaches or
strawberries.

Nutrients per serving:

Calories	51	Cholesterol (mg)	1
Total Fat (g)	0	Sodium (mg)	77
Saturated Fat (g)	0		

Thousand Island Dressing

Makes about 2 cups

⅔ cup PET® Light Evaporated
    Skimmed Milk
⅔ cup bottled chili sauce
⅔ cup safflower oil
¼ cup sweet pickle relish
1 tablespoon lemon juice
1 tablespoon sugar
½ teaspoon salt
⅛ teaspoon ground black pepper

Using a wire whisk, combine all
ingredients in a small bowl.
Refrigerate until well chilled. Serve
over tossed green salad.

Nutrients per serving (1 tablespoon):

Calories	54	Cholesterol (mg)	0
Total Fat (g)	5	Sodium (mg)	129
Saturated Fat (g)	tr		

Bombay Banana Salad

Makes 6 servings

Salad
  2 DOLE® Oranges
  2 firm DOLE® Bananas, peeled,
    sliced
  1 cup seedless red DOLE® Grapes
  ¼ cup DOLE® Whole Almonds,
    toasted
Dressing
  1 ripe DOLE® Banana, peeled
  12 DOLE® Pitted Dates, halved
  ½ cup dairy sour cream
  1 tablespoon brown sugar or
    honey
  1 tablespoon chopped chutney
  ½ teaspoon curry powder

Salad: Grate peel from 1 orange;
reserve peel for dressing. Peel and
slice oranges. In bowl, toss salad
ingredients with dressing.

Dressing: Combine all ingredients
in blender or food processor. Blend
until smooth. Stir in grated orange
peel.

Nutrients per serving:

Calories	240	Cholesterol (mg)	9
Total Fat (g)	9	Sodium (mg)	13
Saturated Fat (g)	3		

Vegetable & Side Dishes

Red, Green & Gold Squash Platter

Makes 8 servings

1 pound red bell peppers (3 medium)
2 tablespoons olive oil
1/4 teaspoon grated lemon peel
1 tablespoon lemon juice
1/2 teaspoon dried dill weed
  Salt and pepper to taste
3 cups *each* sliced zucchini and crookneck squash
1/3 cup BLUE DIAMOND® Sliced Natural Almonds, toasted

Core and quarter red bell peppers. Place in single layer in glass baking dish. Cover; microwave at High power (100%) for 10 minutes. Process peppers and remaining ingredients except squash and almonds in blender container or food processor until smooth. Place squash in 9×9-inch square glass baking dish. Cover; microwave at High power 3 to 4 minutes, until tender-crisp. Spoon squash onto serving platter. Sprinkle with almonds. Drizzle with red pepper sauce to serve.

Nutrients per serving:

Calories	84	Cholesterol (mg)	0
Total Fat (g)	6	Sodium (mg)	140
Saturated Fat (g)	1		

Crispened New Potatoes

Makes 4 servings

1½ pounds very small, scrubbed new potatoes (about 12)
1/2 cup QUAKER® Oat Bran Hot Cereal, uncooked
2 tablespoons grated Parmesan cheese
1 tablespoon snipped fresh parsley *or* 1 teaspoon dried parsley flakes
1/2 teaspoon snipped fresh dill *or* 1/2 teaspoon dried dill weed
1/2 teaspoon paprika
1/4 cup skim milk
1 egg white, slightly beaten
1 tablespoon margarine, melted

Heat oven to 400°F. Lightly spray 11×7-inch dish with vegetable oil cooking spray or oil lightly. Cook whole potatoes in boiling water 15 minutes. Drain; rinse in cold water.

In shallow dish, combine oat bran, cheese, parsley, dill and paprika. In another shallow dish, combine milk and egg white. Coat each potato in oat bran mixture; shake off excess. Dip into egg mixture, then coat again with oat bran mixture. Place into prepared dish; drizzle with margarine. Cover; bake 10 minutes. Uncover; bake an additional 10 minutes or until potatoes are tender.

Nutrients per serving (about 3 potatoes):

Calories	230	Cholesterol (mg)	0
Total Fat (g)	5	Sodium (mg)	110
Saturated Fat (g)	1		

Colorful Cauliflower Bake

Makes 6 servings

1 cup KELLOGG'S® ALL-BRAN®
 cereal
2 tablespoons margarine, melted
¼ teaspoon garlic salt
¼ cup flour
½ teaspoon salt (optional)
⅛ teaspoon white pepper
1⅓ cups skim milk
1 chicken bouillon cube
1 package (16 ounces) frozen,
 cut cauliflower, thawed,
 well drained
½ cup sliced green onions
2 tablespoons drained, chopped
 pimento

1. Combine KELLOGG'S ALL-BRAN cereal, margarine and garlic salt; set aside.

2. In 3-quart saucepan, combine flour, salt and pepper. Gradually add milk, mixing until smooth, using a wire whip if necessary. Add bouillon cube. Cook, stirring constantly, over medium heat until bubbly and thickened. Remove from heat.

3. Add cauliflower, onions and pimento, mixing until combined. Spread evenly in 1½-quart baking dish. Sprinkle with cereal mixture.

4. Bake at 350°F about 20 minutes or until thoroughly heated and sauce is bubbly.

Note: 3½ cups fresh cauliflower flowerets, cooked crisp-tender, may be substituted for frozen cauliflower.

Nutrients per serving:

Calories	120	Cholesterol (mg)	1
Total Fat (g)	4	Sodium (mg)	316
Saturated Fat (g)	1		

Cheese-Crumb Baked Tomatoes

Makes 4 servings

¾ cup finely shredded Wisconsin
 Part-Skim Mozzarella
 Cheese (3 ounces), divided
⅓ cup fine, dry, unseasoned
 bread crumbs
1 to 1½ tablespoons fresh
 chopped herbs (oregano,
 parsley, rosemary) *or* 1 to
 1½ teaspoons dried herbs
1 large clove garlic, pressed
4 tomatoes (about 2½ inches
 in diameter), cored and
 cut into 3 slices *each*

In bowl mix *half* the cheese, the bread crumbs, herbs and garlic until thoroughly blended. Arrange tomato slices on oiled baking sheet. Top each with some of the crumb mixture, then with the remaining cheese, dividing equally. Bake in 475°F oven 10 to 12 minutes until crumbs are lightly browned.

Nutrients per serving:

Calories	112	Cholesterol (mg)	13
Total Fat (g)	4	Sodium (mg)	171
Saturated Fat (g)	2		

Favorite recipe from **Wisconsin Milk Marketing Board © 1992**

Eggplant Italiano

Makes 8 servings

1 eggplant (1 pound), peeled if desired
1 can (6 ounces) low sodium cocktail vegetable juice (¾ cup)
½ cup QUAKER® Oat Bran Hot Cereal, uncooked
2 garlic cloves, minced
1 teaspoon dried basil leaves, crushed
½ teaspoon dried oregano leaves
2 medium tomatoes, chopped
1¼ cups (5 ounces) shredded part-skim mozzarella cheese

Heat oven to 350°F. Line cookie sheet or 15 × 10-inch baking pan with foil. Lightly spray with no-stick cooking spray or oil lightly. Cut eggplant into ½-inch-thick slices; place in single layer on prepared pan. Combine vegetable juice, oat bran, garlic, basil and oregano. Spread evenly over eggplant; top with tomatoes. Sprinkle with mozzarella cheese. Bake 35 to 40 minutes or until eggplant is tender and cheese is melted. Sprinkle with additional basil or oregano, if desired.

Nutrients per serving:

Calories	95	Cholesterol (mg)	10
Total Fat (g)	4	Sodium (mg)	95
Saturated Fat (g)	2		

Almond Ratatouille

Makes 6 servings

¾ pound small new potatoes
2 tomatoes, chopped
1 medium eggplant, cubed (about 4 cups)
2 medium zucchini, sliced (about 2 cups)
1 red pepper, sliced
1 onion, thinly sliced
½ cup vegetable cocktail juice
2 tablespoons *each* chopped fresh cilantro and lime juice
2 tablespoons Balsamic or red wine vinegar
2 cloves garlic, minced
1 tablespoon chopped fresh basil*
1½ teaspoons chopped fresh dill*
⅔ cup blanched slivered almonds, toasted

Cut potatoes in half to form bite-sized pieces. Place in 8 × 12-inch microwave-safe dish. Cover; microwave on High Power (100%) 2 minutes. Stir in remaining ingredients except almonds. Cover; microwave on High Power 15 minutes, stirring every 5 minutes until vegetables are tender-crisp and potatoes are cooked through. Remove from oven; stir in almonds and chill thoroughly before serving.

*Or use 1 teaspoon dried basil *and* ½ teaspoon dried dill.

Note: Hot Almond Ratatouille makes a wonderful topping for baked potatoes or broiled fish.

Nutrients per serving:

Calories	190	Cholesterol (mg)	0
Total Fat (g)	8	Sodium (mg)	86
Saturated Fat (g)	tr		

Favorite recipe from **Almond Board of California**

Holiday Stir-Fry

Makes 4 servings

¾ teaspoon finely chopped fresh
  jalapeño, or to taste
1 clove garlic, minced
2 tablespoons HOLLYWOOD®
  Peanut or Safflower Oil
20 fresh green beans, ends
  trimmed
3 cups fresh spinach, washed
  and trimmed
2 cups finely shredded red
  cabbage
⅓ cup chopped red bell pepper
¾ cup sliced mushrooms

In a large skillet, cook jalapeño and garlic in hot oil for 30 seconds. Add green beans and stir-fry for 1 minute. Cover and cook an additional 2½ minutes. Add remaining ingredients except mushrooms and stir-fry for 2 minutes. Add mushrooms and stir-fry an additional 1½ minutes. Serve hot.

Nutrients per serving:

Calories	89	Cholesterol (mg)	0
Total Fat (g)	7	Sodium (mg)	36
Saturated Fat (g)	1		

Vegetable Soufflé in Pepper Cups

Makes 6 servings

1 cup chopped broccoli
½ cup shredded carrot
¼ cup chopped onion
1 teaspoon dried basil leaves
½ teaspoon ground black pepper
2 teaspoons FLEISCHMANN'S®
  Margarine
2 tablespoons all-purpose flour
1 cup skim milk
1 container (8 ounces)
  EGG BEATERS® 99% Real Egg
  Product
3 large red, green or yellow bell
  peppers, halved lengthwise,
  membrane and seeds removed

In nonstick skillet, over medium-high heat, cook broccoli, carrot, onion, basil and pepper in margarine until tender. Stir in flour until smooth. Gradually add milk, stirring constantly until thickened. Remove from heat; set aside.

In medium bowl, with electric mixer at high speed, beat egg product until foamy, about 3 minutes. Gently fold into broccoli mixture; spoon into pepper halves. Place in 13×9×2-inch baking pan. Bake at 375°F for 30 to 35 minutes or until knife inserted into center comes out clean. Garnish as desired; serve immediately.

Prep time: 15 minutes
Total time: 1 hour

Nutrients per serving:

Calories	75	Cholesterol (mg)	1
Total Fat (g)	2	Sodium (mg)	91
Saturated Fat (g)	tr		

"Lite" Apricot Stuffing

Makes 8 servings

1 cup sliced celery
¾ cup chopped onion
1½ cups turkey broth or reduced-
   sodium chicken bouillon
16 slices reduced-calorie bread,
   cubed and dried
2 tablespoons parsley flakes
1½ teaspoons poultry seasoning
½ teaspoon salt
2 egg whites
¼ cup dried apricots, chopped

In small saucepan, over medium-high heat, combine celery, onion and turkey broth; bring to a boil. Reduce heat to low; cover and simmer 5 minutes or until vegetables are tender.

In large bowl, combine celery mixture and remaining ingredients. Spoon into lightly greased 2-quart casserole dish; cover. Bake at 350°F about 30 minutes or until heated through.

Nutrients per serving:

Calories	164	Cholesterol (mg)	tr
Total Fat (g)	2	Sodium (mg)	566
Saturated Fat (g)	tr		

Favorite recipe from **National Turkey Federation**

Light Italian Spaghetti Primavera

Makes 6 servings

½ of a (1-pound) package
   CREAMETTE® Thin
   Spaghetti, uncooked
½ cup bottled reduced-calorie
   Italian salad dressing
1 medium green bell pepper,
   chopped
1 medium red bell pepper,
   chopped
1 medium yellow squash, cut into
   strips
1 cup sliced fresh mushrooms
¼ cup chopped onion
3 tablespoons sliced pitted olives
¼ cup (1 ounce) shredded part-
   skim mozzarella cheese
3 tablespoons chopped fresh
   parsley

Prepare CREAMETTE® Thin Spaghetti according to package directions; drain. In large skillet, combine salad dressing, vegetables and olives; simmer just until vegetables are tender-crisp. Serve over hot cooked spaghetti; sprinkle with cheese and parsley. Refrigerate leftovers.

Nutrients per serving:

Calories	205	Cholesterol (mg)	8
Total Fat (g)	5	Sodium (mg)	218
Saturated Fat (g)	1		

Desserts

It's the Berries Pie

Makes 8 servings

1 quart fresh strawberries,
    washed and hulled, reserving
    8 for garnish
1 KEEBLER® Ready-Crust® Butter
    Flavored pie crust
1½ cups fresh or frozen raspberries
    (without sugar)
2 tablespoons sugar
1 package (0.3 ounces) triple
    berry or raspberry flavored
    sugar-free gelatin
1 cup boiling water
    Reduced-calorie whipped
    topping (optional)

Place prepared whole strawberries, hullside down, in pie crust. Purée raspberries and sugar in blender container or food processor. Press through a sieve to remove seeds. Set raspberry purée aside. Prepare gelatin according to package directions using 1 cup boiling water. Chill until slightly thickened. Stir raspberry purée into gelatin and pour over strawberries. Chill until firm. Garnish each serving with a dollop of whipped topping and a fresh berry, if desired.

Nutrients per serving:

Calories	164	Cholesterol (mg)	0
Total Fat (g)	5	Sodium (mg)	154
Saturated Fat (g)	1		

Peachy Snack Cake

Makes 12 servings

2 tablespoons margarine, melted
¼ cup firmly packed brown sugar
3 cups KELLOGG'S® RAISIN
    BRAN cereal, divided
1 cup all-purpose flour
¼ teaspoon salt
1 teaspoon baking powder
1 teaspoon ground cinnamon
¼ teaspoon ground nutmeg
¼ cup margarine, softened
½ cup granulated sugar
2 eggs
1 can (16 ounces) sliced cling
    peaches, drained, cut into
    bite-size pieces

1. In small bowl, combine 2 tablespoons margarine, brown sugar and 1½ cups KELLOGG'S RAISIN BRAN cereal; set aside.

2. Combine flour, salt, baking powder and spices; set aside.

3. In medium-size bowl, beat together ¼ cup margarine, granulated sugar and eggs until well combined. Stir in peaches. Add flour mixture and remaining 1½ cups cereal, stirring until combined. Spread evenly in greased 9×9×2-inch baking pan. Sprinkle with cereal mixture.

4. Bake in 350°F oven about 30 minutes or until cake tester inserted in center comes out clean. Serve warm or cold.

Nutrients per serving:

Calories	210	Cholesterol (mg)	46
Total Fat (g)	7	Sodium (mg)	243
Saturated Fat (g)	1		

Peach Yogurt Pie with Almond Melba Sauce

Makes 8 servings

Peach Yogurt Pie
  2 cups fresh, frozen or canned peaches
  2 tablespoons granulated sugar
  1 tablespoon almond-flavored liqueur
  1 quart vanilla-flavored ice milk or frozen yogurt, softened
  1 KEEBLER® Ready-Crust® Butter Flavored pie crust

Almond Melba Sauce
  2 cups fresh or frozen raspberries
  ⅓ cup confectioners' sugar
  2 tablespoons almond-flavored liqueur
  1 tablespoon lemon juice

Optional Garnishes
    Light whipped topping
    Sliced peaches
    Raspberries

To prepare Pie, place peaches, granulated sugar and liqueur in blender container or food processor. (If using fresh peaches, add 1 teaspoon lemon juice.) Cover and blend until smooth. Fold peach purée into softened ice milk or yogurt. Spoon into pie crust and freeze until firm.

To prepare Sauce, place berries, confectioners' sugar, liqueur and lemon juice in blender container or food processor. Cover and process until smooth. Strain to remove seeds. Chill.

To serve, remove pie from freezer and let stand 5 minutes. Slice pie and top each serving with sauce, a dollop of whipped topping and additional peaches and raspberries, if desired.

Nutrients per serving:

Calories	298	Cholesterol (mg)	9
Total Fat (g)	9	Sodium (mg)	203
Saturated Fat (g)	3		

Applesauce Cookies

Makes about 5 dozen cookies

  1 cup all-purpose flour
  1 teaspoon baking powder
  1 teaspoon ground cinnamon
  ½ teaspoon ground nutmeg
  ½ teaspoon ground cloves
  ¼ teaspoon salt
  ½ cup margarine, softened
  ½ cup brown sugar
  2 egg whites
  2 cups rolled oats (uncooked)
  1 cup unsweetened applesauce
  ½ cup chopped raisins

Preheat oven to 375°F. Grease cookie sheet. Mix flour, baking powder, cinnamon, nutmeg, cloves and salt in small bowl; set aside. In large bowl, beat margarine and sugar until creamy. Add egg whites; beat well. Add reserved dry ingredients. Stir in oats, applesauce and raisins, mixing well. Drop by level tablespoonfuls onto prepared cookie sheet. Bake 11 minutes or until edges are lightly browned. Cool on wire rack.

Nutrients per serving (1 cookie):

Calories	45	Cholesterol (mg)	0
Total Fat (g)	2	Sodium (mg)	34
Saturated Fat (g)	tr		

Favorite recipe from **Western New York Apple Growers Association**

Raisin Streusel Bars

Makes 12 bars

Bars

2 cups KELLOGG'S® RAISIN
   BRAN cereal
¾ cup whole wheat flour
¾ cup all-purpose flour
¾ cup firmly packed brown sugar
½ teaspoon baking soda
¼ teaspoon salt
¼ teaspoon ground cinnamon
⅓ cup margarine, softened
2 tablespoons water
½ cup strawberry preserves

Orange Glaze

½ cup powdered sugar
1 teaspoon water
3 tablespoons orange marmalade

1. **To make Bars:** In medium-size bowl, combine KELLOGG'S RAISIN BRAN cereal, flours, brown sugar, baking soda, salt and cinnamon. Using pastry blender, cut in margarine until mixture resembles coarse crumbs. Stir in water. Set aside 1 cup of the cereal mixture. Press remaining mixture in bottom of greased 9×9×2-inch baking pan.

2. Spread strawberry preserves evenly over cereal mixture in bottom of pan. Sprinkle with reserved cereal mixture.

3. Bake in 350°F oven about 25 minutes or until lightly browned; cool completely.

4. **To make Glaze:** In small bowl, combine powdered sugar, water and marmalade until thoroughly combined. Drizzle over cooled bars.

Variation: ½ cup orange marmalade may be substituted for the strawberry preserves.

Nutrients per serving (1 bar):

Calories	240	Cholesterol (mg)	0
Total Fat (g)	5	Sodium (mg)	202
Saturated Fat (g)	1		

Chocolate Chip Cookies

Makes 3 dozen cookies

2 cups all-purpose flour
1 teaspoon baking soda
½ teaspoon salt
1 egg
3 tablespoons water
1 teaspoon vanilla
1 cup firmly packed brown sugar
¼ cup CRISCO® PURITAN® Oil
½ cup semi-sweet chocolate chips

1. Heat oven to 375°F. Grease cookie sheets well.

2. Combine flour, baking soda and salt. Set aside.

3. Combine egg, water and vanilla. Set aside.

4. Blend brown sugar and CRISCO® PURITAN® Oil in large bowl at low speed of electric mixer. Add egg mixture. Beat until smooth. Add flour mixture in three parts at lowest speed. Scrape bowl well after each addition. Stir in chocolate chips.

5. Drop dough by rounded teaspoonfuls onto cookie sheets.

6. Bake at 375°F for 7 to 8 minutes or until lightly browned. Cool on cookie sheets 1 minute. Remove to cooling rack.

Nutrients per serving (1 cookie):

Calories	80	Cholesterol (mg)	10
Total Fat (g)	2	Sodium (mg)	60
Saturated Fat (g)	1		

Chocolate Cake Squares

Makes 20 squares

Chocolate Cake
¾ **cup all purpose flour**
½ **cup cocoa powder**
⅓ **cup cornstarch**
1 **teaspoon baking powder**
½ **teaspoon baking soda**
½ **teaspoon salt**
⅔ **cup granulated sugar**
2 **egg whites**
½ **cup evaporated skim milk**
¾ **cup MOTT'S® Natural Apple Sauce**
½ **cup light corn syrup**
1 **teaspoon vanilla extract**

Cocoa Icing
1½- 2 **cups confectioners sugar**
2 **tablespoons cocoa powder**
½ **teaspoon vanilla extract**
1 **tablespoon cold skim milk or coffee**
Water as needed

Preheat oven to 350°F. Spray 8×8×2-inch baking pan with non-stick cooking spray.

1. **For Cake:** In a medium bowl, sift together flour, cocoa, cornstarch, baking powder, baking soda and salt. Stir in sugar. Set aside.

2. In a separate bowl, whisk together egg whites and milk. Whisk in MOTT'S apple sauce, corn syrup and vanilla. Add dry mixture and stir until blended.

3. Pour batter into prepared pan and bake 35 to 40 minutes, or until knife inserted into center comes out clean. Turn cake onto wire rack and cool completely. Spread with Cocoa Icing and cut into squares.

4. **For Cocoa Icing:** Sift together sugar and cocoa. Add vanilla and cold liquid and beat with a wire whisk until smooth, adding water if needed.

Nutrients per serving (1 square):

Calories	140	Cholesterol (mg)	0.27
Total Fat (g)	0.37	Sodium (mg)	136
Saturated Fat (g)	0.18		

Frozen Apple Sauce 'n Fruit Cup

Makes 7 (½-cup) servings

1 **cup MOTT'S® Chunky or Regular Apple Sauce**
1 **package (10 ounces) frozen strawberries, thawed**
1 **can (11 ounces) mandarin orange segments, drained**
1 **cup grapes, if desired**
2 **tablespoons orange juice concentrate**

In medium bowl, combine all ingredients. Spoon fruit mixture into individual dishes or paper cups. Freeze until firm. Remove from freezer about 30 minutes before serving.

Nutrients per serving:

Calories	107	Cholesterol (mg)	0
Total Fat (g)	0	Sodium (mg)	5
Saturated Fat (g)	0		

Fat and Cholesterol Counter

To help you choose foods that are low in total fat, saturated fat, and cholesterol, we have included this counter. The counter provides calorie, total fat, saturated fat, and cholesterol information for hundreds of generic and brand-name products.

You will find the individual food items grouped into categories, like "Cheese" and "Poultry," which are listed in alphabetical order. After a brief description of each food item, a specific portion size is given.

For an individual food item, you will find the calorie content (CAL.), the total fat (FAT) content in grams (g), the saturated fat (SAT. FAT) content in grams (g), and the cholesterol content (CHOL.) in milligrams (mg). These values apply to the specific portion size listed for that individual food item. The fat values are further broken down to show you what percentage of the food's calories come from fat and from saturated fat, so that you can tell at a glance how well a food item will fit into your dietary plan. The percentage figures can be particularly useful when you are comparing similar foods, because the percentage of fat or saturated fat in a given food item doesn't change, regardless of the portion size. For example, look up buttermilk in the counter. You will find that 18 percent of its calories come from fat. This is true whether you drink a cupful or a cartonful.

In contrast, if you compare foods on the basis of how many grams of fat each one contains, then these components will vary with the quantity eaten (if one cup of buttermilk contains two grams of fat, two cups contain four grams of fat). Using this method, you must consider equal quantities—or estimate them—in order to accurately compare different foods. This can sometimes be difficult, however, because nutritional information comes from a variety of sources that do not necessarily list nutrients in comparable portion sizes.

With a simple formula, you can calculate the fat and saturated fat percentages for foods not included on our list. Multiply the grams of fat (or saturated fat) for an item by 9, divide the result by the total number of calories that item contains, then multiply your answer by 100. This gives the percentage of total calories that comes from fat (or saturated fat). For example, one tablespoon of butter contains 11 grams of fat and has 100 calories. Using the formula, multiply 11 by 9 to get 99, divide 99 by 100 to get 0.99, and multiply 0.99 by 100 to get 99 percent. Thus, 99 percent of the calories in one tablespoon of butter comes from fat.

Some food items have an "na" or a "tr" listed in one of the columns. The "na" means that the content was unavailable to us at the time of printing. The "tr" means that the food item contains only trace amounts of the substance. When trace amounts are shown for grams of fat or saturated fat, it is impossible to calculate exact percentages, so "na" is used. However, as a practical matter, if only trace amounts of these elements are present, the percentage of calories they provide is generally quite low, usually less than ten percent.

The symbol "<" means "less than," so "<1" indicates the presence of less than one unit of whatever is being measured (less than one percent, less than one gram). Fractional amounts have been rounded off.

Values in this counter were obtained from the United States Department of Agriculture and from food labels, manufacturers, and processors. While every effort has been made to ensure that the values listed are accurate and current at the time of printing, changes in the values can occur at the time of food processing.

Baked Goods

FOOD/PORTION SIZE	CAL.	FAT		SAT. FAT		CHOL. (mg)
		Total (g)	As % of Cal.	Total (g)	As % of Cal.	
CAKE						
Angel Food Cake Mix, Duncan Hines, 1/12 of cake	140	0	0	0	0	0
Chocolate Loaf, Fat & Cholesterol Free, Entenmann's, 1 oz. slice	70	0	0	0	0	0
Coffeecake, Butter Streusel, Sara Lee, 1/8 of cake (1.4 oz.)	160	7	39	na	na	na
Cupcakes Lights, Hostess, 1 cupcake, 1½ oz.	130	2	14	0	0	0
Devil's Food Cake Mix, Moist Deluxe, Duncan Hines, 1/12 of cake, regular recipe	280	15	48	4	13	65
Same as above, no-cholesterol recipe	270	14	47	2	7	0
Fudge Marble Supreme Cake Mix, Moist Deluxe, Duncan Hines, 1/12 of cake, regular recipe	260	11	38	3	10	65
Same as above, no-cholesterol recipe	250	10	36	2	7	0
Gingerbread Cake & Cookie Mix, Betty Crocker, 1/9 of cake (1.6 oz.), regular recipe	220	7	29	2	8	30
Same as above, no-cholesterol recipe	210	6	26	0	0	0
Golden Loaf, Fat & Cholesterol Free, Entenmann's, 1 oz. slice	70	0	0	0	0	0
Lemon Supreme Cake Mix, Moist Deluxe, Duncan Hines, 1/12 of cake, regular recipe	260	11	38	3	10	65
Same as above, no-cholesterol recipe	250	10	36	2	7	0
Orange Supreme Cake Mix, Duncan Hines, 1/12 of cake, regular recipe	260	11	38	3	10	65
Same as above, no-cholesterol recipe	250	10	36	2	7	0
Pound Cake, All-Butter, Sara Lee, 1 oz.	130	7	48	0	0	na
Pound Cake, Free & Light, Sara Lee, 1 oz.	70	0	0	0	0	0
Spice Cake Mix, Moist Deluxe, Duncan Hines, 1/12 of cake, regular recipe	260	11	38	3	10	65
Same as above, no-cholesterol recipe	250	10	36	2	7	0
Strawberry Supreme Cake Mix, Moist Deluxe, Duncan Hines, 1/12 of cake, regular recipe	260	11	38	3	10	65
Same as above, no-cholesterol recipe	250	10	36	2	7	0
Twinkies Lights, Hostess, 1 cake, 1½ oz.	130	2	14	0	0	0
White Cake Mix, Lovin' Lites, Pillsbury (using egg whites), 1/12 of cake	170	2	11	<1	na	0

FOOD/PORTION SIZE	CAL.	FAT		SAT. FAT		CHOL. (mg)
		Total (g)	As % of Cal.	Total (g)	As % of Cal.	
White Cake Mix, Moist Deluxe, Duncan Hines, regular recipe, 1/12 of cake	270	12	40	3	11	65
Same as above, no-cholesterol recipe	250	10	36	2	7	0
Yellow Cake Mix, Moist Deluxe, Duncan Hines, 1/12 of cake, regular recipe	260	11	38	3	10	65
Same as above, no-cholesterol recipe	250	10	36	2	7	0
COOKIES						
Chocolate Chip, Chips Ahoy, Nabisco, 1 cookie	50	2	36	tr	<1	0
Chocolate chip, refrigerated dough, 1 cookie	56	3	48	1	16	6
Chocolate Chip Mix, Duncan Hines, 1 cookie	65	3	42	2	28	8
Fig Newtons, Nabisco, 1 cookie	60	1	15	tr	<1	0
Nilla Wafers, Nabisco, 3 cookies	60	2	3	tr	tr	5
Oatmeal Raisin, Fat & Cholesterol Free, Entenmann's, 2 cookies	80	0	0	0	0	0
Oreos, Nabisco, 1 cookie	50	2	36	tr	<1	<2
Peanut Butter Mix, Duncan Hines, 1 cookie	70	4	51	1	13	8
Sandwich (chocolate or vanilla), 1 cookie	49	2	37	1	18	0
Shortbread, commercial, 1 small cookie	39	2	46	1	23	7
Sugar, refrigerated dough, 1 cookie	59	3	46	1	15	7
Teddy Grahams Bearwiches, Nabisco, 4 cookies	70	3	39	tr	<1	0
PASTRY						
Coffeecake, Easy Mix, Aunt Jemima, 1/8 of cake	170	5	26	na	na	na
Danish, fruit, 4¼-in. round, 1 pastry	235	13	50	4	15	56
Danish, plain, 1 oz.	110	6	49	2	16	24
Danish, plain, 4¼-in. round, 1 pastry	220	12	49	4	16	49
Toaster, 1 pastry	210	6	26	2	9	0
PIE						
(All pies include crust made with enriched flour and vegetable shortening.)						
Apple, 1/6 of 9-in. pie	405	18	40	5	11	0
Apple, Homestyle, Sara Lee, 1/6 of pie	433	20	42	na	na	0
Blueberry, 1/6 of 9-in. pie	380	17	40	4	9	0
Cherry, 1/6 of 9-in. pie	410	18	40	5	11	0

FOOD/PORTION SIZE	CAL.	FAT		SAT. FAT		CHOL.
		Total (g)	As % of Cal.	Total (g)	As % of Cal.	(mg)
Custard, ⅛ of 9-in. pie	330	17	46	6	16	169
Lemon meringue, ⅛ of 9-in. pie	355	14	35	4	10	143
Peach, ⅛ of 9-in. pie	405	17	38	4	9	0
Pecan, ⅛ of 9-in. pie	575	32	50	5	8	95
Piecrust, Butter Flavor, Keebler, 1 shell, 6 oz.	880	40	41	8	8	0
Piecrust, Chocolate Flavor, Keebler, 1 shell, 6 oz.	960	40	38	8	8	0
Piecrust, Graham Cracker, Keebler, 1 shell, 6 oz.	960	48	45	8	8	0
Piecrust, Graham Cracker, single serve, Keebler, 1 shell	100	5	45	1	9	0
Piecrust, mix, 9-in., 2-crust pie	1485	93	56	23	14	0
Piecrust, Pet Ritz, 1 shell	720	48	60	12	15	0
Piecrust, Pet Ritz, Deep Dish, all vegetable shortening, 1 shell	780	54	62	12	14	0
Pumpkin, ⅛ of 9-in. pie	320	17	48	6	17	109
MISCELLANEOUS						
Brownies, Fudge, Light, Betty Crocker, ¹⁄₂₄ of package as prepared	100	1	9	na	na	0
Brownies, Fudge Brownie Mix, Duncan Hines, 1 brownie	130	5	35	na	na	0
Doughnuts, cake, plain, 1 doughnut	210	12	51	3	13	20
Doughnuts, yeast, glazed, 1 doughnut	192	13	61	5	23	29
Pizza Crust, All Ready, Pillsbury, ⅛ of crust	90	1	10	0	0	0

Baking Products & Condiments

FOOD/PORTION SIZE	CAL.	FAT		SAT. FAT		CHOL.
		Total (g)	As % of Cal.	Total (g)	As % of Cal.	(mg)
Bacos, 2 tsp.	25	1	36	na	na	0
Baking Powder, Davis, 1 tsp.	8	0	0	0	0	0
Baking soda for home use, 1 tsp.	5	0	0	0	0	0
Barbecue Sauce, Kraft, 1 tbsp.	23	tr	na	tr	na	0
Barbecue Sauce, Original, Open Pit, 1 tbsp.	25	0	0	0	0	0
Barley, pearled, light, uncooked, 1 cup	700	2	3	<1	tr	0
Bulgur, uncooked, 1 cup	600	3	5	1	2	0
Butterscotch Topping, Artificially Flavored, Kraft, 1 tbsp.	60	1	15	0	0	0

FOOD/PORTION SIZE	CAL.	FAT		SAT. FAT		CHOL. (mg)
		Total (g)	As % of Cal.	Total (g)	As % of Cal.	
Cajun Magic Seasoning, K-Paul Enterprises, 1 tsp.	20	0	0	0	0	0
Caramel Topping, Kraft, 1 tbsp.	60	0	0	0	0	0
Catsup, 1 tbsp.	15	tr	na	tr	na	0
Catsup, Weight Watchers, 1 tbsp.	12	0	0	0	0	0
Celery seed, 1 tsp.	10	1	90	tr	na	0
Chili powder, 1 tsp.	10	tr	na	<1	na	0
Chili Sauce, Bennet's, 1 tbsp.	16	0	0	0	0	0
Chili Sauce, Heinz, 1 tbsp.	16	0	0	0	0	0
Chocolate, Semi-Sweet, Baker's, 1 oz.	140	15	96	na	na	0
Chocolate, Unsweetened Chocolate Baking Bar, Baker's, 1 oz.	140	15	96	na	na	0
Chocolate Caramel Topping, Kraft, 1 tbsp.	60	0	0	0	0	0
Chocolate Chips, Mini, Hershey's, ¼ cup	220	12	49	7	29	10
Chocolate Chips, Real, Semi-Sweet, Baker's, ¼ cup	200	12	54	7	32	0
Chocolate Chips, Semi-Sweet, Hershey's, ¼ cup	220	12	49	7	29	8
Chocolate Flavored Chips, Semi-Sweet, Baker's, ¼ cup	200	9	41	7	29	0
Chocolate Topping, Kraft, 1 tbsp.	50	0	0	0	0	0
Cinnamon, 1 tsp.	5	tr	na	tr	na	0
Cocktail Sauce, Sauceworks, 1 tbsp.	14	0	0	0	0	0
Cocoa Powder, Hershey's, ¼ cup	91	3	30	2	20	0
Coconut, Angel Flake, Baker's (bag), ⅓ cup	115	8	63	8	63	0
Coconut, Premium Shred, Baker's, ⅓ cup	140	9	58	9	58	0
Cornmeal, degermed, enriched, dry, 1 cup	500	2	4	<1	na	0
Cornmeal, whole-ground, unbolted, dry, 1 cup	435	5	10	<1	na	0
Curry powder, 1 tsp.	5	tr	na	na	na	0
Flour, buckwheat, light, sifted, 1 cup	340	1	3	<1	na	0
Flour, cake/pastry, enriched, sifted, spooned, 1 cup	350	1	3	<1	na	0
Flour, self-rising, enriched, unsifted, spooned, 1 cup	440	1	2	<1	na	0
Flour, wheat, all-purpose, sifted, spooned, 1 cup	420	1	2	<1	na	0
Flour, wheat, all-purpose, unsifted, spooned, 1 cup	455	1	2	<1	na	0
Flour, whole-wheat from hard wheats, stirred, 1 cup	400	2	5	<1	na	0
Frosting, Chocolate-flavored, Creamy Deluxe, Betty Crocker, ½₂ of tub	160	7	39	2	11	0
Frosting, Chocolate Fudge, Lovin' Lites, Pillsbury, ½₂ of can (1⅓ oz.)	120	2	15	tr	na	0

FOOD/PORTION SIZE	CAL.	FAT		SAT. FAT		CHOL.
		Total (g)	As % of Cal.	Total (g)	As % of Cal.	(mg)
Frosting, Cream Cheese, Duncan Hines, 1 tbsp.	60	3	45	1	15	0
Garlic powder, 1 tsp.	10	tr	na	tr	na	0
Garlic powder with parsley, Lawry's 1 tsp.	12	tr	na	0	0	0
Honey, strained or extracted, 1 tbsp.	65	0	0	0	0	0
Horseradish, Cream Style, Prepared, Kraft, 1 tbsp.	12	1	75	0	0	0
Horseradish, Prepared, Kraft, 1 tbsp.	10	0	0	0	0	0
Horseradish Sauce, Kraft, 1 tbsp.	50	5	90	1	18	5
Hot Fudge Topping, Kraft, 1 tbsp.	70	3	39	1	13	0
Hot Fudge Topping, Light, J.M. Smucker, 1 tbsp.	35	tr	na	0	0	na
Jam, Strawberry, Smucker's, 1 tbsp.	54	0	0	0	0	na
Jams and preserves, 1 tbsp.	55	tr	na	0	0	0
Jellies, 1 tbsp.	50	tr	na	tr	na	0
Marshmallow Creme, Kraft, 1 oz.	90	0	0	0	0	0
Mayonnaise, 1 tbsp.	100	11	99	2	18	8
Mayonnaise, Cholesterol Free, Hellman's, 1 tbsp.	50	5	90	1	18	0
Mayonnaise, Hellmann's, 1 tbsp.	100	11	99	2	18	7
Mayonnaise, Light, Reduced Calorie, Kraft, 1 tbsp.	50	5	90	1	18	5
Mayonnaise, Light Reduced Calorie, Hellman's, 1 tbsp.	50	5	90	1	18	5
Mayonnaise, Nonfat, Kraft Free, 1 tbsp.	12	0	0	0	0	0
Mayonnaise, Real, Kraft, 1 tbsp.	100	12	100	2	18	5
Molasses, Light, Brer Rabbit, 1 tbsp.	56	0	0	0	0	0
Mustard, Dijon, Grey Poupon,1 tbsp.	20	1	45	0	0	0
Mustard, Creamy Spread, French's, 1 tbsp.	8	tr	tr	0	0	0
Mustard, Horseradish, Kraft, 1 tbsp.	14	1	64	0	0	0
Mustard, prepared yellow, 1 tbsp.	15	tr	na	tr	na	0
Mustard, Pure Prepared, Kraft, 1 tbsp.	11	1	82	0	0	0
Onion powder, 1 tsp.	5	tr	na	tr	na	0
Oregano, 1 tsp.	5	tr	na	tr	na	0
Paprika, 1 tsp.	6	tr	na	tr	na	0
Parsley Patch Italian Seasoning, McCormick, 1 tsp.	8	0	0	0	0	0
Pepper, ground, black, 1 tsp.	5	tr	na	tr	na	0
Picante Sauce, Medium, Pace, 2 tbsp.	3	tr	na	na	na	na
Pineapple Topping, Kraft, 1 tbsp.	50	0	0	0	0	0
Preserves, Apricot, Kraft, 1 tbsp.	54	0	0	0	0	0
Relish, sweet, finely chopped, 1 tbsp.	20	tr	na	tr	na	0

FOOD/PORTION SIZE	CAL.	FAT		SAT. FAT		CHOL.
		Total (g)	As % of Cal.	Total (g)	As % of Cal.	(mg)
Salad Dressing, Free Nonfat, Miracle Whip, 1 tbsp.	20	0	0	0	0	0
Salad Dressing, Light, Miracle Whip, 1 tbsp.	45	4	80	1	20	5
Salad Dressing, Miracle Whip, 1 tbsp.	70	7	90	1	13	5
Salsa, Thick & Chunky, Mild, Ortega, 1 tbsp.	4	0	0	0	0	0
Salt, 1 tsp.	0	0	0	0	0	0
Sandwich Spread, Kraft, 1 tbsp.	50	5	90	1	18	5
Seasoning Blend, Mrs. Dash, 1 tsp.	12	0	0	0	0	0
Seasoning Mixture, Original Recipe for Chicken, Shake 'N Bake, ¼ pouch	80	tr	na	tr	na	0
Soy sauce, ready to serve, 1 tbsp.	11	0	0	0	0	0
Steak Sauce, A1, 1 tbsp.	14	0	0	0	0	0
Strawberry Topping, Kraft, 1 tbsp.	50	0	0	0	0	0
Sugar, brown, packed, 1 cup	820	0	0	0	0	0
Sugar, powdered, sifted, spooned into cup, 1 cup	385	0	0	0	0	0
Sugar, white granulated, 1 cup	770	0	0	0	0	0
Sweet 'n Sour Sauce, Sauceworks, 1 tbsp.	25	0	0	0	0	0
Syrup, chocolate-flavored syrup or topping, fudge type, 2 tbsp.	125	5	36	3	22	0
Syrup, chocolate-flavored syrup or topping, thin type, 2 tbsp.	85	tr	na	<1	na	0
Syrup, molasses, cane, blackstrap, 2 tbsp.	85	0	0	0	0	0
Syrup, Regular, Log Cabin, 1 oz. (about 2 tbsp.)	100	tr	na	tr	na	0
Syrup, table (corn & maple), 2 tbsp.	122	0	0	0	0	0
Tabasco Sauce, ¼ tsp.	0	0	0	0	0	0
Tartar sauce, 1 tbsp.	75	8	96	1	12	4
Tartar Sauce, Fat Free, Cholesterol Free, Nonfat, Kraft, 1 tbsp.	16	0	0	0	0	0
Tartar Sauce, Hellmann's, 1 tbsp.	70	8	100	1	13	5
Tartar Sauce, Natural Lemon Herb Flavor, Sauceworks, 1 tbsp.	70	8	100	1	13	5
Tartar Sauce, Sauceworks, 1 tbsp.	50	5	90	1	18	5
Vinegar, Apple Cider, Heinz, 2 tbsp.	4	0	0	0	0	0
Vinegar, Cider, Heinz, 2 tbsp.	4	0	0	0	0	0
Vinegar, Gourmet Wine, Heinz, 2 tbsp.	8	0	0	0	0	0
Vinegar, Wine, Red or White, Heinz, 2 tbsp.	4	0	0	0	0	0
Worcestershire Sauce, Heinz, 1 tbsp.	12	0	0	0	0	0
Yeast, baker's dry active, 1 package	20	tr	na	tr	na	0
Yeast, brewer's dry, 1 tbsp.	25	tr	na	tr	na	0

Beverages

FOOD/PORTION SIZE	CAL.	FAT		SAT. FAT		CHOL. (mg)
		Total (g)	As % of Cal.	Total (g)	As % of Cal.	
ALCOHOL						
Beer, light, 12 fl. oz.	95	0	0	0	0	0
Beer, regular, 12 fl. oz.	150	0	0	0	0	0
Gin, rum, vodka, whiskey, 80-proof, 1½ fl. oz.	97	0	0	0	0	0
Gin, rum, vodka, whiskey, 90-proof, 1½ fl. oz.	110	0	0	0	0	0
Wine, table, red, 3½ fl. oz.	74	0	0	0	0	0
Wine, table, white, 3½ fl. oz.	70	0	0	0	0	0
COFFEE						
Brewed, 6 fl. oz.	tr	tr	na	tr	na	0
Cafe Francais, General Foods International Coffees, 6 fl. oz.	50	3	54	0	0	0
Cafe Francais, General Foods Sugar Free International Coffees, 6 fl. oz.	35	2	51	0	0	0
Coffee Flavor Instant Hot Beverage, Postum, 6 fl. oz.	12	0	0	0	0	0
Instant, Folger's, 1 tbsp.	8	0	0	0	0	0
JUICE						
Apple, bottled or canned, 1 cup	115	tr	na	tr	na	0
Apple, Pure 100%, Kraft, 8 fl. oz.	107	0	0	0	0	0
Apple/Cranberry Fruit Blends, Del Monte, approx. 8 fl. oz.	140	0	0	0	0	0
Cherry, Pure & Light, Dole, 1 cup	120	0	0	0	0	0
Cranberry Juice Cocktail, Ocean Spray, 8 fl. oz.	144	0	0	0	0	0
Grape, canned or bottled, 1 cup	155	tr	na	<1	na	0
Grape, frozen concentrate, sweetened, diluted, 1 cup	125	tr	na	<1	na	0
Grapefruit, canned, sweetened, 1 cup	115	tr	na	tr	na	0
Grapefruit, canned, unsweetened, 1 cup	95	tr	na	tr	na	0
Grapefruit, frozen concentrate, unsweetened, diluted, 1 cup	100	tr	na	tr	na	0
Grapefruit, raw, 1 cup	95	tr	na	tr	na	0
Lemon, canned or bottled, unsweetened, 1 cup	50	1	18	<1	2	0
Lemon, raw, 1 cup	60	tr	na	tr	na	0
Lemon, ReaLemon Juice from Concentrate, Borden, 1 cup	48	0	0	0	0	0

FOOD/PORTION SIZE	CAL.	FAT		SAT. FAT		CHOL.
		Total (g)	As % of Cal.	Total (g)	As % of Cal.	(mg)
Lime, canned or bottled, unsweetened, 1 cup	50	1	18	<1	2	0
Lime, raw, 1 cup	65	tr	na	tr	na	0
Orange, canned, unsweetened, 1 cup	105	tr	na	tr	na	0
Orange, chilled, 1 cup	110	1	8	<1	tr	0
Orange, frozen concentrate, diluted, 1 cup	110	tr	na	tr	na	0
Orange, Minute Maid, 100% pure orange juice from concentrate, 6 fl.oz.	90	0	0	0	0	0
Orange, raw, 1 cup	110	tr	na	<1	<1	0
Orange and grapefruit, canned, 1 cup	105	tr	na	tr	na	0
Peach, Pure & Light, Dole, 8 fl. oz.	120	0	0	0	0	0
Pineapple, Canned, Dole, 8 fl. oz.	133	0	0	0	0	0
Pineapple, unsweetened, canned, 1 cup	140	tr	na	tr	na	0
Pineapple-Orange, Dole, 8 fl. oz.	120	0	0	0	0	0
Pineapple-Orange Fruit Blends, Del Monte, approx. 8 fl. oz.	140	0	0	0	0	0
Pineapple-Orange-Guava, Dole, 8 fl. oz.	133	<1	0	0	0	0
Pineapple-Passion-Banana, Dole, 1 cup	133	0	0	0	0	0
Prune, canned or bottled, 1 cup	180	tr	na	tr	na	0
Raspberry, Pure & Light, Dole 8 fl. oz.	133	0	0	0	0	0
Tomato, canned, 1 cup	40	tr	na	tr	na	0
Vegetable Juice, V-8, 8 fl. oz.	47	0	0	0	0	0
MILK						
Buttermilk, 1 cup	100	2	18	1	9	9
Canned, condensed, sweetened, 1 cup	980	27	25	17	16	104
Canned, evaporated, skim, 1 cup	200	1	5	<1	1	9
Canned, evaporated, whole, 1 cup	340	19	50	12	32	74
Chocolate, lowfat (1%), 1 cup	160	3	17	2	11	7
Chocolate, lowfat (2%), 1 cup	180	5	25	3	15	17
Chocolate Malt Flavor, Ovaltine Classic, ¾ oz.	80	0	0	0	0	0
Cocoa Mix, Milk Chocolate, Carnation, 1 envelope	110	1	8	tr	<1	1
Cocoa Mix, Rich Chocolate, Carnation, 1 envelope	110	1	8	1	8	1
Cocoa Mix, Rich Chocolate with Marshmallows, Carnation, 1 envelope	110	1	8	1	8	2
Dried, nonfat, instant, 1 cup	245	tr	na	<1	1	12
Dried, nonfat, instant, 1 envelope (3⅕ oz.) (makes 1 quart liquid milk)	325	1	3	<1	1	17
Eggnog (commercial), 1 cup	340	19	50	11	29	149
Evaporated Filled Milk, Milnot, 2 tbsp.	37	2	49	tr	<1	na
Evaporated Milk, Carnation, 2 tbsp.	43	3	63	na	na	na

BEVERAGES

FOOD/PORTION SIZE	CAL.	FAT		SAT. FAT		CHOL.
		Total (g)	As % of Cal.	Total (g)	As % of Cal.	(mg)
Evaporated Milk, Pet, 2 tbsp.	43	3	63	2	42	9
Evaporated Skim Milk, Light, Pet, 2 tbsp.	25	0	0	0	0	3
Evaporated Skim Milk, Lite, Carnation, 2 tbsp.	25	0	0	0	0	3
Fudge Drink, Chocolate, Slender, 10 fl. oz.	220	4	16	na	na	4
Lowfat (2%), milk solids added, 1 cup	125	5	36	3	22	18
Lowfat (2%), no milk solids, 1 cup	120	5	38	3	23	18
Malt Drink, Chocolate, Slender, 10 fl. oz.	220	4	16	na	na	4
Malted, chocolate, powder, ¾ oz.	84	1	11	<1	5	1
Malted, chocolate, powder, prepared with 8 oz. whole milk	235	9	34	6	23	34
Malted, natural, powder, prepared with 8 oz. whole milk	235	10	38	6	23	37
Malt Flavor, Classic, Ovaltine, ¾ oz. dry	80	tr	na	tr	na	0
Nonfat (skim), milk solids added, 1 cup	90	1	10	<1	4	5
Nonfat (skim), no milk solids, 1 cup	86	tr	na	<1	3	4
Quik, Chocolate, Nestle, ¾ oz. dry (2½ tsp.)	90	1	10	0	0	0
Shake Mix, Alba 77 Fit n' Frosty, all flavors, 1 envelope	70	0	0	0	0	3
Skim Milk, Fortified, Lite-line or Viva, Borden, 1 cup	100	1	9	tr	<1	5
Whole (3.3% fat), 1 cup	150	8	48	5	30	33
Whole, Borden, 1 cup	150	8	48	na	na	na

SOFT DRINKS, CARBONATED

7-Up, Diet, 6 fl. oz.	2	0	0	0	0	na
7-Up, Diet Cherry, 6 fl.oz.	2	0	0	0	0	na
Club soda, 6 fl. oz.	0	0	0	0	0	0
Coca-Cola Classic, 6 fl. oz.	72	0	0	0	0	0
Diet Coke, 6 fl. oz.	0	0	0	0	0	na
Diet Coke, Caffeine Free, 6 fl.oz.	0	0	0	0	0	na
Diet Pepsi, Caffeine Free, 6 fl. oz.	0	0	0	0	0	na
Diet-Rite, Black Cherry, 6 fl. oz.	2	0	0	0	0	na
Diet-Rite, Cola, 6 fl. oz.	2	0	0	0	0	na
Diet-Rite, Pink Grapefruit, 6 fl. oz.	2	0	0	0	0	na
Diet-Rite, Red Raspberry, 6 fl. oz.	2	0	0	0	0	na
Dr. Pepper (Diet), 6 fl. oz.	2	0	0	0	0	na
Fresca, 6 fl. oz.	2	0	0	0	0	na
Ginger Ale, Canada Dry, Diet, 6 fl. oz.	2	0	0	0	0	na
Grape, carbonated, 6 fl. oz.	90	0	0	0	0	0
Orange, carbonated, 6 fl. oz.	90	0	0	0	0	0

BEVERAGES

FOOD/PORTION SIZE	CAL.	FAT		SAT. FAT		CHOL. (mg)
		Total (g)	As % of Cal.	Total (g)	As % of Cal.	
Pepsi-Cola, Diet, 6 fl. oz.	0	0	0	0	0	na
Root beer, 6 fl. oz.	83	0	0	0	0	0
Root Beer, Dad's, Diet, 6 fl. oz.	2	0	0	0	0	na

SOFT DRINKS, NONCARBONATED

FOOD/PORTION SIZE	CAL.	FAT		SAT. FAT		CHOL. (mg)
Country Time Drink Mix, Sugar Sweetened, Lemonade/Pink Lemonade, 8 fl. oz.	80	0	0	0	0	0
Country Time Drink Mix, Sugar Sweetened, Lemon-Lime, 8 fl. oz.	80	0	0	0	0	0
Country Time Sugar Free Drink Mix, Lemonade/Pink Lemonade, 8 fl. oz.	4	0	0	0	0	0
Country Time Sugar Free Drink Mix, Lemon-Lime, 8 fl. oz.	4	0	0	0	0	0
Crystal Light Sugar Free Drink Mix, all flavors, 8 fl. oz.	4	0	0	0	0	0
Grape drink, noncarbonated, canned, 6 fl. oz.	100	0	0	0	0	0
Hi-C Cherry Drink, 6 fl. oz.	100	0	0	0	0	0
Hi-C Citrus Cooler Drink, 6 fl. oz.	100	0	0	0	0	0
Hi-C Double Fruit Cooler Drink, 6 fl. oz.	90	0	0	0	0	0
Hi-C Fruit Punch Drink, 6 fl. oz.	100	0	0	0	0	0
Hi-C Hula Punch Drink, 6 fl. oz.	80	0	0	0	0	0
Kool-Aid Koolers Juice Drink, all flavors, approx. 8 fl. oz.	130	0	0	0	0	0
Kool-Aid Soft Drink Mix, Sugar-Sweetened, all flavors, 8 fl. oz.	80	0	0	0	0	0
Kool-Aid Soft Drink Mix, Unsweetened, all flavors, 8 fl. oz.	2	0	0	0	0	0
Kool-Aid Soft Drink Mix, Unsweetened, all flavors, with sugar added, 8 fl. oz.	100	0	0	0	0	0
Kool-Aid Sugar-Free Soft Drink Mix, all flavors, 8 fl. oz.	4	0	0	0	0	0
Lemonade concentrate, frozen, diluted, 6 fl. oz.	80	tr	na	tr	na	0
Lemon Lime, Gatorade, 8 fl. oz.	50	0	0	0	0	na
Limeade concentrate, frozen, diluted, 6 fl. oz.	75	tr	na	tr	na	0
Ocean Spray, Cran-Apple Drink, 6 oz.	130	0	0	0	0	na
Ocean Spray, Cran-Grape Drink, 6 oz.	130	0	0	0	0	na
Ocean Spray, Cran-Raspberry Drink, 6 oz.	110	0	0	0	0	na
Pineapple-grapefruit juice drink, 6 fl. oz.	90	tr	<1	0	0	0
Wyler's Punch Mix, Sweetened, all flavors, 8 fl. oz.	90	0	0	0	0	na
Wyler's Punch Mix, Unsweetened, all flavors, 8 fl. oz.	2	0	0	0	0	na

120

FOOD/PORTION SIZE	CAL.	FAT		SAT. FAT		CHOL.
		Total (g)	As % of Cal.	Total (g)	As % of Cal.	(mg)
TEA						
Berry, Crystal Light Fruit-Tea Sugar Free Drink Mix, 8 fl. oz.	4	0	0	0	0	0
Brewed, Lipton, 8 fl. oz.	3	tr	<1	0	0	0
Citrus, Crystal Light Fruit-Tea Sugar Free Drink Mix, 8 fl. oz.	4	0	0	0	0	0
Iced Tea, Crystal Light Sugar Free Drink Mix, 8 fl. oz.	4	0	0	0	0	0
Instant, powder, sweetened, 8 fl. oz.	85	tr	na	tr	na	0
Instant, powder, unsweetened, 8 fl.oz.	tr	tr	na	tr	na	0
Natural Brew, Crystal Light Fruit-Tea Sugar Free Drink Mix, 8 fl. oz.	4	0	0	0	0	0
Tropical Fruit, Crystal Light Fruit-Tea Sugar Free Drink Mix, 8 fl. oz.	4	0	0	0	0	0

Breads & Cereals

FOOD/PORTION SIZE	CAL.	FAT		SAT. FAT		CHOL.
		Total (g)	As % of Cal.	Total (g)	As % of Cal.	(mg)
BISCUITS						
Baking powder, home recipe, 1 biscuit	100	5	45	1	9	tr
Baking powder, refrigerated dough, 1 biscuit	65	2	28	1	14	1
BREAD						
Boston brown, canned, 3¼ × ½-in. slice	95	1	9	<1	3	3
Cracked-wheat, 1 slice	65	1	14	<1	3	0
Crumbs, enriched, dry, grated, 1 cup	390	5	12	2	5	5
French, enriched, 5 × 2½ × 1-in. slice	100	1	9	<1	3	0
Frozen Bread Dough, Honey Wheat, Rhodes, 1 slice, approx. 28 g (1 oz.)	69	1	13	tr	<1	0
Frozen Bread Dough, Texas White Roll, Rhodes, 2 oz.	150	4	24	1	6	0
Frozen Bread Dough, Texas Whole Wheat, Rhodes, 2 oz.	129	1	7	tr	<1	0
Italian, enriched, 4½ × 3¼ × ¾-in. slice	85	tr	na	tr	na	0
Oat, Hearty Slices Crunchy Oat Bread, Pepperidge Farm, 1 slice	95	2	19	1	5	0
Oat, Oat Bran Bread, Roman Meal, 1 slice	70	tr	<1	na	na	0
Pita, enriched, white, 6-in. diameter, 1 pita	165	1	5	<1	<1	0
Pumpernickel, ⅔ rye, ⅓ wheat, 1 slice	80	1	11	<1	2	0

FOOD/PORTION SIZE	CAL.	FAT		SAT. FAT		CHOL. (mg)
		Total (g)	As % of Cal.	Total (g)	As % of Cal.	
Raisin, enriched, 1 slice	65	1	14	<1	3	0
Rye, ⅔ wheat, ⅓ rye, 4¾ × 3¾ × ⁷⁄₁₆-in. slice	65	1	14	<1	3	0
Vienna, enriched, 4¾ × 4 × ½-in. slice	70	1	13	<1	3	0
Wheat, Soft, Brownberry, 1 slice	70	1	13	tr	<1	0
Wheat, Stoneground 100% Wheat, Wonder, 1 slice	70	1	13	na	na	0
White, Country White Hearty Slices, Pepperidge Farm, 1 slice	95	1	9	1	5	0
White, enriched, soft crumbs, 1 cup	120	2	15	<1	5	0
White, Home Pride Buttertop, 1 slice	70	1	13	tr	<1	1
White, Wonder, 1 slice	70	1	13	tr	<1	0
Whole-wheat, 16-slice loaf, 1 slice	70	1	13	<1	5	0
CEREALS, COLD						
40% Bran Flakes, Post, 1 oz. (⅔ cup)	90	tr	<1	tr	<1	0
100% Bran, Nabisco, 1 oz. (⅓ cup)	70	1	8	tr	<1	0
100% Natural, Oats & Honey, Quaker, 1 oz. (¼ cup)	130	6	40	4	27	0
All-Bran, Kellogg's, 1 oz. (⅓ cup)	70	1	13	tr	<1	0
Alpha-Bits, Post, 1 oz.	110	1	8	tr	<1	0
Apple Jacks, Kellogg's, 1 oz.	110	0	0	0	0	0
Bran Flakes, Kellogg's, 1 oz. (¾ cup)	90	0	0	0	0	0
Bran Flakes, Post, 1 oz.	90	0	0	0	0	0
Cap'n Crunch, Quaker, 1 oz. (¾ cup)	120	3	23	2	15	0
Cap'n Crunch Peanut Butter, Quaker, 1 oz.	127	3	21	2	14	na
Cheerios, General Mills, 1 oz. (1¼ cups)	110	2	16	tr	<1	0
Cheerios, Honey-Nut, General Mills, 1 oz. (¾ cup)	110	1	8	tr	<1	0
Cocoa Krispies, Kellogg's, 1 oz.	110	0	0	0	0	0
Cocoa Pebbles, Post, 1 oz.	110	1	8	1	8	0
Cocoa Puffs, General Mills, 1 oz.	110	1	8	tr	<1	0
Common Sense Oat Bran, Kellogg's, 1 oz.	100	1	9	tr	<1	0
Complete Bran Flakes, Kellogg's, 1 oz.	90	0	0	0	0	0
Corn Chex, Ralston, 1 oz.	110	0	0	0	0	0
Corn Flakes, Kellogg's, 1 oz. (1¼ cups)	100	0	0	0	0	0
Corn Flakes, Post Toasties, 1 oz. (1¼ cups)	110	tr	<1	tr	<1	0
Corn Flakes, Total, 1 oz. (1 cup)	110	1	8	tr	<1	0
Cracklin' Oat Bran, Kellogg's, 1 oz.	110	4	33	tr	<1	0
Froot Loops, Kellogg's, 1 oz. (1 cup)	110	1	8	tr	<1	0
Frosted Mini-Wheats, Kellog's, 1 oz.	100	0	0	0	0	0

FOOD/PORTION SIZE	CAL.	FAT		SAT. FAT		CHOL.
		Total (g)	As % of Cal.	Total (g)	As % of Cal.	(mg)
Fruit & Fibre—Dates, Raisins, Walnuts, Post, 1 oz.	90	1	10	tr	<1	0
Fruit & Fibre—Harvest Medley, Post, 1 oz.	92	1	10	tr	<1	0
Fruit & Fibre—Mountain Trail, Post, 1 oz.	90	1	10	tr	<1	0
Fruit & Fibre—Tropical Fruit, Post, 1 oz.	90	1	10	tr	<1	0
Fruity Pebbles, Post, 1 oz.	113	1	8	1	8	0
Golden Grahams, General Mills, 1 oz. (¾ cup)	110	1	8	tr	<1	0
Granola, Nature Valley, 1 oz. (⅓ cup)	125	5	36	3	22	tr
Granola with Almonds, Sun Country, 1 oz.	130	5	35	1	7	0
Granola with Raisins, Hearty, C.W. Post, 1 oz.	125	4	29	3	32	0
Granola with Raisins, Sun Country, 1 oz.	125	5	36	1	7	0
Grape-Nuts, Post, 1 oz.	110	0	0	0	0	0
Grape-Nuts Flakes, Post, 1 oz.	105	1	9	tr	<1	0
Honeycomb, Post, 1 oz.	110	0	0	0	0	0
Just Right with Fiber Nuggets, Kellogg's, 1 oz.	100	1	9	tr	<1	0
Just Right with Fruit & Nuts, Kellogg's, 1 oz.	140	1	8	tr	<1	0
Kix, General Mills, 1 oz.	110	0	0	0	0	0
Life, Quaker Oats, 1 oz.	111	2	16	tr	<1	na
Life, Cinnamon, Quaker Oats, 1 oz.	101	2	18	tr	<1	0
Lucky Charms, General Mills, 1 oz. (1 cup)	110	1	8	tr	<1	0
Mueslix Five Grain, Kellogg's, 1 oz.	96	1	9	tr	<1	0
Natural Raisin Bran, Post, 1 oz.	87	0	0	0	0	0
Nutri Grain Almonds & Raisins, Kellogg's, 1 oz.	100	2	18	0	0	0
Nutri Grain Biscuits, Kellogg's, 1 oz.	90	0	0	0	0	0
Nutri Grain Wheat, Kellogg's, 1 oz.	100	0	0	0	0	0
Nutri Grain Wheat & Raisins, Kellogg's, 1 oz.	130	0	0	0	0	0
Oat Bran, Quaker, 1 oz.	110	2	16	tr	<1	0
Product 19, Kellogg's, 1 oz. (¾ cup)	110	tr	<1	0	0	0
Puffed Rice, Quaker Oats, ½ oz.	54	tr	<1	tr	<1	0
Puffed Wheat, Quaker Oats, ½ oz.	54	tr	<1	tr	<1	0
Raisin Bran, Kellogg's, 1 oz. (¾ cup)	120	1	8	tr	<1	0
Raisin Bran, Post, 1 oz. (½ cup)	85	1	11	0	0	0
Rice Chex, Ralston, 1 oz.	110	1	11	0	0	0
Rice Krispies, Kellogg's, 1 oz. (1 cup)	110	0	0	0	0	0
Shredded Wheat, Nabisco, 1 biscuit, ⅚ oz.	80	<1	na	tr	<1	0
Shredded Wheat, Spoon Size, Nabisco, 1 oz.	90	<1	na	tr	<1	0
Special K, Kellogg's, 1 oz. (1⅓ cups)	110	tr	<1	0	0	tr
Sugar Frosted Flakes, Kellogg's, 1 oz. (¾ cup)	110	tr	<1	0	0	0
Super Golden Crisp, Post, 1 oz.	110	0	0	0	0	0
Trix, General Mills, 1 oz. (1 cup)	110	1	8	tr	<1	0

FOOD/PORTION SIZE	CAL.	FAT Total (g)	FAT As % of Cal.	SAT. FAT Total (g)	SAT. FAT As % of Cal.	CHOL. (mg)
Wheat Chex, Ralston Purina, 1 oz.	100	0	0	0	0	0
Wheat Germ, Honey Crunch, Kretschmer, 1 oz.	105	3	26	tr	<1	0
Wheaties, General Mills, 1 oz. (1 cup)	100	tr	<1	tr	<1	0
CEREALS, HOT						
Corn grits, regular/quick, enriched, 1 cup	145	tr	na	tr	na	0
Cream of Rice, 1 oz.	100	0	0	na	na	0
Cream of Wheat, Mix 'n Eat, plain, 1 packet	100	tr	<1	0	0	0
Cream of Wheat, regular/quick/instant, 1 cup	149	tr	<1	0	0	0
Malt-O-Meal, Chocolate, 1 oz.	100	0	0	0	0	na
Oat Bran, Quaker Oats, 1 oz.	92	2	20	na	na	0
Oats, Instant, Apple Cinnamon, Quaker Oats, 1¼ oz.	134	2	13	1	7	0
Oats, Instant, Bananas & Cream, Quaker Oats, 1¼ oz.	160	2	11	1	6	0
Oats, Instant, Blueberries & Cream, Quaker Oats, 1¼ oz.	130	2	14	tr	<1	0
Oats, Instant, Cinnamon Spice, Quaker Oats, 1⅔ oz.	160	2	11	tr	<1	0
Oats, Instant, Maple & Brown Sugar, Quaker Oats, 1½ oz.	163	2	11	tr	<1	0
Oats, Instant, Peaches & Cream, Quaker Oats, 1¼ oz.	136	2	13	tr	<1	0
Oats, Instant, Raisin Date Walnut, Quaker Oats, 1⅓ oz.	130	2	14	tr	<1	0
Oats, Instant, Raisin Spice, Quaker Oats, 1½ oz.	159	2	11	tr	<1	0
Oats, Instant, Regular, Quaker Oats, dry, 1 oz.	109	2	17	tr	<1	0
Oats, Instant, Strawberries & Cream, Quaker Oats, 1¼ oz.	136	2	13	tr	<1	0
Oats, Quick or Old Fashioned, Quaker Oats, dry, 1 oz.	100	2	17	tr	<1	0
Wheateena, 1 oz.	100	1	9	na	na	na
Whole Wheat Hot Natural, Quaker Oats, 1 oz.	92	1	10	tr	<1	0
CRACKERS						
Cheese, plain, 1-in. square, 10 crackers	50	3	54	<1	16	6
Cheese, sandwich/peanut butter, 1 sandwich	40	2	45	<1	9	1
Graham, Nabisco, 1 sheet	60	1	15	<1	na	0
Graham, plain, 2½-in. square, 2 crackers	60	1	15	<1	6	0

FOOD/PORTION SIZE	CAL.	FAT		SAT. FAT		CHOL.
		Total (g)	As % of Cal.	Total (g)	As % of Cal.	(mg)
Oat Bran, Sunshine, 8 crackers (½ oz.)	80	4	45	1	11	0
Ritz, Nabisco, ½ oz. (4 crackers)	70	4	51	<1	na	0
Rye-Bran Crispbread, Kavli, 1 slice	30	0	0	0	0	0
Rye wafers, whole-grain, 2 wafers	55	1	16	<1	5	0
Rykrisp, (Natural), ½ cracker	40	0	0	0	0	0
Saltines, 4 crackers	50	1	18	<1	9	4
Snack-type, standard, 1 round cracker	15	1	60	<1	12	0
Town House, Low Sodium, Keebler, 4 crackers	70	4	51	3	39	0
Wheat, thin, 4 crackers	35	1	26	<1	13	0
Wheat Thins, Original, Nabisco, 8 crackers (½ oz.)	70	3	39	na	na	0
Whole Wheat Wafers, Triscuit, Nabisco, ½ oz. (3 wafers)	60	2	30	na	na	0
MUFFINS						
Apple Streusel, Breakfast, Hostess, 1 muffin	100	1	9	tr	<1	0
Banana Nut, Frozen, Healthy Choice, 1 muffin	180	6	30	tr	<1	0
Blueberry, Bakery Style Muffin Mix, Duncan Hines, 1 muffin	180	5	25	na	na	na
Blueberry, Frozen, Healthy Choice, 1 muffin	190	4	19	tr	<1	0
Blueberry, mix, 1 muffin	140	5	32	1	6	45
Blueberry, Wild, Light, Betty Crocker, regular recipe, 1 muffin	70	tr	na	na	na	20
Same as above, no-cholesterol recipe	70	tr	na	na	na	0
Bran, mix, 1 muffin	140	4	26	1	6	28
Bran, with Raisins, Pepperidge Farm, 1 muffin (2 oz.)	170	6	32	1	5	0
Cinnamon Swirl, Bakery Style Muffin Mix, Duncan Hines, 1 muffin	200	7	32	na	na	na
English, plain, enriched, 1 muffin	140	1	6	<1	2	0
English, Thomas', 1 muffin, 57 g (2 oz.)	130	1	7	na	na	0
ROLLS						
Dinner, enriched commercial, 1 roll	85	2	21	<1	5	tr
Frankfurter/hamburger, enriched commercial, 1 roll	115	2	16	<1	4	tr
Hard, enriched commercial, 1 roll	155	2	12	<1	2	tr
Hoagie/submarine, enriched commercial, 1 roll	400	8	18	2	5	tr

FOOD/PORTION SIZE	CAL.	FAT Total (g)	FAT As % of Cal.	SAT. FAT Total (g)	SAT. FAT As % of Cal.	CHOL. (mg)
MISCELLANEOUS						
Bagel, plain/water, enriched, 1 bagel	200	2	9	<1	1	0
Bagels, Egg, Lender's, 1 bagel (2 oz.)	150	1	6	na	na	0
Bagels, Plain, Lender's, 1 bagel (2 oz.)	150	1	6	na	na	0
Bran, unprocessed, Quaker Oats, ¼ oz.	21	tr	<1	tr	<1	0
Breadsticks, Pillsbury, 1 stick	100	2	18	tr	na	0
Croissant, with enriched flour, 1 croissant	235	12	46	4	15	13
Melba toast, plain, 1 piece	20	tr	na	<1	5	0
Pancake & Waffle Mix, Extra Light, Hungry Jack, regular recipe, three 4-in. pancakes	190	6	28	1	47	55
Same as above, no-cholesterol recipe	170	4	21	<1	<1	0
Pancakes & Waffle Mix, Original, Aunt Jemima, regular recipe, 3 to 4 pancakes	190	6	28	na	na	65
Same as above, no-cholesterol recipe	170	3	16	na	na	0
Stuffing, Herb Seasoned, Pepperidge Farm, 1 oz.	110	1	8	na	na	na
Stuffing Mix, Chicken Flavored, Stove Top One Step, 1 oz.	120	3	23	na	na	0
Stuffing Mix, Croutettes, Kellogg's, 1 oz.	93	3	29	na	na	0
Stuffing mix, moist, prepared from mix, 1 cup	420	26	56	5	11	67
Taco Shell, Ortega, 1 shell	70	3	39	0	0	0
Tortilla, corn, 1 tortilla	65	1	14	<1	1	0
Tortilla, Corn, Azteca, 1 tortilla	45	0	0	0	0	0
Tortillas, Flour, Azteca, 7-inch, 1 tortilla	80	2	23	0	0	0
Waffles, Home Style, Aunt Jemima (frozen), 1 waffle (1¼ oz.)	90	3	30	na	na	na
Wheat Bran, Kretschmer, 1 oz.	57	2	32	na	na	0

Candy

FOOD/PORTION SIZE	CAL.	FAT Total (g)	FAT As % of Cal.	SAT. FAT Total (g)	SAT. FAT As % of Cal.	CHOL. (mg)
Almond Joy, 1 bar (1.76 oz.)	250	14	50	na	na	na
Baby Ruth, 1 bar (2.1 oz.)	290	14	43	8	25	0
Butterfinger Bar, 1 bar (2.1 oz.)	280	12	39	5	16	0
Butter Mints, Kraft, 1 mint	8	0	0	0	0	0
Caramels, Kraft, 1 caramel	30	1	30	0	0	0
Chocolate, sweet dark, 1 oz.	152	10	59	6	36	0
Chocolate Fudgies, Kraft, 1 fudgie	35	1	26	0	0	0

FOOD/PORTION SIZE	CAL.	FAT Total (g)	FAT As % of Cal.	SAT. FAT Total (g)	SAT. FAT As % of Cal.	CHOL. (mg)
Crunch, Nestlé, 1.4 oz.	200	10	45	na	na	na
Fudge, chocolate, plain, 1 oz.	117	3	23	2	15	1
Gum drops, 1 oz.	100	tr	na	tr	na	0
Hard candy, 1 oz.	110	0	0	0	0	0
Jelly beans, 1 oz.	105	tr	na	tr	na	0
Jet-Puffed Marshmallows, Kraft, 1 marshmallow	25	0	0	0	0	0
Kisses, Hershey's, 9 pieces	220	13	53	8	33	10
Kit-Kat, 1 3/25 oz.	172	9	47	6	31	8
M & M's Peanut Chocolate Candies, 1 oz.	150	7	42	na	na	na
M & M's Plain Chocolate Candies, 1 oz.	140	6	39	na	na	na
Milk chocolate, plain, 1 oz.	147	9	55	5	31	6
Milk chocolate, with almonds, 1 oz.	152	9	53	5	30	5
Milk chocolate, with peanuts, 1 oz.	154	10	58	4	23	5
Milk chocolate, with rice cereal, 1 oz.	140	7	45	4	26	6
Milk Chocolate Bar, Hershey's, 1 bar	250	12	43	7	25	12
Milky Way Bar, 1 bar (2.15 oz.)	280	11	35	na	na	na
Miniature Marshmallows, Kraft, 10 marshmallows	18	0	0	0	0	0
Mr. Goodbar, Hershey's, 1.65 oz.	240	15	56	na	na	na
Party Mints, Kraft, 1 mint	8	0	0	0	0	0
Peanut Brittle, Kraft, 1 oz.	130	5	35	1	7	0
Peanut Butter Cups, Reese's, 2 cups	280	17	55	6	19	8
Snickers, 1 bar (2.7 oz.)	280	13	42	na	na	na
Special Dark, Hershey's, 1.75 oz.	280	16	51	9	29	4

Cheese

FOOD/PORTION SIZE	CAL.	FAT Total (g)	FAT As % of Cal.	SAT. FAT Total (g)	SAT. FAT As % of Cal.	CHOL. (mg)
American, Pasteurized Process Cheese Slices, Deluxe, Kraft, 1 oz.	110	9	74	5	41	25
American, Sharp, Pasteurized Process Slices, Old English, Kraft, 1 oz.	110	9	74	5	41	30
American Flavor, Imitation Pasteurized Process Cheese Food, Golden Image, 1 oz.	90	6	60	2	20	5
American Flavored, Singles Pasteurized Process Cheese Product, Light n' Lively, 1 oz.	70	4	51	3	39	13

FOOD/PORTION SIZE	CAL.	FAT		SAT. FAT		CHOL.
		Total (g)	As % of Cal.	Total (g)	As % of Cal.	(mg)
American Flavor Process Cheese, Low Sodium, Weight Watchers, 1 slice	35	1	26	1	26	5
American Process Cheese, Borden Lite-Line, 1 oz.	50	2	36	1	18	5
American Singles Pasteurized Process Cheese Food, Kraft, 1 oz.	90	7	70	4	40	25
Blue, 1 oz.	100	8	72	6	54	21
Blue, Natural, Kraft, 1 oz.	100	9	81	5	45	30
Brick, Natural, Kraft, 1 oz.	110	9	74	5	41	30
Camembert, 1 wedge (⅓ of 4-oz. container)	115	9	70	6	47	27
Cheddar, Extra Sharp, Cold Pack Cheese Food, Cracker Barrel, 1 oz.	90	7	70	4	40	20
Cheddar, Free 'n Lean, Alpine Lace, 1 oz.	35	0	0	0	0	5
Cheddar, Light Naturals Reduced Fat, Kraft, 1 oz.	80	5	56	3	34	20
Cheddar, Mild, Imitation, Golden Image, 1 oz.	110	9	74	2	16	5
Cheddar, Natural, Kraft, 1 oz.	110	9	74	5	41	30
Cheddar, Port Wine, Cheese Log with Almonds, Cracker Barrel, 1 oz.	90	6	60	3	30	15
Cheddar, Port Wine, Cold Pack Cheese Food, Cracker Barrel, 1 oz.	100	7	63	4	36	20
Cheddar, Preferred Light, Fancy Supreme Shredded, Sargento, 1 oz.	90	5	50	3	30	15
Cheddar, Reduced Fat, Dorman's Light, 1 oz.	80	5	56	3	34	20
Cheddar, Sharp, Cheese Ball with Almonds, Cracker Barrel, 1 oz.	100	7	63	3	27	20
Cheddar, Sharp, Cold Pack Cheese Food, Cracker Barrel, 1 oz.	100	7	63	4	36	20
Cheddar, Sharp, Process Cheese, Borden Lite-Line, 1 oz.	50	2	36	1	18	5
Cheddar, shredded, 1 cup	455	34	67	23	45	120
Cheddar, Smokey, Cheese Log with Almonds, Cracker Barrel, 1 oz.	90	6	60	3	30	15
Cheddar Flavored, Sharp, Singles Pasteurized Process Cheese Product, Light n' Lively, 1 oz.	70	4	51	2	26	15
Cheese Food, Cold Pack with Real Bacon, Cracker Barrel, 1 oz.	90	7	70	4	40	20
Cheese Food, Pasteurized Process Sharp Singles, Kraft, 1 oz.	100	8	72	5	45	25
Cheese Spread, Hot Mexican, Pasteurized Process, Velveeta, 1 oz.	80	6	68	3	34	20
Cheese Spread, Mild Mexican, Pasteurized Process, Velveeta, 1 oz.	80	6	68	3	34	20
Cheese Spread, Pasteurized Process, Velveeta, 1 oz.	80	6	68	4	45	20

FOOD/PORTION SIZE	CAL.	FAT		SAT. FAT		CHOL.
		Total (g)	As % of Cal.	Total (g)	As % of Cal.	(mg)
Cheese Spread, Slices, Pasteurized Process, Velveeta, 1 oz.	90	6	60	4	40	20
Cheez Whiz, Mild Mexican, Pasteurized Process Cheese Spread, 1 oz.	80	6	68	4	45	20
Cheez Whiz, Pasteurized Process Cheese Spread, 1 oz.	80	6	68	3	34	20
Cheez Whiz with Jalapeño Pepper, Pasteurized Process Cheese Spread, 1 oz.	80	6	68	4	45	20
Colby, Imitation, Golden Image, 1 oz.	110	9	74	2	16	5
Cottage, creamed, Borden, 1 cup	240	10	38	na	na	na
Cottage, creamed, large curd, 1 cup	235	10	38	6	23	34
Cottage, creamed, small curd, 1 cup	215	9	35	6	25	31
Cottage, Lite n' Lively, 1 cup	160	2	11	2	11	10
Cottage, low-fat (2%), 1 cup	205	4	18	3	13	19
Cottage, Lowfat, Lite-line or Viva, Borden, 1 cup	90	1	10	tr	na	5
Cottage, uncreamed, dry curd, 1 cup	125	1	7	<1	3	10
Cream Cheese, Philadelphia Brand, 1 oz.	100	10	90	6	54	30
Cream Cheese, Whipped, with Chives, Philadelphia Brand, 1 oz.	90	8	80	5	50	30
Cream Cheese, Whipped, with Onions, Philadelphia Brand, 1 oz.	90	8	80	5	50	25
Cream Cheese, Whipped, with Smoked Salmon, Philadelphia Brand, 1 oz.	90	8	80	5	50	30
Cream Cheese Product, Pasteurized Process, Light, Philadelphia Brand, 1 oz.	60	5	75	3	45	10
Cream Cheese with Chives, Philadelphia Brand, 1 oz.	90	9	90	5	50	30
Cream Cheese with Chives & Onion, Soft, Philadelphia Brand, 1 oz.	100	9	81	5	45	30
Cream Cheese with Herbs & Garlic, Soft Philadelphia Brand, 1 oz.	100	9	81	5	45	25
Cream Cheese with Olives & Pimento, Soft, Philadelphia Brand, 1 oz.	90	8	80	5	50	25
Cream Cheese with Pimentos, Philadelphia Brand, 1 oz.	90	9	90	5	50	30
Cream Cheese with Pineapple, Soft, Philadelphia Brand, 1 oz.	90	8	80	5	50	25
Cream Cheese with Smoked Salmon, Soft, Philadelphia Brand, 1 oz.	90	9	90	5	50	25
Cream Cheese with Strawberries, Soft, Philadelphia Brand, 1 oz.	90	8	80	5	50	20
Edam, Natural, Kraft, 1 oz.	90	7	70	4	40	20
Feta, 1 oz.	75	6	72	4	48	25
Feta, Churny Athenos, 1 oz.	75	7	84	4	48	25

FOOD/PORTION SIZE	CAL.	FAT		SAT. FAT		CHOL.
		Total (g)	As % of Cal.	Total (g)	As % of Cal.	(mg)
Gouda, Natural, Kraft, 1 oz.	110	9	74	5	41	30
Hickory Smoke Flavor Pasteurized Process Cheese Spread, Squeez-A-Snak, 1 oz.	80	7	79	4	45	20
Jalapeño Pasteurized Process Cheese Spread, Kraft, 1 oz.	80	6	68	4	45	20
Jalapeño Pepper Spread, Kraft, 1 oz.	70	5	64	3	39	15
Jalapeño Singles Pasteurized Process Cheese Food, Kraft, 1 oz.	90	7	70	4	40	25
Limburger, Natural, Little Gem Size, Mohawk Valley, 1 oz.	90	8	80	5	50	25
Limburger Pasteurized Process Cheese Spread, Mohawk Valley, 1 oz.	70	6	77	3	39	20
Monterey Jack, Natural, Kraft, 1 oz.	110	9	74	5	41	30
Monterey Jack Singles Pasteurized Process Cheese Food, Kraft, 1 oz.	90	7	70	4	40	25
Monti-Jack-Lo, Alpine Lace, 1 oz.	80	5	56	3	34	15
Mozzarella, Low Moisture, Casino, 1 oz.	90	7	70	4	40	25
Mozzarella, made with part-skim milk, 1 oz.	72	5	63	3	38	16
Mozzarella, made with whole milk, 1 oz.	80	6	68	4	45	22
Mozzarella, Part-Skim, Low Moisture, Kraft, 1 oz.	80	5	56	3	34	15
Mozzarella, Preferred Light Fancy Supreme Shredded, Sargento, 1 oz.	60	3	45	na	na	10
Mozzarella, Preferred Light Sliced, Sargento, 1 oz.	60	3	45	2	30	10
Mozzarella, Truly Lite, Frigo, 1 oz.	60	2	30	na	na	8
Mozzarella String with Jalapeño Pepper, Part-Skim, Low Moisture, Kraft, 1 oz.	80	5	56	3	34	20
Muenster, 1 oz.	104	8	69	4	35	27
Munster, Lo-Chol Cheese Alternative, Dorman's, 1 oz.	100	7	63	1	9	5
Neufchatel Light, Philadelphia Brand, 1 oz.	80	7	79	4	45	25
Olives & Pimento Spread, Kraft, 1 oz.	60	5	75	3	45	15
Parmesan, Grated, 1 tbsp.	25	2	72	1	36	4
Parmesan, Grated, Kraft, 1 oz.	130	9	62	5	35	30
Parmesan, Natural, Kraft, 1 oz.	100	7	63	4	36	20
Parmesan, Preferred Light Grated Gourmet, Sargento, 1 tbsp.	25	2	72	tr	na	4
Pimento Cheese Spread, Pasteurized Process, Velveeta, 1 oz.	80	6	68	3	34	20
Pimento Pasteurized Process Cheese Slices, Deluxe, Kraft, 1 oz.	100	8	72	5	45	25
Pimento Singles Pasteurized Process Cheese Food, Kraft, 1 oz.	90	7	70	4	40	25

FOOD/PORTION SIZE	CAL.	FAT		SAT. FAT		CHOL.
		Total (g)	As % of Cal.	Total (g)	As % of Cal.	(mg)
Pimento Spread, Kraft, 1 oz.	70	5	64	3	39	15
Provolone, 1 oz.	100	8	72	5	45	20
Ricotta, made with part-skim milk, 1 cup	340	19	50	12	32	76
Ricotta, made with whole milk, 1 cup	430	30	63	20	42	126
Ricotta, Natural Nonfat, Polly-O Free, 1 oz.	25	0	0	0	0	0
Ricotta, Reduced Fat, Polly-O Lite, 1 oz.	35	2	51	1	26	5
Romano, Grated, Kraft, 1 oz.	130	9	62	6	42	30
Romano, Natural, Casino, 1 oz.	100	7	63	4	36	20
Sandwich Slices with Vegetable Oil, Lunch Wagon, 1 oz.	90	7	70	2	20	5
Swiss, 1 oz.	105	8	69	5	43	26
Swiss, Light, No Salt, Dorman's, 1 oz.	90	5	50	3	30	15
Swiss, Natural, Kraft, 1 oz.	110	8	65	5	41	25
Swiss, Preferred Light, Sargento, 1 oz.	90	5	50	3	30	15
Swiss Flavor Process Cheese, Lite-Line, Borden, 1 oz.	50	2	36	1	18	10
Swiss Pasteurized Process Cheese Slices, Deluxe, 1 oz.	90	7	70	4	40	25
Swiss Singles Pasteurized Process Cheese Food, Kraft, 1 oz.	90	7	70	4	40	25

Cream & Creamers

FOOD/PORTION SIZE	CAL.	FAT		SAT. FAT		CHOL.
		Total (g)	As % of Cal.	Total (g)	As % of Cal.	(mg)
Coffee Rich, ½ oz.	20	2	90	tr	na	0
Cool Whip Extra Creamy Dairy Recipe Whipped Topping, Birds Eye, 1 tbsp.	14	1	64	1	64	0
Cool Whip Lite Whipped Topping, Birds Eye, 1 tbsp.	8	tr	na	na	na	0
Cool Whip Non-Dairy Whipped Topping, Birds Eye, 1 tbsp.	12	1	75	tr	na	0
Cream, sour, 1 tbsp.	25	3	100	2	72	5
Cream, Sour, Land O Lakes, 1 tbsp.	30	3	90	2	60	5
Cream, Sour, Light, Land O Lakes, 1 tbsp.	20	1	45	1	45	3
Cream, Sour, Light n' Lively Free, Kraft, 1 tbsp.	10	0	0	0	0	0
Cream, Sour Half and Half, Breakstone's Light Choice, 1 tbsp.	20	1	45	1	45	5
Cream, sweet, half-and-half, 1 tbsp.	20	2	90	2	90	6
Cream, sweet, light/coffee/table, 1 tbsp.	30	3	90	2	60	10

FOOD/PORTION SIZE	CAL.	FAT Total (g)	FAT As % of Cal.	SAT. FAT Total (g)	SAT. FAT As % of Cal.	CHOL. (mg)
Cream, sweet, whipping, unwhipped, heavy, 1 cup	832	84	91	55	59	336
Cream, sweet, whipping, unwhipped, heavy, 1 tbsp.	52	6	100	3	52	21
Cream, sweet, whipping, unwhipped, light, 1 cup	700	69	89	46	59	272
Cream, sweet, whipping, unwhipped, light, 1 tbsp.	44	5	100	3	61	17
Creamer, sweet, imitation, liquid, 1 tbsp.	20	1	45	1	45	0
Creamer, Sweet, Powdered, Cremora Lite, 1 tsp.	8	tr	na	0	0	0
Cream Topping, Real, Kraft, 1 tbsp.	8	tr	56	tr	56	3
Whipped topping, cream, pressurized, 1 tbsp.	10	1	90	<1	36	2
Whipped Topping, Kraft, 1 tbsp.	9	tr	77	tr	77	0
Whipped topping, sweet, imitation, frozen, 1 tbsp.	15	1	60	1	60	0
Whipped topping, sweet, imitation, pressurized, 1 tbsp.	10	1	90	<1	72	2
Whipped topping, sweet, powdered, prepared with whole milk, 1 tbsp.	10	1	90	<1	72	tr
Whipped Topping Mix, Dream Whip, prepared with water, 1 tbsp.	5	0	0	0	0	0
Whipped Topping Mix, Reduced Calorie, D-Zerta, prepared, 1 tbsp.	8	1	100	tr	na	0

Eggs

FOOD/PORTION SIZE	CAL.	FAT Total (g)	FAT As % of Cal.	SAT. FAT Total (g)	SAT. FAT As % of Cal.	CHOL. (mg)
Cholesterol Free Egg Product, Healthy Choice, ¼ cup	30	<1	na	na	na	0
Egg Beaters, Fleischmann's, ¼ cup	25	0	0	0	0	0
Egg Substitute, Scramblers, ¼ cup	60	3	45	tr	na	0
Large, fried in butter, 1 egg	95	7	76	3	33	278
Large, hard-cooked, 1 egg	80	6	68	2	23	213
Large, poached, 1 egg	80	6	68	2	23	213
Large, raw, white only, 1 white	15	0	0	0	0	0
Large, raw, whole, 1 egg	80	6	68	2	23	213
Large, raw, yolk only, 1 yolk	65	6	83	2	28	213
Scrambled, with milk, cooked in margarine, 1 egg	100	7	63	2	18	215

Fast Foods

FOOD/PORTION SIZE	CAL.	FAT		SAT. FAT		CHOL.
		Total (g)	As % of Cal.	Total (g)	As % of Cal.	(mg)
ARBY'S						
Dressing, Blue Cheese, 2 oz.	295	31	95	6	18	50
Dressing, Buttermilk Ranch, 2 oz.	349	40	100	6	15	6
Dressing, Honey French, 2 oz.	322	27	75	4	11	0
Dressing, Light Italian, 2 oz.	23	1	39	tr	na	0
Dressing, Weight Watchers Creamy French, 1 oz.	48	3	56	1	19	0
Dressing, Weight Watchers Creamy Italian, 1 oz.	29	3	93	1	31	0
Light Roast Beef Deluxe Sandwich	294	10	31	4	12	42
Light Roast Chicken Deluxe Sandwich	263	6	21	2	7	39
Light Roast Turkey Deluxe Sandwich	260	5	17	2	7	30
Salad, Chef	205	10	44	4	18	126
Salad, Garden	109	5	41	3	25	12
Salad, Roast Chicken	184	7	34	3	15	36
Salad, Side	25	tr	na	0	0	0
BURGER KING						
Bacon Double Cheeseburger	507	30	53	14	25	108
Cheeseburger	318	15	42	7	20	50
Chicken BK Broiler Sandwich	267	8	27	2	7	45
Chunky Chicken Salad	142	4	25	1	6	49
Croissan'wich with Bacon	353	23	59	8	20	230
Croissan'wich with Ham	351	22	56	7	18	236
Croissan'wich with Sausage	534	40	67	14	24	258
French Fries, lightly salted, medium	372	20	48	5	12	0
French Toast Sticks, 1 order	538	32	54	8	13	52
Hamburger	272	11	36	4	13	37
Ocean Catch Fish Fillet	479	33	62	8	15	45
Onion Rings, 1 order	339	19	50	5	13	0
Pie, Apple	311	14	41	4	12	4
Salad, Chef	178	9	46	4	20	103
Whopper	614	36	53	12	18	91
Whopper with Cheese	706	44	56	16	20	116
DAIRY QUEEN						
Banana Split	510	11	19	8	14	30
Fish Fillet sandwich	370	16	39	3	7	45

FOOD/PORTION SIZE	CAL.	FAT		SAT. FAT		CHOL.
		Total (g)	As % of Cal.	Total (g)	As % of Cal.	(mg)
Fish Fillet with Cheese sandwich	420	21	45	6	13	60
Grilled Chicken Fillet sandwich	300	8	24	2	6	50
Hamburger, Single	310	13	38	6	17	45
"Heath" "Blizzard," small	560	23	37	11	18	40
Malt, Regular Vanilla	610	14	21	8	12	45
Parfait, Peanut Buster	710	32	41	10	13	30
Shake, Regular Chocolate	540	14	23	8	13	45
Sundae, Regular Chocolate	300	7	21	5	15	20
DOMINO'S						
Pizza, Cheese, 2 slices	376	10	24	6	14	19
Pizza, Deluxe, 2 slices	498	20	36	9	16	40
Pizza, Double Cheese/Pepperoni, 2 slices	545	25	44	13	21	48
Pizza, Ham, 2 slices	417	11	24	6	13	26
Pizza, Pepperoni, 2 slices	460	18	35	8	16	28
Pizza, Sausage/Mushroom, 2 slices	430	16	33	8	17	28
Pizza, Veggie, 2 slices	498	19	34	10	18	36
DUNKIN' DONUTS						
Apple Filled Cinnamon	190	9	43	2	9	0
Boston Kreme	240	11	41	2	8	0
Chocolate Frosted Yeast Ring	200	10	45	2	9	0
Glazed Yeast Ring	200	9	41	2	9	0
Honey Dipped Cruller	260	11	38	2	7	0
Jelly Filled	220	9	37	2	8	0
Plain Cake Ring	262	18	62	4	14	0
Powdered Cake Ring	270	16	53	3	10	0
KENTUCKY FRIED CHICKEN						
Buttermilk Biscuit, 2.3 oz.	235	12	46	3	11	1
Coleslaw, 3.2 oz.	114	6	47	1	8	4
Corn On-the-Cob, 2.6 oz.	90	2	20	1	10	tr
Extra Tasty Crispy, center breast, 3.9 oz.	344	21	55	5	13	80
Extra Tasty Crispy, drumstick, 2.4 oz.	205	14	61	3	13	72
Extra Tasty Crispy, wing, 2 oz.	231	17	66	4	16	63
French Fries, 2.7 oz.	244	12	44	3	11	2
Hot & Spicy, center breast, 4.3 oz.	382	25	59	6	14	84
Hot & Spicy, drumstick, 2.5 oz.	207	14	61	3	13	75
Hot & Spicy, wing, 2.2 oz.	244	18	66	4	15	65

FOOD/PORTION SIZE	CAL.	FAT		SAT. FAT		CHOL.
		Total (g)	As % of Cal.	Total (g)	As % of Cal.	(mg)
Hot Wings, six wings, 4.8 oz.	471	33	63	8	15	150
Kentucky Nuggets, six, 3.4 oz.	284	18	57	4	13	66
Mashed Potatoes & Gravy, 3.5 oz.	71	2	25	0	0	tr
Sauce, Barbeque, 1 oz.	35	1	26	0	0	tr
Sauce, Sweet 'N Sour, 1 oz.	58	1	16	0	0	tr
Skinfree Crispy, center breast, 4 oz.	296	16	49	3	9	59
Skinfree Crispy, thigh, 3 oz.	256	17	60	4	14	68
LONG JOHN SILVER'S						
Baked Chicken, Light Herb	130	4	28	na	na	65
Baked Fish, Lemon Crumb, 3 pieces	150	1	6	na	na	110
Baked Fish, Lemon Crumb, 2 pieces, Rice, and Small Salad (w/o dressing)	320	4	11	na	na	75
Baked Shrimp, Scampi Sauce	120	5	38	na	na	205
Cole Slaw	140	6	39	na	na	15
Rice Pilaf	210	2	9	na	na	0
Salad, Small (w/o dressing)	8	0	0	0	0	0
McDONALD'S						
Big Mac	500	26	47	9	16	100
Biscuit with Bacon, Egg, and Cheese	440	26	53	8	16	240
Biscuit with Sausage	420	28	60	8	17	44
Biscuit with Sausage and Egg	505	33	59	10	18	260
Cheeseburger	305	13	38	5	15	50
Chicken McNuggets (6 pieces)	270	15	50	<4	12	55
Cone, Low fat Frozen Yogurt, Vanilla	105	1	9	<1	4	3
Cookies, Chocolaty Chip, 1 box	330	15	41	4	11	4
Cookies, McDonaldland, 1 box	290	9	28	1	3	0
Danish, Apple	390	17	39	4	9	25
Danish, Cinnamon Raisin	440	21	43	5	10	34
Danish, Iced Cheese	390	21	48	6	14	47
Danish, Raspberry	410	16	35	3	7	26
Dressing, Lite Vinaigrette, 1 oz.	24	1	38	<1	8	0
Dressing, Ranch, 1 oz.	110	10	82	2	16	10
Egg McMuffin	280	11	35	4	13	235
Eggs, Scrambled, 2 eggs	140	10	64	3	19	425
Filet-O-Fish sandwich	370	18	44	4	10	50
French Fries, small	220	12	49	<3	10	9
Hamburger	255	9	32	3	11	37
Hashbrowns	130	7	48	1	7	0

FOOD/PORTION SIZE	CAL.	FAT Total (g)	As % of Cal.	SAT. FAT Total (g)	As % of Cal.	CHOL. (mg)
Hotcakes with 2 pats margarine and 1½ oz. syrup	440	12	25	2	4	8
McLean Deluxe	320	10	28	4	11	60
Milk Shake, Chocolate Low-fat	320	<2	5	<1	2	10
Milk Shake, Strawberry Low-fat	320	<2	4	<1	2	10
Milk Shake, Vanilla Low-fat	290	<2	4	<1	2	10
Pie, Apple	260	15	52	4	14	6
Quarter Pounder	410	20	44	8	18	85
Quarter Pounder with Cheese	510	28	49	11	19	115
Salad, Chef	170	9	48	4	21	111
Salad, Chicken, Chunky	150	4	24	1	6	78
Salad, Garden	50	2	36	<1	11	65
Sauce, Barbecue, 1 serving	50	<1	9	<1	2	0
Sauce, Hot Mustard, 1 serving	70	4	51	<1	6	5
Sauce, Sweet-n-Sour, 1 serving	60	<1	3	0	0	0
Sausage	160	15	84	5	28	43
Sausage McMuffin	345	20	52	7	18	57
Sausage McMuffin with Egg	430	25	52	8	17	270
Sundae, Hot Caramel Low-fat Frozen Yogurt	270	3	10	<2	5	13
Sundae, Hot Fudge Low-fat Frozen Yogurt	240	3	11	2	8	6
Sundae, Strawberry Low-fat Frozen Yogurt	210	1	4	<1	2	5
PIZZA HUT						
Hand-Tossed, Cheese, 2 slices medium (15-inch), 7.9 oz.	518	20	35	14	24	55
Hand-Tossed, Supreme, 2 slices medium (15-inch), 8.5 oz.	540	26	43	14	23	55
Pan, Super Supreme, 2 slices medium (15-inch), 9.2 oz.	563	26	42	12	19	55
Pan, with cheese, 2 slices medium (15-inch), 7.3 oz.	492	18	33	9	16	34
Personal Pan, Pepperoni, whole (5-inch), 9.1 oz.	675	29	39	12	16	53
Personal Pan, Supreme, whole (5-inch), 9.4 oz.	647	28	39	11	15	49
Thin 'n Crispy, Pepperoni, 2 slices medium (15-inch), 5.2 oz.	413	20	44	11	24	46
Thin 'n Crispy, Supreme, 2 slices medium (15-inch), 7.1 oz.	459	22	43	11	22	42

FOOD/PORTION SIZE	CAL.	FAT		SAT. FAT		CHOL.
		Total (g)	As % of Cal.	Total (g)	As % of Cal.	(mg)
SUBWAY						
BMT Salad, small	369	30	73	10	24	66
BMT Sub, Italian Roll, 6-inch	491	28	51	10	18	66
Club Salad, small	225	13	52	3	12	42
Club Sub, Italian Roll, 6-inch	346	11	29	4	10	42
Cold Cut Combo Salad, small	305	26	77	6	18	83
Cold Cut Combo Sub, Italian Roll, 6-inch	427	20	42	6	13	83
Ham & Cheese Salad, small	200	12	54	3	14	36
Ham & Cheese Sub, Italian Roll, 6-inch	322	9	25	3	8	36
Meatball Sub, Italian Roll, 6-inch	459	22	43	8	16	44
Roast Beef Salad, small	222	10	41	4	16	38
Roast Beef Sub, Italian Roll, 6-inch	345	12	31	4	10	38
Seafood & Crab Salad, small	371	30	73	5	12	28
Seafood & Crab Sub, Italian Roll, 6-inch	493	28	51	5	9	28
Steak & Cheese Sub, Italian Roll, 6-inch	383	16	38	6	14	41
Tuna Salad, small	430	38	80	6	13	43
Tuna Sub, Italian Roll, 6-inch	551	36	59	7	11	43
Turkey Breast Salad, small	201	11	49	3	13	33
Turkey Breast Sub, Italian Roll, 6-inch	322	10	28	3	8	33
Veggies & Cheese Sub, Italian Roll, 6-inch	268	9	30	3	10	9
TACO BELL						
Burrito, Bean	447	14	28	4	8	9
Burrito, Beef	493	21	38	8	15	57
Burrito, Chicken	334	12	32	4	11	52
Burrito, Combo	407	16	35	5	11	33
Burrito Supreme	503	22	39	8	14	33
Cinnamon Twists	171	8	42	3	16	0
Meximelt, Beef	266	15	51	8	27	38
Meximelt, Chicken	257	15	53	7	25	48
Nachos	346	18	47	6	16	9
Nachos Bellgrande	649	35	49	12	17	36
Pintos & Cheese	190	9	43	4	19	16
Pizza, Mexican	575	37	58	11	17	52
Salad, Taco	905	61	61	19	19	80
Salad, Taco, w/o shell	484	31	58	14	26	80
Salsa	18	0	0	0	0	0
Sauce, Hot Taco, 1 packet	3	0	0	0	0	0
Sauce, Taco, 1 packet	2	0	0	0	0	0
Taco	183	11	54	5	25	32
Taco Bellgrande	335	23	62	11	30	56

FAST FOODS

FOOD/PORTION SIZE	CAL.	FAT Total (g)	As % of Cal.	SAT. FAT Total (g)	As % of Cal.	CHOL. (mg)
Taco, Soft	225	12	48	5	20	32
Taco, Soft, Chicken	213	10	42	4	17	52
Taco, Soft, Steak	218	11	45	5	21	30
WENDY'S						
Big Classic Sandwich, with Kaiser Bun	570	33	52	6	9	90
Chicken Nuggets, Crispy, 6 pieces	280	20	64	5	16	50
Chicken Sandwich	430	19	40	3	6	60
Chili, Regular, 9 oz.	220	7	29	3	12	45
Cookie, Chocolate Chip, 1 cookie	275	13	43	4	13	15
Fish Fillet Sandwich	460	25	49	5	10	55
Fries, small (3⅕ oz.)	240	12	45	3	11	0
Frosty Dairy Dessert, small	400	14	32	5	11	50
Grilled Chicken Sandwich	340	13	34	3	8	60
Hamburger, Kid's Meal, with White Bun	260	9	31	3	10	35
Hamburger, Single, Plain, ¼-lb.	340	15	40	6	16	65
Nuggets Sauce, Barbeque, 1 packet	50	<1	na	tr	na	0
Nuggets Sauce, Honey, 1 packet	45	<1	na	tr	na	0
Nuggets Sauce, Sweet & Sour, 1 packet	45	<1	na	tr	na	0
Nuggets Sauce, Sweet Mustard, 1 packet	50	1	18	<1	na	0
Potato, Hot Stuffed Baked, Bacon & Cheese	520	18	31	5	9	20
Potato, Hot Stuffed Baked, Broccoli & Cheese	400	16	36	3	7	tr
Potato, Hot Stuffed Baked, Cheese	420	15	32	4	9	10
Potato, Hot Stuffed Baked, Chili & Cheese	500	18	32	4	7	25
Potato, Hot Stuffed Baked, Plain	270	<1	na	tr	na	0
Potato, Hot Stuffed Baked, Sour Cream & Chives	500	23	41	9	16	25
Salad, Chef (take-out)	180	9	45	na	na	120
Salad, Garden (take-out)	102	5	44	na	na	0
Salad, Taco	660	37	50	na	na	35
Swiss Deluxe Sandwich, Jr.	360	18	45	3.3	8	40

Fats & Oils

FOOD/PORTION SIZE	CAL.	FAT Total (g)	As % of Cal.	SAT. FAT Total (g)	As % of Cal.	CHOL. (mg)
Butter, approx. 1 tbsp.	100	11	99	7	63	31
Butter, Land O Lakes, 1 tbsp.	100	11	99	7	63	30

FOOD/PORTION SIZE	CAL.	FAT		SAT. FAT		CHOL.
		Total (g)	As % of Cal.	Total (g)	As % of Cal.	(mg)
Butter, Whipped, Land O Lakes, 1 tbsp.	60	7	100	4	60	20
Butter Buds, ½ teaspoon	4	0	0	0	0	0
Lard, 1 tbsp.	115	13	100	5	39	12
Margarine, Blue Bonnet, 1 tbsp.	100	11	99	2	18	0
Margarine, Extra Light, Promise, 1 tbsp.	50	6	98	<1	na	0
Margarine, imitation, soft, 1 tbsp.	50	5	90	1	18	0
Margarine, Light, Parkay, stick, 1 tbsp.	70	7	90	1	13	0
Margarine, Parkay, 1 tbsp.	100	11	99	2	18	0
Margarine, regular, hard, 1 tbsp. (⅛ stick)	100	11	99	2	18	0
Margarine, regular, hard, approx. 1 tsp.	35	4	100	1	26	0
Margarine, regular, soft, 1 tbsp.	100	11	99	2	18	0
Margarine, Soft, Parkay, 1 tbsp.	100	11	99	2	18	0
Margarine, Soft, Parkay Corn Oil, 1 tbsp.	100	11	99	2	18	0
Margarine, Soft Diet, Parkay Reduced Calorie, 1 tbsp.	50	6	100	1	18	0
Margarine, spread, hard, 1 tbsp. (⅛ stick)	75	9	100	2	24	0
Margarine, spread, hard, approx. 1 tsp.	25	3	100	1	36	0
Margarine, Squeezable, Shedd's Spread Country Crock, 1 tbsp.	80	9	100	1	11	0
Margarine, Squeeze Parkay, 1 tbsp.	90	10	100	2	20	0
Margarine, Stick, Corn, Mazola, 1 tbsp.	100	11	99	2	18	0
Margarine, Stick, Corn Oil, Fleischmann's, 1 tbsp.	100	11	99	2	18	0
Margarine, Stick, Corn Oil, Mazola, 1 tbsp.	100	11	99	2	18	0
Margarine, Stick, Soy Oil, Chiffon, 1 tbsp.	100	11	99	2	18	0
Margarine, Stick, Soy Oil, Weight Watchers Reduced-Calorie, 1 tbsp.	60	7	100	1	15	0
Margarine, Stick, Sunflower Oil, Promise, 1 tbsp.	90	10	100	2	20	0
Margarine, Tub, Soy Oil, Chiffon, 1 tbsp.	90	10	100	1	10	0
Margarine, Tub, Soy Oil, Weight Watchers Reduced-Calorie Light Spread, 1 tbsp.	50	6	100	1	18	0
Margarine, Tub, Sunflower Oil, Promise, 1 tbsp.	90	10	100	2	20	0
Oil, Canola, Crisco Puritan, 1 tbsp.	120	13	98	1	18	0
Oil, Corn, Mazola, 1 tbsp.	120	14	100	2	15	0
Oil, Olive, Bertolli, 1 tbsp.	120	14	100	2	15	0
Oil, Olive, Filippo Berio, 1 tbsp.	120	14	100	2	15	0
Oil, peanut, 1 tbsp.	125	14	100	2	14	0
Oil, Peanut, Hollywood, 1 tbsp.	120	14	100	4	30	0
Oil, Safflower, Hollywood, 1 tbsp.	120	14	100	1	8	0
Oil, Soybean, Crisco, 1 tbsp.	120	13	98	2	15	0
Oil, soybean-cottonseed blend, hydrogenated, 1 tbsp.	125	14	100	3	22	0

FOOD/PORTION SIZE	CAL.	FAT		SAT. FAT		CHOL.
		Total (g)	As % of Cal.	Total (g)	As % of Cal.	(mg)
Oil, sunflower, 1 tbsp.	125	14	100	1	7	0
Oil, Sunflower, Sunlite, 1 tbsp.	120	14	100	1	7	0
Oil, Vegetable, Crisco, 1 tbsp.	120	14	100	1	7	0
Shortening, Vegetable, Crisco, 1 tbsp.	110	12	98	3	25	0
Shortening, Vegetable, Crisco Butter Flavor, 1 tbsp.	110	12	98	3	25	0
Spray, Cooking (Vegetable Oil), Pam, 2½-second spray	14	2	100	tr	na	0
Spray, No-Stick (Vegetable), Mazola, 2½-second spray	6	1	100	tr	na	0
Spread, 50% Fat, Parkay, 1 tbsp.	60	7	100	1	15	0
Spread, Parkay (50% vegetable oil), 1 tbsp.	60	7	100	1	15	0
Spread, Stick, Touch of Butter, Kraft, 1 tbsp.	90	10	90	2	20	0
Spread, Tub, (Vegetable), Shedd's, 1 tbsp.	70	7	90	1	13	0

Fish & Shellfish

FOOD/PORTION SIZE	CAL.	FAT		SAT. FAT		CHOL.
		Total (g)	As % of Cal.	Total (g)	As % of Cal.	(mg)
Catfish, breaded, fried, 3 oz.	194	11	52	na	na	69
Catfish, skinless, baked w/o fat, 3 oz.	120	5	38	1	8	60
Clams, Canned, Liquid and Solids, Doxsee, ½ cup	59	tr	na	0	0	38
Clams, raw, meat only, 3 oz.	65	1	14	<1	4	43
Cod, fillets (frozen), Booth, 4 oz.	90	1	10	na	na	na
Cod, skinless, broiled w/o fat, 3 oz.	90	1	10	0	0	50
Crabmeat, canned, 1 cup	135	3	20	<1	3	135
Fish sticks (frozen), reheated, 4 × ½-in. stick	70	3	39	1	13	26
Flounder, baked, with lemon juice, w/o added fat, 3 oz.	80	1	11	<1	4	59
Haddock, breaded, fried, 3 oz.	175	9	46	2	10	75
Haddock, skinless, baked w/o fat, 3 oz.	90	1	10	0	0	60
Halibut, broiled, with butter, with lemon juice, 3 oz.	140	6	39	3	19	62
Herring, pickled, 3 oz.	190	13	62	4	19	85
Lobster, boiled, 3 oz.	100	1	9	0	0	100
Mackerel, skinless, broiled w/o fat, 3 oz.	190	12	57	3	14	60
Orange roughy, broiled, 3 oz.	130	7	48	0	0	20
Oysters, breaded, fried, 1 oyster	90	5	50	1	10	35
Oysters, raw, meat only, 1 cup	160	4	23	1	6	120

FOOD/PORTION SIZE	CAL.	FAT Total (g)	FAT As % of Cal.	SAT. FAT Total (g)	SAT. FAT As % of Cal.	CHOL. (mg)
Perch, ocean, breaded, fried, 1 fillet	185	11	54	3	15	66
Perch, Ocean, Natural Fillets (frozen), Taste O'Sea, 4 oz.	100	3	27	na	na	na
Pollock, skinless, broiled w/o fat, 3 oz.	100	1	9	0	0	80
Salmon, Pink, Bumble Bee, 3½ oz.	138	6	39	2	13	40
Salmon, Pink (in spring water), Chicken of the Sea, 3½ oz.	105	4	30	na	na	na
Salmon, red, baked, 3 oz.	140	5	32	1	6	60
Salmon, smoked, 3 oz.	150	8	48	3	18	51
Sardines, canned in oil, drained, 3 oz.	175	11	57	2	10	121
Sardines (in olive oil), King Oscar, 3¾ oz.	460	16	31	3	6	na
Scallops, breaded (frozen), reheated, 6 scallops	195	10	46	3	14	70
Scallops, broiled, 3 oz. (5.7 large or 14 small)	150	1	6	0	0	60
Shrimp, boiled, 3 oz.	110	2	16	0	0	160
Shrimp, canned, drained solids, 3 oz.	103	1	9	tr	na	148
Shrimp, French fried, 3 oz. (7 medium)	189	9	43	2	10	137
Snapper, cooked by dry heat, 3 oz.	109	2	17	na	na	40
Sole, baked, with lemon juice, w/o added fat, 3 oz.	90	1	10	tr	na	49
Surimi seafood, crab flavored, chunk style, ½ cup	84	tr	na	tr	na	25
Trout, Rainbow, skinless, broiled w/o fat, 3 oz.	130	4	28	1	7	60
Tuna, Albacore (in water), Bumble Bee, 2 oz.	70	1	13	tr	na	24
Tuna, Chunk Light (in spring water), StarKist, ½ cup	77	1	12	tr	na	26
Tuna, Chunk Light (in vegetable oil), Bumble Bee, 2 oz.	160	12	68	2	11	24
Tuna, Chunk Light (in water), Bumble Bee, 2 oz.	70	1	13	1	13	27

Frozen Appetizers & Entrées

FOOD/PORTION SIZE	CAL.	FAT Total (g)	FAT As % of Cal.	SAT. FAT Total (g)	SAT. FAT As % of Cal.	CHOL. (mg)
APPETIZERS						
Chicken Nuggets, Weight Watchers, approx. 6 oz.	270	12	40	4	13	50
Ravioli, Baked Cheese, Weight Watchers, 9 oz.	290	12	37	5	16	85

FOOD/PORTION SIZE	CAL.	FAT		SAT. FAT		CHOL.
		Total (g)	As % of Cal.	Total (g)	As % of Cal.	(mg)
MEAT ENTRÉES						
Beef Pot Pie, Swanson, 7 oz.	370	19	46	na	na	na
Lasagna with Meat Sauce, Weight Watchers, 11 oz.	330	11	30	5	14	60
Pizza, Cheese Party, Totino's, 5 oz. (½ pizza)	290	10	31	3	9	15
Pizza, Sausage, Pepperoni, & Mushroom, Stouffer's French Bread Deluxe, 1 piece, about 6 oz.	420	19	41	na	na	na
Pizza, Sausage French Bread, Lean Cuisine, 6 oz.	350	11	28	3	8	40
Pizza, Vegetable, Tombstone Light, ⅕ pizza (4⅓ oz.)	200	7	32	na	na	10
Salisbury Steak, Hungry Man, Swanson, 16¼ oz.	630	32	46	na	na	na
Salisbury Steak, Lean Cuisine, 9½ oz.	240	7	26	2	8	45
Salisbury Steak Dinner, Healthy Choice, 11½ oz.	300	7	21	3	9	50
Sirloin Beef with Barbecue Sauce Dinner, Healthy Choice, 11 oz.	300	6	18	3	9	50
Spaghetti, Lean Cuisine, 11½ oz.	270	6	20	2	7	30
Szechwan Beef with Noodles, Lean Cuisine, 8⅝ oz.	259	9	31	3	10	83
MISCELLANEOUS						
Macaroni & Cheese, Lean Cuisine, 9 oz.	290	9	28	4	12	30
Pasta Classic, Healthy Choice, 12½ oz.	310	3	9	tr	na	35
POULTRY ENTRÉES						
Breast of Chicken Marsala, Lean Cuisine, 8⅛ oz.	190	5	24	2	9	65
Chicken, Broccoli & Cheddar Turnovers, Quaker Ovenstuffs, 4¾ oz.	350	16	41	na	na	na
Chicken, Fried, Plump & Juicy, Swanson, 3¼ oz.	270	16	53	na	na	na
Chicken a la King, Weight Watchers, 9 oz.	220	8	33	2	8	55
Chicken Burritos, Weight Watchers, 7⅗ oz.	310	13	38	4	12	60
Chicken Cacciatore, Lean Cuisine, 10⅞ oz.	280	10	32	2	6	45
Chicken Dijon Dinner, Healthy Choice, 11 oz.	260	3	10	1	3	45
Chicken Fettucini, Weight Watchers, 8¼ oz.	280	9	29	3	10	40
Chicken Parmigiana Dinner, Healthy Choice, 11½ oz.	270	3	10	2	7	50

FOOD/PORTION SIZE	CAL.	FAT		SAT. FAT		CHOL.
		Total (g)	As % of Cal.	Total (g)	As % of Cal.	(mg)
Mesquite Chicken Dinner, Healthy Choice, 10½ oz.	340	1	3	tr	na	45
Pot Pie, Chicken, Swanson, 7 oz.	390	23	53	na	na	na
SEAFOOD ENTRÉES						
Filet of Fish Divan, Lean Cuisine, 12⅜ oz.	270	9	30	2	7	90
Fish Dijon, Light Entrée, Mrs. Paul's, 8¾ oz.	200	5	23	na	na	60
Fish Fillet Au Gratin, Booth, 9½ oz.	280	8	26	na	na	72
Fish Fillet Florentine, Booth, 9½ oz.	260	8	28	na	na	82
Fish Florentine, Light Entree, Mrs. Paul's, 8 oz.	220	8	33	na	na	95
Fish Mornay, Light Entrée, Mrs. Paul's, 9 oz.	230	10	39	na	na	80
Seafood Linguini, Weight Watchers, 9 oz.	210	7	30	1	4	5
Shrimp Primavera with Fettuccine, Booth, 10 oz.	200	3	14	na	na	0
Shrimp with Lobster Sauce, Fresh & Lite, La Choy, 10 oz.	210	7	30	na	na	na
Tuna Lasagna, Lean Cuisine, 9¾ oz.	280	10	32	4	13	25

Frozen Desserts

FOOD/PORTION SIZE	CAL.	FAT		SAT. FAT		CHOL.
		Total (g)	As % of Cal.	Total (g)	As % of Cal.	(mg)
DAIRY						
Frozen Dairy Dessert, Strawberry, Healthy Choice, ½ cup	110	1	8	1	8	5
Frozen Dessert, Nonfat, Chocolate Flavor, Sealtest Free, ½ cup	110	0	0	na	na	0
Frozen Yogurt, Peach, Borden, ½ cup	100	2	18	na	na	na
Frozen Yogurt, Peach, Sealtest, ½ cup	100	0	0	na	na	0
Ice Cream, Butter Pecan, Breyers, ½ cup	150	8	48	7	42	na
Ice Cream, Chocolate, Breyers, ½ cup	160	8	45	5	28	na
Ice Cream, Chocolate, Sealtest, ½ cup	140	7	45	na	na	na
Ice Cream, Peach, Natural, Breyers, ½ cup	140	12	77	4	26	na
Ice Cream, Strawberry, Natural, Breyers, ½ cup	130	6	42	4	28	na
Ice Cream, Vanilla, Natural, Breyers, ½ cup	180	12	60	5	25	na
Ice Cream, Vanilla, Sealtest, ½ cup	140	7	45	5	32	na

FOOD/PORTION SIZE	CAL.	FAT		SAT. FAT		CHOL.
		Total (g)	As % of Cal.	Total (g)	As % of Cal.	(mg)
Ice Cream, Vanilla/Chocolate/ Strawberry, Sealtest, ½ cup	140	6	39	na	na	na
Ice Milk, Chocolate, Weight Watchers, ½ cup	110	3	25	1	8	10
Ice Milk, Neapolitan, Weight Watchers, ½ cup	110	3	25	1	8	10
Ice milk, vanilla, soft serve, ½ cup	113	3	20	2	12	7
Ice Milk, Vanilla, Weight Watchers, ½ cup	100	3	27	1	9	10
Sherbet, ½ cup	135	2	13	1	7	7
Sherbet, Orange, Borden, ½ cup	120	1	8	na	na	na
Sherbet, Raspberry Real Fruit, Dean Foods, ½ cup	110	1	7	na	na	na

SPECIALTY BARS

	CAL.	FAT		SAT. FAT		CHOL.
Fruit Bars, all flavors, Jell-O, 1 bar	45	0	0	0	0	0
Fruit n' Juice Bars, Pineapple, Dole, 1 bar	70	1	13	na	na	na
Gelatin Pops, all flavors, Jell-O, 1 bar	35	0	0	0	0	0
Popsicle, 3-fl.-oz. size, 1 popsicle	70	0	0	0	0	0
Pudding Pops, Chocolate, Jell-O, 1 bar	80	2	23	2	23	0
Pudding Pops, Chocolate-Caramel Swirl, Jell-O, 1 bar	80	2	23	2	23	0
Pudding Pops, Chocolate-Covered Chocolate, Jell-O, 1 bar	130	7	48	5	35	0
Pudding Pops, Chocolate-Covered Vanilla, Jell-O, 1 bar	130	7	48	5	35	0
Pudding Pops, Vanilla, Jell-O, 1 bar	70	2	26	2	26	0
Pudding Pops, Vanilla with Chocolate Chips, Jell-O, 1 bar	80	3	34	2	23	0
Pudding Snacks, Chocolate, Jell-O, 4 oz.	160	5	28	2	11	0
Pudding Snacks, Chocolate, Jello-O Free, 4 oz.	100	0	0	0	0	0
Vanilla Ice Cream, Dark Chocolate Coating, Eskimo Pie, 1 bar (3 fl. oz.)	180	12	60	na	na	na

Fruit

FOOD/PORTION SIZE	CAL.	FAT		SAT. FAT		CHOL.
		Total (g)	As % of Cal.	Total (g)	As % of Cal.	(mg)
Apples, dried, sulfured, 10 rings	155	tr	na	tr	na	0
Apples, raw, unpeeled, 3¼-in. diameter, 1 apple	125	1	7	<1	<1	0
Apple Sauce, Natural, Mott's, 1 cup	100	0	0	0	0	0

FOOD/PORTION SIZE	CAL.	FAT Total (g)	As % of Cal.	SAT. FAT Total (g)	As % of Cal.	CHOL. (mg)
Apple Sauce, Canned, Regular or Chunky, Mott's, 1 cup	114	0	0	0	0	0
Applesauce, canned, sweetened, 1 cup	195	tr	na	<1	<1	0
Applesauce, canned, unsweetened, 1 cup	105	tr	na	tr	na	0
Apricots, canned, heavy syrup pack, 3 halves	70	tr	na	tr	na	0
Apricots, canned, juice pack, 3 halves	40	tr	na	tr	na	0
Apricots, dried, cooked, unsweetened, 1 cup	210	tr	na	tr	na	0
Apricots, dried, uncooked, 1 cup	310	1	3	tr	na	0
Apricots, raw, 3 apricots	50	tr	na	tr	na	0
Avocados, raw, whole, California, 1 avocado	305	28	83	5	15	0
Avocados, raw, whole, Florida, 1 avocado	340	23	61	5	13	0
Bananas, raw, 1 banana	105	1	9	<1	2	0
Blackberries, raw, 1 cup	75	1	12	<1	2	0
Blueberries, frozen, sweetened, 10 oz.	230	tr	na	tr	na	0
Blueberries, raw, 1 cup	80	1	11	tr	<1	0
Cantaloupe, raw, ½ melon	95	1	9	<1	<1	0
Cherries, sour, red, pitted, canned water pack, 1 cup	90	tr	<1	<1	1	0
Cherries, sweet, raw, 10 cherries	50	1	18	<1	2	0
Cranberry sauce, sweetened, canned, strained, 1 cup	420	tr	na	tr	na	0
Dates, chopped, ½ cup	245	<1	2	<1	<1	0
Dates, whole, w/o pits, 10 dates	230	tr	na	<1	<1	0
Figs, dried, 10 figs	475	2	4	<1	<1	0
Fruit, Mixed, in Syrup, Birds Eye Quick Thaw Pouch, 5 oz.	120	0	0	na	na	0
Fruit, Mixed, Libby's Chunky, Lite, ½ cup	50	0	0	na	na	na
Fruit Cocktail, Del Monte, ½ cup	80	0	0	na	na	na
Fruit Cocktail, Del Monte Lite, ½ cup	50	0	0	na	na	na
Fruit Cocktail, Libby's Lite, ½ cup	50	0	0	na	na	na
Grapefruit, canned, with syrup, 1 cup	150	tr	na	tr	na	0
Grapefruit, raw, ½ grapefruit	40	tr	na	tr	na	0
Grapes, Thompson seedless, 10 grapes	35	tr	na	<1	3	0
Grapes, Tokay/Emperor, seeded, 10 grapes	40	tr	na	<1	2	0
Honeydew melon, raw, ¹⁄₁₀ melon	45	tr	na	tr	na	0
Kiwifruit, raw, w/o skin, 1 kiwifruit	45	tr	na	tr	na	0
Lemons, raw, 1 lemon	15	tr	na	tr	na	0
Mandarin Orange Segments, Dole, ½ cup	70	<1	<1	0	0	0
Mangos, raw, 1 mango	135	1	7	<1	<1	0
Nectarines, raw, 1 nectarine	65	1	14	<1	1	0
Olives, canned, green, 4 medium or 3 extra large	15	2	100	<1	12	0

145

FOOD/PORTION SIZE	CAL.	FAT		SAT. FAT		CHOL.
		Total (g)	As % of Cal.	Total (g)	As % of Cal.	(mg)
Olives, ripe, mission, pitted, 3 small or 2 large	15	2	100	<1	18	0
Oranges, raw, whole, w/o peel and seeds, 1 orange	60	tr	na	tr	na	0
Papayas, raw, ½-in. cubes, 1 cup	65	tr	na	<1	1	0
Peaches, canned, heavy syrup, 1 cup	190	tr	na	tr	na	0
Peaches, canned, juice pack, 1 cup	110	tr	na	tr	na	0
Peaches, dried, uncooked, 1 cup	380	1	2	<1	<1	0
Peaches, frozen, sliced, sweetened, 1 cup	235	tr	na	tr	na	0
Peaches, raw, whole, 2½-in. diameter, 1 peach	35	tr	na	tr	na	0
Peaches, Sliced, Lite, Libby's, 1 cup	100	0	0	na	na	na
Pears, Bartlett, raw with skin, 1 pear	100	1	9	tr	na	0
Pears, Bosc, raw with skin, 1 pear	85	1	11	tr	na	0
Pears, canned, heavy syrup, 1 cup	190	tr	na	tr	na	0
Pears, canned, juice pack, 1 cup	125	tr	na	tr	na	0
Pears, D'Anjou, raw with skin, 1 pear	120	1	8	tr	na	0
Pears, Halves, Lite, Libby's, ½ cup	60	0	0	na	na	na
Pineapple, Canned, Heavy Syrup Dole, (all cuts), ½ cup	91	0	0	0	0	0
Pineapple, canned, heavy syrup, sliced, 1 slice	45	tr	na	tr	na	0
Pineapple, Canned, Juice Pack Dole, (all cuts), ½ cup	70	0	0	0	0	0
Pineapple, canned, juice pack slices, 1 slice	35	tr	na	tr	na	0
Pineapple, raw, diced, ½ cup	38	tr	12	tr	na	0
Plums, canned, purple, juice pack, 3 plums	55	tr	na	tr	na	0
Plums, raw, 1½-in. diameter, 1 plum	15	Tr	na	Total	na	0
Plums, raw, 2⅛-in. diameter, 1 plum	35	tr	na	tr	na	0
Prunes, dried, cooked, unsweetened, 1 cup	225	tr	na	tr	na	0
Prunes, dried, uncooked, 4 extra large or 5 large	115	tr	na	tr	na	0
Raisins, seedless, ½-oz. packet, 1 packet	40	tr	na	tr	na	0
Raisins, seedless, 1 cup	435	1	12	<1	<1	0
Raspberries, frozen, sweetened, 1 cup	255	tr	na	tr	na	0
Raspberries, in Lite Syrup, Birds Eye Quick Thaw Pouch, 5 oz.	100	1	9	na	na	0
Raspberries, raw, 1 cup	60	1	15	tr	na	0
Rhubarb, cooked, added sugar, 1 cup	280	tr	na	tr	na	0
Strawberries, frozen, sweetened, sliced, 1 cup	245	tr	<1	tr	<1	0
Strawberries, Halved, in Lite Syrup, Birds Eye Quick Thaw Pouch, 5 oz.	90	0	0	0	0	0

FOOD/PORTION SIZE	CAL.	FAT		SAT. FAT		CHOL.
		Total (g)	As % of Cal.	Total (g)	As % of Cal.	(mg)
Strawberries, Halved, in Syrup, Birds Eye Quick Thaw Pouch, 5 oz.	120	tr	<1	tr	<1	0
Strawberries, raw, whole, 1 cup	45	1	20	tr	na	0
Tangerines, raw, 2⅜-in. diameter, 1 tangerine	35	tr	na	tr	na	0
Watermelon, raw, 4 × 8-in. wedge, 1 piece	155	2	12	<1	2	0
Watermelon, raw, diced, 1 cup	50	1	18	<1	2	0

Gelatin, Pudding & Pie Filling

FOOD/PORTION SIZE	CAL.	FAT		SAT. FAT		CHOL.
		Total (g)	As % of Cal.	Total (g)	As % of Cal.	(mg)
All flavors, Gelatin, Jell-O, ½ cup (average)	80	0	0	0	0	0
All flavors, Gelatin, Low Calorie, D-Zerta, ½ cup (average)	8	0	0	0	0	0
All flavors, Gelatin, Sugar Free, Jell-O, ½ cup (average)	8	0	0	0	0	0
Banana, Pudding & Pie Filling, Instant, Sugar Free Jell-O, with 2% milk, ½ cup	80	2	23	1	11	10
Banana Cream, Pudding & Pie Filling, Instant, Jell-O, with whole milk, ½ cup	160	4	23	3	17	15
Banana Cream, Pudding & Pie Filling, Jell-O, with whole milk, ⅙ pie (excluding crust)	100	3	27	2	18	10
Butter Pecan, Pudding & Pie Filling, Instant, Jell-O, with whole milk, ½ cup	170	5	26	3	16	15
Butterscotch, Pudding, Reduced Calorie, D-Zerta, with skim milk, ½ cup	70	0	0	0	0	0
Butterscotch, Pudding & Pie Filling, Instant, Jell-O, with whole milk, ½ cup	160	4	23	3	17	15
Butterscotch, Pudding & Pie Filling, Instant, Sugar Free, Jell-O, with 2% milk, ½ cup	90	2	20	1	10	10
Butterscotch, Pudding & Pie Filling, Jell-O, with whole milk, ½ cup	170	4	21	3	16	15
Chocolate, pudding, canned, 5-oz. can	205	11	48	9	40	1
Chocolate, Pudding, Reduced Calorie, D-Zerta, with skim milk, ½ cup	70	tr	na	tr	na	2
Chocolate, Pudding & Pie Filling, Instant, Jell-O, with whole milk, ½ cup	180	4	20	3	15	15
Chocolate, Pudding & Pie Filling, Instant, Sugar Free, Jell-O, with 2% milk, ½ cup	90	3	30	2	20	10
Chocolate, Pudding & Pie Filling, Jell-O, with whole milk, ½ cup	160	4	23	2	11	15

GELATIN, PUDDING & PIE FILLING

FOOD/PORTION SIZE	CAL.	FAT		SAT. FAT		CHOL.
		Total (g)	As % of Cal.	Total (g)	As % of Cal.	(mg)
Chocolate, Pudding & Pie Filling, Sugar Free, Jell-O, with 2% milk, ½ cup	90	3	30	2	20	10
Chocolate, Rich & Luscious Mousse, Jell-O, with whole milk, ½ cup	150	6	36	4	24	9
Chocolate Fudge, Pudding & Pie Filling, Instant, Jell-O, with whole milk, ½ cup	180	5	25	3	15	15
Chocolate Fudge, Pudding & Pie Filling, Instant, Sugar Free, Jell-O, with 2% milk, ½ cup	100	3	27	2	18	10
Chocolate Fudge, Pudding & Pie Filling, Jell-O, with whole milk, ½ cup	160	4	23	2	11	15
Chocolate Fudge, Rich & Luscious Mousse, Jell-O, with whole milk, ½ cup	140	6	39	4	26	10
Coconut Cream, Pudding & Pie Filling, Instant Jell-O, with whole milk, ½ cup	180	6	30	4	20	15
Coconut Cream, Pudding & Pie Filling, Jell-O, with whole milk, ⅙ pie (excluding crust)	110	4	33	2	16	10
Custard, baked, 1 cup	305	13	38	7	21	278
Custard, Golden Egg, Mix, Jell-O Americana, with whole milk, ½ cup	160	5	28	3	17	80
Lemon, Pudding & Pie Filling, Instant, Jell-O, with whole milk, ½ cup	170	4	21	3	16	15
Lemon, Pudding & Pie Filling, Jell-O, with whole milk, ⅙ pie (excluding crust)	170	2	11	na	na	90
Milk Chocolate, Pudding & Pie Filling, Instant, Jell-O, with whole milk, ½ cup	180	5	25	3	15	17
Milk Chocolate, Pudding & Pie Filling, Jell-O, with whole milk, ½ cup	160	4	23	2	11	17
Pineapple Cream, Pudding & Pie Filling, Instant, Jell-O, with whole milk, ½ cup	160	4	23	2	11	17
Pistachio, Pudding & Pie Filling, Instant, Jell-O, with whole milk, ½ cup	170	5	26	3	16	17
Pistachio, Pudding & Pie Filling, Instant, Sugar Free, Jell-O, with 2% milk, ½ cup	100	3	27	2	3	10
Rice Pudding, Jell-O Americana, with whole milk, ½ cup	170	4	21	2	11	17
Tapioca, pudding, prepared with whole milk, ½ cup	145	4	25	2	12	17
Vanilla, French, Pudding & Pie Filling, Instant, Jell-O, with whole milk, ½ cup	160	4	23	2	11	17
Vanilla, French, Pudding & Pie Filling, Jell-O, with whole milk, ½ cup	170	4	21	3	16	17

FOOD/PORTION SIZE	CAL.	FAT Total (g)	FAT As % of Cal.	SAT. FAT Total (g)	SAT. FAT As % of Cal.	CHOL. (mg)
Vanilla, pudding, canned, 5-oz. can	220	10	41	10	41	1
Vanilla, Pudding, Reduced Calorie, D-Zerta, with skim milk, ½ cup	70	0	0	0	0	0
Vanilla, pudding, regular (cooked) dry mix, made with whole milk, ½ cup	145	4	25	2	12	15
Vanilla, Pudding & Pie Filling, Instant, Jell-O, with whole milk, ½ cup	170	4	21	3	16	17
Vanilla, Pudding & Pie Filling, Instant, Sugar Free, Jell-O, with 2% milk, ½ cup	90	2	20	1	10	9
Vanilla, Pudding & Pie Filling, Jell-O, with whole milk, ½ cup	160	4	23	3	17	17
Vanilla, Pudding & Pie Filling, Sugar Free, Jell-O, with 2% milk, ½ cup	80	2	23	0	0	10
Vanilla, Tapioca, Pudding, Jell-O Americana, with whole milk, ½ cup	160	4	23	3	17	17

Gravies & Sauces

FOOD/PORTION SIZE	CAL.	FAT Total (g)	FAT As % of Cal.	SAT. FAT Total (g)	SAT. FAT As % of Cal.	CHOL. (mg)
GRAVIES						
Beef, canned, 1 cup	125	5	36	3	22	7
Beef, Franco-American, 2 oz.	35	2	51	na	na	na
Brown, from dry mix, 1 cup	80	2	23	1	11	2
Brown, with onions, Heinz, HomeStyle, 2 oz.	25	1	36	na	na	na
Chicken, canned, 1 cup	190	14	66	4	19	5
Chicken, Franco-American, 2 oz.	45	4	80	na	na	na
Chicken, from dry mix, 1 cup	85	2	21	<1	5	tr
Turkey, Canned, Heinz HomeStyle, 2 oz.	25	1	36	0	0	0
SAUCES						
Barbecue sauce, *see* BAKING PRODUCTS & CONDIMENTS						
Cheese, from dry mix, prepared with milk, 2 tbsp.	38	2	47	1	24	7
Hollandaise, prepared with water, 2 tbsp.	30	3	90	2	60	7
Picante Sauce, Old El Paso, 2 tbsp.	12	0	0	0	0	0
Picante Sauce, Pace, 2 tbsp.	9	0	0	0	0	0

FOOD/PORTION SIZE	CAL.	FAT		SAT. FAT		CHOL. (mg)
		Total (g)	As % of Cal.	Total (g)	As % of Cal.	
Soy sauce, *see* BAKING PRODUCTS & CONDIMENTS						
Spaghetti, Chunky Garden Style, with Mushrooms and Green Peppers, Ragu, 4 oz.	70	3	39	na	na	0
Spaghetti, Extra Chunky, Garden Tomato with Mushrooms, Prego, 4 oz.	100	6	54	tr	na	52
Spaghetti, Extra Chunky, Mushroom and Tomato, Prego, 4 oz.	110	5	41	na	na	na
Spaghetti, Extra Chunky, Tomato and Onion, Prego, 4 oz.	140	6	39	na	na	na
Spaghetti, Plain, Prego, 4 oz.	140	5	32	1	6	0
Spaghetti, Ragu, 4 oz.	80	3	34	tr	na	0
Spaghetti, Thick & Hearty, Ragu, 4 oz.	140	5	32	tr	na	0
Spaghetti, with Meat, Homestyle, Ragu, 4 oz.	70	2	26	tr	na	2
Spaghetti, with Meat, Prego, 4 oz.	150	6	36	2	12	4
Spaghetti, with Meat, Ragu, 4 oz.	80	3	34	tr	na	2
Spaghetti, with Mushrooms, Prego, 4 oz.	140	5	32	1	6	0
Spaghetti, with Mushrooms, Ragu, 4 oz.	80	4	45	tr	na	0
Spaghetti, with Mushrooms, Thick & Hearty, Ragu, 4 oz.	140	5	32	tr	na	0
White, prepared with milk, 2 tbsp.	30	2	49	1	23	5

Legumes & Nuts

FOOD/PORTION SIZE	CAL.	FAT		SAT. FAT		CHOL. (mg)
		Total (g)	As % of Cal.	Total (g)	As % of Cal.	
BEANS						
Black, dry, cooked, drained, 1 cup	225	1	4	tr	<1	0
Chickpeas, dry, cooked, drained, 1 cup	270	4	13	tr	<1	0
Great Northern, dry, cooked, drained, 1 cup	210	1	4	tr	<1	0
Lentils, dry, cooked, 1 cup	215	1	4	tr	<1	0
Lima, dry, cooked, drained, 1 cup	216	1	4	tr	<1	0
Lima, immature seeds, frozen, cooked, drained: thick-seeded types (Fordhooks), 1 cup	170	1	5	tr	<1	0
Lima, immature seeds, frozen, cooked, drained: thin-seeded types (baby limas), 1 cup	188	1	5	tr	<1	0
Peas (Navy), dry, cooked, drained, 1 cup	258	1	3	tr	<1	0
Pinto, dry, cooked, drained, 1 cup	234	1	4	tr	<1	0

FOOD/PORTION SIZE	CAL.	FAT		SAT. FAT		CHOL. (mg)
		Total (g)	As % of Cal.	Total (g)	As % of Cal.	
Pork and Beans, Van Camp's, 1 cup	227	1	5	na	na	0
Red kidney, canned, 1 cup	216	1	4	tr	<1	0
Refried, canned, 1 cup	268	3	10	1	3	15
Refried, Vegetarian, Old El Paso, 1 cup	140	2	13	na	na	0
Snap, canned, drained, solids (cut), 1 cup	25	tr	na	tr	na	0
Snap, cooked, drained, from frozen (cut), 1 cup	35	tr	na	tr	na	0
Snap, cooked, drained, from raw (cut and French style), 1 cup	45	tr	na	<1	2	0
Sprouts, (mung), raw, 1 cup	30	tr	na	tr	na	0
Tahini, 1 tbsp.	95	7	66	1	9	0
Vegetarian Beans in Tomato Sauce, Heinz, 1 cup	250	2	7	na	na	0
White, with sliced frankfurters, canned, 1 cup	365	18	44	7	17	30
NUTS						
Almonds, shelled, whole, 1 oz.	165	15	82	1	5	0
Almonds, sliced, 1 oz.	170	13	69	1	5	0
Almonds, Sliced, Blue Diamond, 1 oz.	150	13	78	1	6	0
Almonds, Whole, Blue Diamond, 1 oz.	150	13	78	1	6	0
Brazil, shelled, 1 oz.	185	19	92	4	19	0
Cashews, salted, dry roasted, 1 cup	869	65	67	14	14	0
Cashews, salted, roasted in oil, 1 cup	869	67	69	14	14	0
Chestnuts, European, roasted, shelled, 1 cup	350	3	8	tr	<1	0
Coconut, raw, piece, 45 g (1.6 oz.)	160	15	84	13	73	0
Filberts (hazelnuts), chopped, 1 cup	955	84	79	7	7	0
Macadamia, salted, roasted in oil, 1 cup	1088	103	85	16	13	0
Mixed, with peanuts, salted, dry roasted, 1 oz.	170	13	69	2	11	0
Mixed, with peanuts, salted, roasted in oil, 1 oz.	175	14	72	2	10	0
Peanut Butter, 2 tbsp.	190	16	76	2	9	0
Peanut Butter, Creamy, Skippy, 2 tbsp.	190	17	81	3	14	0
Peanut Butter, Extra Crunchy, Jif, 2 tbsp.	180	16	80	na	na	0
Peanuts, Dry Roasted, Planter's, 1 oz.	160	14	79	2	11	0
Peanuts, salted, roasted in oil, 1 cup	869	64	66	9	9	0
Pecans, halves, 1 cup	760	68	81	6	7	0
Pistachios, dried, shelled, 1 oz.	165	13	71	2	11	0
Walnuts, black, chopped, 1 cup	760	62	73	4	5	0

FOOD/PORTION SIZE	CAL.	FAT		SAT. FAT		CHOL. (mg)
		Total (g)	As % of Cal.	Total (g)	As % of Cal.	
Walnuts, English or Persian, pieces/chips, 1 cup	770	66	77	6	7	0
PEAS						
Black-eyed, dry, cooked, 1 cup	190	1	5	<1	1	0
Split, dry, cooked, 1 cup	230	1	4	<1	<1	0
SEEDS						
Pumpkin/squash kernels, dry, hulled, 1 oz.	155	13	75	2	12	0
Sesame, dry, hulled, 1 tbsp.	45	4	80	<1	12	0
Sunflower, dry, hulled, 1 oz.	160	14	79	<2	8	0
SOY PRODUCTS						
Miso, 1 cup	568	14	22	2	3	0
Soybeans, dry, cooked, drained, 1 cup	298	13	39	2	6	0
Tofu, firm, 2 oz.	82	5	55	tr	na	0

Meat

FOOD/PORTION SIZE	CAL.	FAT		SAT. FAT		CHOL. (mg)
		Total (g)	As % of Cal.	Total (g)	As % of Cal.	
BEEF						
Chipped, dried, 2½ oz.	118	3	23	1	8	50
Chuck blade, lean only, braised/simmered/ pot roasted, approx. 2¼ oz.	168	9	48	4	21	66
Corned, canned, 3 oz.	213	16	68	5	21	83
Corned, lean, Carl Buddig, 1 oz.	40	2	45	na	na	na
Ground, Extra Lean, Healthy Choice, 3 oz.	98	3	28	2	7	55
Ground, patty, lean, broiled, 3 oz.	230	16	63	6	27	74
Ground, patty, regular, broiled, 3 oz.	245	18	66	7	26	76
Heart, lean, braised, 3 oz.	150	5	30	2	12	164
Liver, fried, 3 oz.	185	7	34	3	15	410
Roast, eye of round, lean only, oven cooked, approx. 2½ oz.	135	5	33	2	13	52
Roast, rib, lean only, oven cooked, approx. 2¼ oz.	150	9	54	4	24	49
Roast, tip, lean only, oven cooked, approx. 2½ oz.	135	5	33	2	13	52

FOOD/PORTION SIZE	CAL.	FAT		SAT. FAT		CHOL.
		Total (g)	As % of Cal.	Total (g)	As % of Cal.	(mg)
Round, bottom, lean only, braised/simmered/ pot roasted, 2⅘ oz.	175	8	41	3	15	75
Steak, cubed, lean only, broiled, 2½ oz.	170	9	48	4	21	66
Steak, sirloin, lean only, broiled, 2½ oz.	150	6	36	3	18	64
FRANKS & SAUSAGES						
Frankfurter, Chicken, Health Valley, 1 frank	145	12	74	4	25	27
Franks, Beef, Oscar Mayer, 1 link	144	14	88	6	38	28
Franks, Eckrich, 1 frank	190	17	81	na	na	na
Franks, Healthy Choice, 1 frank	50	1	18	<1	na	15
Franks, Jumbo Beef, Eckrich, 1 frank	190	17	81	na	na	na
Franks, Lite, Eckrich, 1 frank	120	10	75	na	na	25
Sausage, beef and pork, frankfurters, cooked, 1 frank	183	16	79	6	30	29
Sausage, pork, brown/serve, browned, 1 link	50	5	90	2	36	9
Sausage, pork, links, 1 link (1 oz.)	50	4	72	2	36	11
Sausage, Pork, Regular, Jimmy Dean, 1 patty (1⅕ oz.)	140	13	84	na	na	na
Turkey Breakfast Sausage, Louis Rich, 1 oz.	54	4	67	2	33	22
Turkey Smoked Sausage, Louis Rich, 1 oz.	43	2	50	6	13	18
Wieners, Oscar Mayer, 1 link	144	13	81	5	31	27
GAME						
Buffalo, roasted, 3 oz.	111	2	16	<1	na	52
Venison, roasted, 3 oz.	134	3	20	1	7	95
LAMB						
Chops, shoulder, lean only, braised, approx. 1¾ oz.	135	7	47	3	20	44
Leg, lean only, roasted, approx. 2⅔ oz.	140	6	39	3	19	65
Loin, chop, lean only, broiled, approx. 2⅓ oz.	182	10	49	4	20	60
Rib, lean only, roasted, 2 oz.	130	7	48	4	28	50
LUNCHEON MEATS						
Bologna, Beef, Oscar Mayer, 28 g (1 oz.)	90	8	80	4	40	20
Bologna, Lite, Oscar Mayer, 28 g (1 oz.)	70	6	77	na	na	15
Bologna, Oscar Mayer, 15 g (½ oz.)	50	4	72	2	36	9
Braunschweiger sausage, 2 oz.	205	18	79	7	31	88
Chicken, roll, light, 2 oz.	90	4	40	1	10	28

MEAT

FOOD/PORTION SIZE	CAL.	FAT Total (g)	FAT As % of Cal.	SAT. FAT Total (g)	SAT. FAT As % of Cal.	CHOL. (mg)
Ham, chopped, 8-slice (6-oz.) pack, 2 slices	98	7	64	3	28	23
Ham, Cooked, Eckrich Lite, 1 oz.	25	1	36	na	na	15
Ham, extra lean, cooked, 2 slices (2 oz.)	75	3	36	1	12	27
Ham, regular, cooked, 2 slices (2 oz.)	105	6	51	2	17	32
Pork, canned lunch meat, spiced/unspiced, 2 slices, 42 g (1½ oz.)	140	13	84	5	32	26
Salami sausage, cooked, 2 oz.	141	11	70	5	32	37
Salami sausage, dry, 12-slice (4-oz.) pack, 2 slices	84	6	64	2	21	16
Sandwich spread, pork/beef, 1 tbsp.	35	3	77	<1	23	6
Turkey, breast meat, loaf, 8-slice (6-oz.) pack, 2 slices	45	1	20	<1	4	17
Turkey, Oscar Mayer, ¾ oz.	22	1	41	tr	na	8
Turkey, Salami, 1 slice, 28 grams	54	4	67	1	17	20
Turkey, thigh meat, ham cured, 2 oz.	75	3	36	1	12	32
Turkey Bologna, Louis Rich Turkey Cold Cuts, 28 g (1 oz.)	61	5	74	2	30	22
Turkey Breast, Healthy Choice, 2 oz.	60	1	15	na	na	25
Turkey Breast, Light, Eckrich, 1 oz.	30	1	30	0	0	10
Turkey Breast, Oven Roasted, Deli Thin Louis Rich, 22 grams	24	1	38	tr	tr	8
Turkey Breast, Oven Roasted, Eckrich Lite, 1 oz.	30	1	31	na	na	10
Turkey Ham, Louis Rich Turkey Cold Cuts, 21 g (¾ oz.)	25	1	36	0	0	14
Turkey Ham, Smoked, Louis Rich Turkey Cold Cuts, 28 g (1 oz.)	34	1	26	1	26	19
Turkey Pastrami, Louis Rich Turkey Cold Cuts, 23 g (⅘ oz.)	24	1	38	0	0	14
Vienna sausage, 7 per 4-oz. can, 1 sausage, 16 g (approx. ½ oz.)	45	4	80	2	40	8

PORK

FOOD/PORTION SIZE	CAL.	FAT Total (g)	FAT As % of Cal.	SAT. FAT Total (g)	SAT. FAT As % of Cal.	CHOL. (mg)
Bacon, Canadian, cured, cooked, 2 slices	86	4	42	1	10	27
Bacon, Low Salt, Armour, 2 slices	76	8	95	2	24	12
Bacon, regular, cured, cooked, 3 medium slices	108	9	75	3	25	16
Chop, loin, fresh, lean only, broiled, 2½ oz.	163	7	39	3	17	69
Chop, loin, fresh, lean only, pan fried, approx. 2½ oz.	181	10	50	4	20	73
Ham, Baked, Oscar Mayer, 21 g (¾ oz.)	21	1	43	tr	na	11
Ham, Boiled, Oscar Mayer, 21 g (¾ oz.)	26	1	35	tr	na	12
Ham, Breakfast Slice, Oscar Mayer, 1 slice	50	2	36	tr	na	20

154

FOOD/PORTION SIZE	CAL.	FAT		SAT. FAT		CHOL.
		Total (g)	As % of Cal.	Total (g)	As % of Cal.	(mg)
Ham, canned, roasted, 3 oz.	140	7	45	2	13	35
Ham, leg, fresh, lean only, roasted, 2½ oz.	156	8	46	3	17	67
Ham, light cure, lean only, roasted, approx. 2½ oz.	107	4	34	1	8	38
Ham, Lower Salt, Light, Eckrich, 1 oz.	25	1	36	0	0	15
Ham, Low Salt, Armour, 1 oz.	40	3	68	1	23	15
Rib, fresh, lean only, roasted, 2½ oz.	173	8	42	3	16	56
Shoulder cut, fresh, lean only, braised, 2⅖ oz.	169	8	43	3	16	78
Tenderloin, roasted, lean, 3 oz.	139	4	26	1	6	67
Turkey Bacon, Louis Rich, 1 slice	32	2	56	tr	na	10
VEAL						
Cubed, lean only, braised, 3½ oz.	188	4	19	1	5	145
Cutlet, leg, lean only, braised, 3½ oz.	203	6	27	2	9	135
Rib, lean only, roasted, 3½ oz.	177	7	36	2	10	115

Packaged Entrées

FOOD/PORTION SIZE	CAL.	FAT		SAT. FAT		CHOL.
		Total (g)	As % of Cal.	Total (g)	As % of Cal.	(mg)
Beef Noodle, Hamburger Helper, prepared with meat, 1 cup	320	15	42	7	20	79
Beef Stew, Dinty Moore, 10 oz.	270	13	43	na	na	na
Cheeseburger Macaroni, Hamburger Helper, prepared with meat, 1 cup	370	19	46	na	na	na
Chicken, Sweet & Sour, La Choy, ¾ cup	230	2	8	tr	<1	103
Chili con carne with beans, canned, 1 cup	286	13	41	6	19	43
Chow Mein, Beef, La Choy, ¾ cup	60	1	15	tr	na	25
Chow Mein, Chicken, La Choy, ¾ cup	80	3	34	na	na	na
Egg Noodle and Cheese Dinner, Kraft, ¾ cup	340	17	45	4	11	50
Egg Noodle with Chicken Dinner, Kraft, ¾ cup	240	9	34	2	8	45
Lasagna, Hamburger Helper, prepared with meat, 1 cup	340	14	37	na	na	na
Macaroni and Cheese Deluxe Dinner, Kraft, ¾ cup	260	8	28	4	14	20
Macaroni and Cheese Dinner, Original, Kraft, ¾ cup	290	13	40	na	na	na
Shells and Cheese Dinner, Velveeta, ½ cup	210	8	34	4	17	20

FOOD/PORTION SIZE	CAL.	FAT		SAT. FAT		CHOL.
		Total (g)	As % of Cal.	Total (g)	As % of Cal.	(mg)
Spaghetti, Mild American Style Dinner, Kraft, 1 cup	300	7	21	2	6	0
Spaghetti Dinner, Tangy Italian Style, Kraft, 1 cup	310	48	23	2	6	5
Spaghetti in tomato sauce with cheese, canned, 1 cup	190	2	9	<1	2	3
Spaghetti with Meat Sauce, Top Shelf 2-Minute Entrée, Hormel, 10 oz.	260	6	21	na	na	20
Spaghetti with Meat Sauce Dinner, Kraft, 1 cup	360	14	35	4	10	15

Pasta

FOOD/PORTION SIZE	CAL.	FAT		SAT. FAT		CHOL.
		Total (g)	As % of Cal.	Total (g)	As % of Cal.	(mg)
Egg Noodles, Creamette, 2 oz.	210	3	13	na	na	55
Egg Noodles Substitute, Cholesterol Free, No Yolks, 2 oz. dry	200	1	5	na	na	0
Linguine, Fresh, Di Giorno, Cholesterol Free, 3 oz.	250	3	11	na	na	0
Macaroni, enriched, cooked, firm, hot, 1 cup	190	1	5	<1	<1	0
Macaroni, enriched, cooked, tender, cold, 1 cup	115	tr	na	<1	<1	0
Macaroni, enriched, cooked, tender, hot, 1 cup	155	1	6	<1	<1	0
Macaroni and cheese dishes, see PACKAGED ENTRÉES						
Noodle Roni Fettucini, prepared with margarine and 2% milk, ½ cup	291	17	53	5	15	28
Noodle Roni Parmesano, prepared with margarine and 2% milk, ½ cup	250	14	50	4	14	21
Noodle Roni Romanoff, prepared with margarine and 2% milk, ½ cup	213	8	34	3	13	25
Noodle Roni Stroganoff, prepared with margarine and 2% milk, ½ cup	290	11	34	4	12	47
Noodles, chow mein, canned, 1 cup	220	11	45	2	8	5
Noodles, Creamette, all types except egg, 2 oz.	210	1	4	na	na	0
Noodles, egg, enriched, cooked, 1 cup	200	2	9	1	5	50
Spaghetti, enriched, cooked, firm, hot, 1 cup	190	1	5	<1	<1	0
Spaghetti, enriched, cooked, tender, hot, 1 cup	155	1	6	0	0	0

FOOD/PORTION SIZE	CAL.	FAT		SAT. FAT		CHOL. (mg)
		Total (g)	As % of Cal.	Total (g)	As % of Cal.	
Spaghetti with sauce/meat, *see* PACKAGED ENTRÉES						

Poultry

FOOD/PORTION SIZE	CAL.	FAT		SAT. FAT		CHOL. (mg)
		Total (g)	As % of Cal.	Total (g)	As % of Cal.	
Chicken, boneless, canned, 5 oz.	235	11	42	3	11	88
Chicken, boneless, skinless, Perdue, Fit 'n Easy, Oven Stuffer Roaster Breast, 1 oz.	30	<1	<1	<1	<1	17
Chicken, boneless, skinless, Perdue, Fit 'n Easy, Pick of the Chick, 1 oz.	30	<1	<1	<1	<1	17
Chicken, breast, flesh only, roasted, 3 oz.	140	3	19	<1	6	73
Chicken, broiler-fryer, breast, w/o skin, roasted, 3½ oz.	165	4	22	1	5	85
Chicken, drumstick, roasted, approx. 1.6 oz.	75	2	24	<1	8	26
Chicken, light and dark meat, flesh only, stewed, 1 cup	332	17	46	1	3	117
Chicken, liver, cooked, 1 liver	30	1	30	<1	12	120
Chicken, white and dark meat, w/o skin, roasted, 3½ oz.	190	7	33	2	9	89
Cold cuts, chicken or turkey, *see* LUNCHEON MEATS *in* MEAT section						
Duck, flesh only, roasted, ½ duck, approx. 7¾ oz.	445	24	49	11	22	197
Frankfurters, chicken, *see* FRANKS & SAUSAGES in MEAT section						
Turkey, dark meat only, w/o skin, roasted, 3½ oz.	187	7	34	2	10	85
Turkey, flesh only, 1 light and 2 dark slices, 85 g (3 oz.)	145	4	25	1	6	65
Turkey, flesh only, light and dark meat, chopped or diced, roasted, 1 cup, 140 g (5 oz.)	240	7	26	2	8	106
Turkey, flesh only, light meat, roasted, 2 pieces, 85 g (3 oz.)	135	3	20	1	7	59
Turkey, frozen, boneless, light and dark meat, seasoned, chunked, roasted, 3 oz.	130	5	35	2	14	45

FOOD/PORTION SIZE	CAL.	FAT		SAT. FAT		CHOL.
		Total (g)	As % of Cal.	Total (g)	As % of Cal.	(mg)
Turkey, Ground, Lean, Louis Rich, cooked, 1 oz.	52	2	35	1	17	25
Turkey, Ground, Louis Rich, cooked, 1 oz.	60	4	60	1	15	25
Turkey, patties, breaded, battered, fried, 1 patty	180	12	60	3	15	40
Turkey, smoked, 1 slice, 28 grams	32	1	28	.4	11	12
Turkey, white meat only, w/o skin, roasted, 3½ oz.	157	3	17	1	6	69
Turkey and gravy, frozen, 5 oz. pkg.	95	3	28	1	9	18
Turkey Breast Steaks, Louis Rich, 1 oz.	39	tr	tr	.2	5	18

Rice

FOOD/PORTION SIZE	CAL.	FAT		SAT. FAT		CHOL.
		Total (g)	As % of Cal.	Total (g)	As % of Cal.	(mg)
Beef Flavor, Rice-A-Roni, prepared with margarine, ½ cup	170	5	26	1	5	0
Boil-in-Bag, Uncle Ben's, about ½ cup cooked	80	<1	<1	na	na	na
Brown, cooked, hot, ½ cup	115	tr	4	<1	1	0
Brown & Wild, Mushroom Recipe, Uncle Ben's, ½ cup cooked	130	1	7	na	na	na
Chicken Flavor, Rice-A-Roni, prepared with margarine, ½ cup	171	5	26	1	5	tr
Chicken Vegetable, Rice-A-Roni, prepared with margarine, ½ cup cooked	139	3	19	1	6	0
Extra-Long-Grain, Riceland, ½ cup cooked	100	0	0	0	0	na
Fast Cook, Uncle Ben's, about ⅔ cup cooked	110	<1	<1	na	na	na
Herb Rice Au Gratin, Country Inn, Uncle Ben's, prepared with margarine, ½ cup	170	5	26	2	11	11
Instant, ready-to-serve, cooked, hot, ½ cup	90	0	0	0	0	0
Long Grain, Natural, Converted, Uncle Ben's, ⅔ cup cooked	120	0	0	0	0	na
Long Grain & Wild, Minute Rice, ½ cup cooked	120	0	0	0	0	0
Long Grain & Wild, Original Recipe, Uncle Ben's, about ½ cup cooked	100	<1	<9	na	na	na
Long Grain & Wild, Rice-A-Roni, prepared with margarine, ½ cup cooked	137	3	20	1	7	0
Minute Rice, w/o salt or butter, ⅔ cup cooked	120	0	0	na	na	0

FOOD/PORTION SIZE	CAL.	FAT		SAT. FAT		CHOL. (mg)
		Total (g)	As % of Cal.	Total (g)	As % of Cal.	
Parboiled, cooked, hot, ½ cup	93	tr	na	tr	na	0
Parboiled, raw, ½ cup	343	tr	1	<1	<1	0
Savory Broccoli Au Gratin, Rice-A-Roni, prepared with margarine, ½ cup cooked	178	10	51	3	15	4
Savory Rice Pilaf, Rice-A-Roni, prepared with margarine, ½ cup cooked	186	5	24	1	5	tr
White, enriched, cooked, hot, ½ cup	113	tr	na	<1	<1	0

Salad Dressings

FOOD/PORTION SIZE	CAL.	FAT		SAT. FAT		CHOL. (mg)
		Total (g)	As % of Cal.	Total (g)	As % of Cal.	
Bacon, Creamy, Reduced Calorie, Kraft, 1 tbsp.	30	2	60	0	0	0
Bacon & Tomato, Kraft, 1 tbsp.	70	7	90	1	13	0
Blue Cheese, Chunky, Healthy Sensation!, 1 tbsp.	20	0	0	na	na	0
Blue Cheese, Chunky, Kraft, 1 tbsp.	60	6	90	1	15	5
Blue Cheese, Chunky, Reduced Calorie, Kraft, 1 tbsp.	30	2	60	1	30	5
Blue Cheese, Lite, Less Oil, Wish-Bone, 1 tbsp.	40	4	90	tr	na	0
Blue Cheese and Herb, Good Seasons, prepared with oil and vinegar, 1 tbsp.	70	8	100	na	na	0
Buttermilk, Creamy, Kraft, 1 tbsp.	80	8	90	1	11	5
Buttermilk, Creamy, Reduced Calorie, Kraft, 1 tbsp.	30	3	90	0	0	5
Buttermilk, Farm Style, Good Seasons, with whole milk and mayonnaise, 1 tbsp.	58	6	93	na	na	0
Caesar, Weight Watchers, 1 tbsp.	4	0	0	0	0	na
Cheese Garlic, Good Seasons, with vinegar and oil, 1 tbsp.	7	8	100	na	na	0
Cheese Italian, Good Seasons, with vinegar and oil, 1 tbsp.	70	8	100	na	na	0
Coleslaw, Kraft, 1 tbsp.	70	6	77	1	13	10
Cucumber, Creamy, Kraft, 1 tbsp.	70	8	100	1	13	0
Cucumber, Creamy, Reduced Calorie, Kraft, 1 tbsp.	25	2	72	0	0	0
French, Catalina Brand, Kraft, 1 tbsp.	60	5	75	1	15	0
French, Kraft, 1 tbsp.	60	6	90	1	15	0

FOOD/PORTION SIZE	CAL.	FAT		SAT. FAT		CHOL.
		Total (g)	As % of Cal.	Total (g)	As % of Cal.	(mg)
French, Lite, Less Oil, Wish-Bone, 1 tbsp.	30	2	60	0	0	0
French, No Oil, Pritikin, 1 tbsp.	10	0	0	0	0	0
French, Reduced Calorie, Kraft, 1 tbsp.	20	1	45	0	0	0
French, Sweet 'n Spicy Lite, Wish-Bone, 1 tbsp.	16	0	0	0	0	0
French, Weight Watchers, 1 tbsp.	10	0	0	0	0	na
Garlic, Creamy, Kraft, 1 tbsp.	50	5	90	1	18	0
Garlic and Herbs, Good Seasons, with oil and vinegar, 1 tbsp.	70	8	100	na	na	0
Golden Caesar, Kraft, 1 tbsp.	70	7	90	1	13	0
Herb, Classic, Good Seasons, with vinegar and oil, 1 tbsp.	70	8	100	na	na	0
Honey Dijon, Healthy Sensation!, 1 tbsp.	25	0	0	na	na	0
Italian, Creamy, Lite, Less Oil, Wish-Bone, 1 tbsp.	6	0	0	0	0	0
Italian, Creamy, Reduced Calorie, Kraft, 1 tbsp.	25	2	72	0	0	0
Italian, Good Seasons, with oil and vinegar, 1 tbsp.	71	8	100	na	na	0
Italian, Healthy Sensation!, 1 tbsp.	6	0	0	na	na	0
Italian, Lite, Good Seasons, with oil and vinegar, 1 tbsp.	26	3	100	na	na	0
Italian, Lite, Wish-Bone, 1 tbsp.	6	1	100	0	0	0
Italian, Mild, Good Seasons, with oil and vinegar, 1 tbsp.	73	8	99	na	na	0
Italian, No Oil, Good Seasons, with vinegar and water, 1 tbsp.	7	0	0	na	na	0
Italian, No Oil, Pritikin, 1 tbsp.	10	0	0	0	0	0
Italian, Oil-Free, Kraft, 1 tbsp.	4	0	0	0	0	0
Italian, Olive Oil Classics, Wishbone, 1 tbsp.	33	3	82	4	11	0
Italian, Weight Watchers, 1 tbsp.	6	0	0	0	0	na
Italian, Wishbone, 1 tbsp.	45	5	100	1	20	0
Italian, Zesty, Good Seasons, with oil and vinegar, 1 tbsp.	71	8	100	na	na	0
Italian, Zesty, Kraft, 1 tbsp.	50	5	90	1	18	0
Italian, Zesty, Reduced Calorie, Kraft, 1 tbsp.	20	2	90	0	0	0
Lemon Herb, Good Seasons, with oil and vinegar, 1 tbsp.	70	8	100	na	na	0
Miracle Whip, Free Nonfat, 1 tbsp.	5	0	0	0	0	0
Miracle Whip Light Reduced Calorie Salad Dressing with No Cholesterol, 1 tbsp.	45	4	80	1	20	0
Miracle Whip Salad Dressing, 1 tbsp.	70	7	90	1	13	5
Oil & Vinegar, Kraft, 1 tbsp.	70	8	100	1	13	0
Ranch, Original, Hidden Valley Ranch, 1 tbsp.	80	8	90	na	na	10

FOOD/PORTION SIZE	CAL.	FAT		SAT. FAT		CHOL.
		Total (g)	As % of Cal.	Total (g)	As % of Cal.	(mg)
Ranch, Original, Take Heart, Hidden Valley Ranch, 1 tbsp.	20	1	45	na	na	0
Reduced Calorie, Catalina Brand, Kraft, 1 tbsp.	18	1	50	0	0	0
Red Wine, Vinegar and Oil, Kraft, 1 tbsp.	60	4	60	1	15	0
Russian, Reduced Calorie, Kraft, 1 tbsp.	30	1	30	0	0	0
Thousand Island, Kraft, 1 tbsp.	60	5	75	1	15	5
Thousand Island, Lite, Less Oil, Wish-Bone, 1 tbsp.	40	0	0	na	na	0
Thousand Island, Reduced Calorie, Kraft, 1 tbsp.	20	2	90	0	0	0
Thousand Island & Bacon, Kraft, 1 tbsp.	60	6	90	1	10	0
Tomato Vinaigrette, Weight Watchers, 1 tbsp.	8	0	0	0	0	na

Snacks

FOOD/PORTION SIZE	CAL.	FAT		SAT. FAT		CHOL.
		Total (g)	As % of Cal.	Total (g)	As % of Cal.	(mg)
CORN CHIPS						
Bugles, 1 oz.	150	8	48	7	42	0
Doritos, Cool Ranch, 1 oz.	144	7	44	2	13	0
Doritos, Nacho Cheese, 1 oz.	143	7	44	2	13	0
Fritos Corn Chips, 1 oz.	154	9	53	3	18	0
Tortilla Chips, Restaurant Style, Tostitos, 1 oz.	140	7	45	na	na	0
Tostitos, Traditional, 1 oz.	145	8	50	1	6	0
DIPS						
Avocado (guacamole), Kraft, 2 tbsp.	50	4	72	2	36	0
Bacon & Horseradish, Kraft, 2 tbsp.	60	5	75	3	45	0
Blue Cheese, Kraft Premium, 2 tbsp.	50	4	72	2	36	10
Clam, Kraft, 2 tbsp.	60	4	60	1	15	10
Cucumber, Creamy, Kraft Premium, 2 tbsp.	50	4	72	3	54	10
French Onion, Kraft, 2 tbsp.	60	4	60	2	30	0
Green Onion, Kraft, 2 tbsp.	60	4	60	2	30	0
Jalapeño Pepper, Kraft, 2 tbsp.	50	4	72	2	36	0
Nacho Cheese, Kraft Premium, 2 tbsp.	55	4	65	2	33	10
Onion, Creamy, Kraft Premium, 2 tbsp.	45	4	80	2	40	10

FOOD/PORTION SIZE	CAL.	FAT		SAT. FAT		CHOL.
		Total (g)	As % of Cal.	Total (g)	As % of Cal.	(mg)
FRUIT SNACKS						
Fruit Roll-Ups, Cherry, ½ oz.	50	1	18	0	0	0
Fruit Roll-Ups, Grape, ½ oz.	50	1	18	0	0	0
Fruit Roll-Ups, Watermelon, ½ oz.	60	1	15	tr	na	0
Fruit Wrinkles, Orange, Betty Crocker, 1 pouch	100	2	18	tr	na	0
Fruit Wrinkles, Strawberry, Betty Crocker, 1 pouch	100	2	18	tr	na	0
Fun Fruits, Fantastic Fruit Punch, Sunkist, 1 oz.	100	1	9	na	na	na
Fun Fruits, Grape, Sunkist, 1 oz.	100	1	9	na	na	na
GRANOLA						
Apple, Chewy Granola Bar, Quaker Oats, 1 oz.	120	3	23	tr	na	tr
Chocolate Chip, Chewy Granola Bar, Quaker Oats, 1 oz.	130	5	35	tr	na	tr
Chocolate Covered Caramel Nut Dipps, Quaker Oats, 1 bar	140	6	39	3	19	4
Chocolate Covered Chocolate Chip Dipps, Quaker Oats, 1 bar	138	7	46	4	26	4
Chocolate Covered Peanut Butter Dipps, Quaker Oats, 1 bar	141	7	45	4	26	3
Chocolate Graham & Marshmallow, Chewy Granola Bar, Quaker Oats, 1 oz.	126	4	29	2	14	tr
Nut & Raisin, Chunky, Chewy Granola Bar, Quaker Oats, 1 oz.	133	6	41	2	14	tr
Oats n' Honey, Granola Bar, Nature Valley, 1 bar	120	5	38	2	15	0
Peanut Butter Chocolate Chip, Chewy Granola Bar, Quaker Oats, 1 oz.	131	5	34	2	14	tr
POPCORN						
Air-popped, unsalted, 1 cup	30	tr	na	tr	na	0
Microwave, Butter, Orville Redenbacher, 1 cup	28	2	49	tr	na	0
Microwave, Natural, Orville Redenbacher, 1 cup	28	2	57	1	8	0
Popped in vegetable oil, salted, 1 cup	55	3	49	<1	8	0
Sugar syrup coated, 1 cup	135	1	6	<1	<1	0
POTATO CHIPS						
Lays, 1 oz.	152	9	53	2	12	0

FOOD/PORTION SIZE	CAL.	FAT		SAT. FAT		CHOL.
		Total (g)	As % of Cal.	Total (g)	As % of Cal.	(mg)
Lays, Bar-B-Que, 1 oz.	149	9	54	2	12	0
O'Grady's, 1 oz.	150	9	54	2	12	0
O'Grady's, Au Gratin, 1 oz.	147	8	49	2	12	1
Pringles, 1 oz.	170	13	69	2	11	0
Pringles, Sour Cream n' Onion, 1 oz.	170	13	69	2	11	0
Pringles Light, Ranch, 1 oz.	150	8	48	2	12	0
Ruffles, 1 oz.	151	10	60	2	12	0
Ruffles, Cajun Spice, 1 oz.	154	10	58	2	12	0
Ruffles, Sour Cream & Onion, 1 oz.	150	9	54	2	12	1
PRETZELS						
Enriched flour, 2¼-in. sticks, 10 pretzels	10	tr	na	tr	na	0
Enriched flour, twisted, dutch, 1 pretzel	65	1	14	<1	1	0
Enriched flour, twisted, thin, 10 pretzels	240	2	8	<1	1	0
Mister Salty, Sticks, 1 oz.	110	1	18	tr	na	0
Mister Salty, Twists, 1 oz.	110	2	16	tr	na	0
Pretzel Chips, Mr. Phipps, ½ oz. (8 chips)	60	1	15	na	na	0
Rold Gold, Thin, 1 oz.	110	1	8	na	na	0

Soups

FOOD/PORTION SIZE	CAL.	FAT		SAT. FAT		CHOL.
		Total (g)	As % of Cal.	Total (g)	As % of Cal.	(mg)
Asparagus, Cream of, Campbell's, 4 oz. condensed, 8 oz. as prepared	80	4	45	na	na	<5
Bean with bacon, canned, condensed, prepared with water, 1 cup	173	6	31	2	10	3
Beef broth bouillon consommé, canned, condensed, prepared with water, 1 cup	29	0	0	0	0	0
Beef noodle, canned, condensed, prepared with water, 1 cup	85	3	32	1	11	5
Bouillon (beef or chicken), Wylers, 1 tsp.	6	0	0	0	0	0
Chicken, broth, College Inn, 7 oz.	35	3	77	1	26	5
Chicken, cream of, canned, condensed, prepared with milk, 1 cup	190	11	52	5	24	27
Chicken, cream of, canned, condensed, prepared with water, 1 cup	115	7	55	2	16	10
Chicken noodle, canned, condensed, prepared with water, 1 cup	75	2	24	<1	8	7

FOOD/PORTION SIZE	CAL.	FAT		SAT. FAT		CHOL.
		Total (g)	As % of Cal.	Total (g)	As % of Cal.	(mg)
Chicken noodle, dehydrated, prepared with water, 6 oz.	40	1	23	<1	5	3
Chicken Noodle, Hearty, Campbell's Healthy Request, 8 oz.	80	2	23	na	na	25
Chicken Noodle, Old Fashioned, Healthy Choice, 7½ oz.	90	3	30	1	na	20
Chicken Noodle, Progresso, 9.5 oz.	120	4	30	na	na	40
Chicken rice, canned, condensed, prepared with water, 1 cup	60	2	30	<1	8	7
Clam chowder, Manhattan, canned, condensed, prepared with water, 1 cup	80	2	23	<1	5	2
Clam chowder, New England, canned, condensed, prepared with milk, 1 cup	163	6	33	3	17	22
Minestrone, canned, condensed, prepared with water, 1 cup	80	3	34	<1	7	2
Minestrone, Progresso, 9½ oz.	130	4	28	na	na	0
Mushroom, cream of, canned, condensed, prepared with milk, 1 cup	203	13	58	5	22	20
Mushroom, cream of, canned, condensed, prepared with water, 1 cup	129	9	63	3	21	2
Mushroom, Cream of, Healthy Request, Campbell's, 4 oz. condensed, 8 oz. as prepared	60	2	30	na	na	<5
Noodle Soup Mix with Real Chicken Broth, Lipton, 8 oz.	70	2	26	na	na	na
Onion, dehydrated, prepared with water, 1 packet	20	tr	na	<1	5	0
Onion-Mushroom Recipe Soup Mix, Lipton, 8 oz.	40	<1	<1	na	na	na
Onion Soup Recipe Mix, Lipton, 8 oz.	20	0	0	na	na	na
Pea, green, canned, condensed, prepared with water, 1 cup	164	3	16	1	5	0
Tomato, canned, condensed, prepared with milk, 1 cup	160	6	34	3	17	17
Tomato, canned, condensed, prepared with water, 1 cup	85	2	21	<1	4	9
Tomato vegetable, dehydrated, prepared with water, 6 oz.	40	1	23	<1	7	0
Turkey Noodle, Campbell's, 4 oz. condensed, 8 oz. as prepared	70	2	26	na	na	15
Vegetable, Vegetarian, Campbell's, 4 oz. condensed, 8 oz. as prepared	80	2	23	na	na	0
Vegetable beef, canned, condensed, prepared with water, 1 cup	80	2	23	<1	10	5

Vegetables

FOOD/PORTION SIZE	CAL.	FAT		SAT. FAT		CHOL. (mg)
		Total (g)	As % of Cal.	Total (g)	As % of Cal.	
ALFALFA						
Seeds, sprouted, raw, 1 cup	10	tr	na	tr	na	0
ARTICHOKES						
Globe or French, cooked, drained, 1 artichoke	53	tr	na	tr	na	0
Jerusalem, red, sliced, 1 cup	114	tr	na	0	0	0
ASPARAGUS						
Canned, spears, 4 spears	10	tr	na	tr	na	0
Cuts & tips, cooked, drained, from raw, 1 cup	45	1	20	<1	2	0
Cuts & tips, from frozen, 1 cup	50	1	18	<1	4	0
Spears, cooked, drained, from raw, 4 spears	15	tr	na	tr	na	0
Spears, from frozen, 4 spears	15	tr	na	<1	6	0
BAMBOO SHOOTS						
Canned, drained, 1 cup	25	1	36	<1	4	0
BEANS						
Baby Lima, Birds Eye Regular Vegetables, approx. 3⅓ oz.	98	0	0	0	0	0
Fordhook Lima, Birds Eye Regular Vegetables, approx. 3⅓ oz.	94	0	0	0	0	0
Green, Blue Lake, Del Monte, ½ cup	20	0	0	0	0	0
Green, Cut, Birds Eye Regular Vegetables, 3 oz.	23	0	0	0	0	0
Green, French Cut, Birds Eye Deluxe, 3 oz.	25	0	0	0	0	0
Green, Whole, Birds Eye Deluxe Vegetables, 3 oz.	25	0	0	0	0	0
Sprouts (mung), cooked, drained, 1 cup	25	tr	na	tr	na	0
BEETS						
Canned, drained, solids, diced or sliced, 1 cup	55	tr	na	tr	na	0
Cooked, drained, diced or sliced, 1 cup	55	tr	na	tr	na	0
Cooked, drained, whole, 2 beets	30	tr	na	tr	na	0
Greens, leaves and stems, cooked, drained, 1 cup	40	tr	na	tr	na	0

FOOD/PORTION SIZE	CAL.	FAT Total (g)	FAT As % of Cal.	SAT. FAT Total (g)	SAT. FAT As % of Cal.	CHOL. (mg)
BROCCOLI						
Cooked, drained, from frozen, 1 piece (4½-5 in. long)	10	tr	tr	tr	tr	0
Cooked, drained, from frozen, chopped, 1 cup	50	tr	tr	tr	tr	0
Raw, 1 spear	40	1	23	<1	2	0
Spears, cooked, drained, from raw, 1 cup (½-in. pieces)	45	tr	tr	<1	2	0
BRUSSELS SPROUTS						
Cooked, drained, from frozen, 1 cup	65	1	14	<1	1	0
Cooked, drained, from raw, 1 cup	60	1	15	<1	3	0
CABBAGE						
Chinese pak-choi, cooked, drained, 1 cup	20	tr	na	tr	na	0
Chinese pe-tsai, raw, 1-in. pieces, 1 cup	10	tr	na	tr	na	0
Common varieties, cooked, drained, 1 cup	30	tr	na	tr	na	0
Red, raw, coarsely shredded or sliced, 1 cup	20	tr	na	tr	na	0
Savoy, raw, coarsely shredded or sliced, 1 cup	20	tr	na	tr	na	0
CARROTS						
Canned, sliced, drained, solids, 1 cup	35	tr	na	<1	3	0
Cooked, sliced, drained, from frozen, 1 cup	55	tr	na	tr	na	0
Cooked, sliced, drained, from raw, 1 cup	70	tr	na	<1	1	0
Raw, w/o crowns or tips, scraped, grated, 1 cup	45	tr	na	tr	na	0
CAULIFLOWER						
Cooked, drained, from frozen (flowerets), 1 cup	35	tr	na	<1	3	0
Cooked, drained, from raw (flowerets), 1 cup	30	tr	na	tr	na	0
CELERY						
Pascal type, raw, large outer stalk, 1 stalk	5	tr	na	tr	na	0
Pascal type, raw, pieces, diced, 1 cup	20	tr	na	tr	na	0

FOOD/PORTION SIZE	CAL.	FAT Total (g)	As % of Cal.	SAT. FAT Total (g)	As % of Cal.	CHOL. (mg)
COLLARDS						
Cooked, drained, from frozen (chopped), 1 cup	60	1	15	<1	2	0
Cooked, drained, from raw (leaves w/o stems), 1 cup	25	tr	<1	<1	5	0
CORN						
Sweet, canned, cream style, 1 cup	185	1	5	<1	1	0
Sweet, cooked, drained, from frozen, 1 ear (3½ in.)	60	tr	na	<1	2	0
Sweet, cooked, drained, from raw, 1 ear (5 × 1¾ in.)	85	1	11	<1	2	0
Sweet, cooked, drained, kernels, 1 cup	135	tr	na	tr	na	0
Sweet, vacuum packed, whole kernel, 1 cup	165	1	5	<1	1	0
CUCUMBER						
Peeled slices, ⅛ in. thick (large 2⅛-in. diameter, small 1¾ in. diameter), 6 large or 8 small	5	tr	na	tr	na	0
EGGPLANT						
Cooked, steamed, 1 cup	25	tr	na	tr	na	0
ENDIVE						
Curly (including escarole), raw, small pieces, 1 cup	10	tr	na	tr	na	0
GARLIC						
Clove, 1 medium	4	tr	na	0	0	0
GREENS						
Dandelion, cooked, drained, 1 cup	34	1	26	<1	3	0
Mustard, w/o stems and midribs, cooked, drained, 1 cup	20	tr	na	tr	na	0
Turnip, cooked, drained, from frozen (chopped), 1 cup	50	1	19	<1	4	0
Turnip, cooked, drained, from raw (leaves & stems), 1 cup	30	tr	na	<1	3	0

FOOD/PORTION SIZE	CAL.	FAT		SAT. FAT		CHOL. (mg)
		Total (g)	As % of Cal.	Total (g)	As % of Cal.	
KALE						
Cooked, drained, from frozen, chopped, 1 cup	40	1	23	<1	2	0
Cooked, drained, from raw, chopped, 1 cup	40	1	21	<1	2	0
KOHLRABI						
Thickened bulblike stem, cooked, drained, diced, 1 cup	50	tr	na	tr	na	0
LETTUCE						
Butterhead, as Boston types, raw, leaves, 1 outer or 2 inner leaves	tr	tr	na	tr	na	0
Crisphead, as iceberg, raw, ¼ of head, 1 wedge	20	tr	na	tr	na	0
Crisphead, as iceberg, raw, pieces, chopped, shredded, 1 cup	5	tr	na	tr	na	0
Looseleaf (bunching varieties including romaine or cos), chopped or shredded, 1 cup	10	tr	na	tr	na	0
MIXED VEGETABLES						
Baby Carrots, Peas, Pearl Onions, Birds Eye Deluxe Vegetables, 3⅓ oz.	50	0	0	0	0	0
Bavarian Style Vegetables, Birds Eye International Recipe, 3⅓ oz.	109	6	50	1	8	14
Broccoli, Baby Carrots, Water Chestnuts, Birds Eye Farm Fresh Mix, 3⅕ oz.	28	0	0	0	0	0
Broccoli, Carrots, Pasta, Birds Eye Combination Vegetables, 3⅓ oz.	89	4	40	tr	na	0
Broccoli, Cauliflower, Carrots, Birds Eye Farm Fresh Mix, 3⅕ oz.	20	0	0	0	0	0
Broccoli, Corn, Red Pepper, Birds Eye Farm Fresh Mix, 3⅕ oz.	40	0	0	0	0	0
Broccoli, Green Beans, Pearl Onions, Red Peppers, Birds Eye Farm Fresh Mix, 3⅕ oz.	20	0	0	0	0	0
Broccoli, Red Peppers, Bamboo Shoots, and Straw Mushrooms, Birds Eye Farm Fresh Mix, 3⅕ oz.	20	0	0	0	0	0
Brussels Sprouts, Cauliflower, Carrots, Birds Eye Farm Fresh Mix, 3⅕ oz.	24	0	0	0	0	0
Cauliflower, Baby Carrots, Snow Pea Pods, Birds Eye Farm Fresh Mix, 3⅕ oz.	24	0	0	0	0	0
Chinese Style, Birds Eye International Recipe, 3⅓ oz.	79	5	57	tr	na	0

FOOD/PORTION SIZE	CAL.	FAT		SAT. FAT		CHOL. (mg)
		Total (g)	As % of Cal.	Total (g)	As % of Cal.	
Chinese Style, Birds Eye Stir-Fry Vegetables, prepared with soybean oil, 3⅓ oz.	107	8	67	1	8	tr
Chow Mein Style, Birds Eye International Recipe, 3⅓ oz.	89	3	30	1	10	tr
Corn, Green Beans, Pasta, Birds Eye Combination Vegetables, 3⅓ oz.	109	5	41	1	8	1
Green Beans, French, Toasted Almond, Birds Eye Combination Vegetables, prepared with margarine, 3 oz.	93	5	48	tr	na	0
Green Peas, Pearl Onions, Birds Eye Combination Vegetables, prepared with margarine, 3⅓ oz.	98	3	28	tr	na	0
Italian Style, Birds Eye International Recipe, 3⅓ oz.	109	6	50	1	8	0
Japanese Style, Birds Eye International Recipe, 3⅓ oz.	99	5	45	1	9	tr
Japanese Style, Birds Eye Stir-Fry Vegetables, prepared with soybean oil, 3⅓ oz.	120	8	60	1	8	0
Mandarin Style, Birds Eye International Recipe, 3⅓ oz.	89	4	40	tr	na	tr
New England Style Vegetables, Birds Eye International Recipe, 3⅓ oz.	129	7	49	1	78	tr
Pasta Primavera Style, Birds Eye International Recipe, prepared with 2% milk, 3⅓ oz.	103	4	35	1	9	5
Rice, Green Peas, Mushrooms, Birds Eye Combination Vegetables, prepared with margarine, 2⅓ oz.	72	0	0	0	0	0
San Francisco Style, Birds Eye International Recipe, 3⅓ oz.	99	5	45	tr	na	tr
Spinach, Creamed, Birds Eye Combination Vegetables, 3 oz.	60	4	60	tr	na	0
MIXED VEGETABLES WITH SAUCE						
Broccoli, Cauliflower, Carrots, Cheese Sauce, Birds Eye Cheese Sauce Combination Vegetables, 5 oz.	100	4	36	1	9	5
Broccoli, Cauliflower, Creamy Italian Cheese Sauce, Birds Eye Cheese Sauce Combination Vegetables, 4½ oz.	90	6	60	3	30	14
Green Peas, Potatoes, Cream Sauce, Birds Eye Combination Vegetables, prepared with 2% milk and margarine, 2⅗ oz.	99	5	45	1	9	3

FOOD/PORTION SIZE	CAL.	FAT		SAT. FAT		CHOL.
		Total (g)	As % of Cal.	Total (g)	As % of Cal.	(mg)
Mixed Vegetables with Onion Sauce, Birds Eye Combination Vegetables, prepared with margarine, 2⅗ oz.	44	2	41	tr	na	0
Peas, Pearl Onions, Cheese Sauce, Birds Eye Cheese Sauce Combination Vegetables, prepared with margarine, 5 oz.	140	4	26	1	6	5
MUSHROOMS						
Canned, drained, solids, 1 cup	35	tr	na	<1	3	0
Cooked, drained, 1 cup	40	1	23	<1	2	0
Raw, sliced or chopped, 1 cup	20	tr	na	tr	na	0
OKRA						
Pods, 3 × ⅝ in., cooked, 8 pods	27	tr	na	tr	na	0
ONIONS						
Cooked (whole or sliced), drained, 1 cup	60	tr	na	<1	2	0
Raw, chopped, 1 cup	55	tr	na	<1	2	0
Raw, sliced, 1 cup	40	tr	na	<1	2	0
Rings, breaded par-fried, frozen, prepared, 2 rings	80	5	56	2	23	0
Spring, raw, bulb (⅜-in. diameter) and white portion of top, 6 onions	10	tr	na	tr	na	0
PARSLEY						
Raw, 10 sprigs	5	tr	na	tr	na	0
PARSNIPS						
Cooked, (diced or 2-in. lengths), drained, 1 cup	125	tr	na	<1	<1	0
PEAS						
Black-eyed, immature seeds, cooked, drained, from frozen, 1 cup	225	1	4	<1	1	0
Black-eyed, immature seeds, cooked, drained, from raw, 1 cup	180	1	5	<1	2	0
Green, canned, drained, solids, 1 cup	115	1	8	<1	1	0
Green, frozen, cooked, drained, 1 cup	125	tr	na	<1	1	0

FOOD/PORTION SIZE	CAL.	FAT		SAT. FAT		CHOL.
		Total (g)	As % of Cal.	Total (g)	As % of Cal.	(mg)
Pods, edible, cooked, drained, 1 cup	65	tr	na	<1	1	0
PEPPERS						
Hot chili, raw, 1 pepper	20	tr	na	tr	na	0
Sweet (about 5 per lb., whole), stem and seeds removed, 1 pepper	20	tr	na	tr	na	0
Sweet (about 5 per lb., whole), stem and seeds removed, cooked, drained, 1 pepper	15	tr	na	tr	na	0
PICKLES						
Bread and Butter Sticks, Vlasic, 2 sticks	18	0	0	0	0	0
Cucumber, dill, medium whole, 1 pickle (3¾-in. long, 1¼-in. diameter)	5	tr	na	tr	na	0
Cucumber, Dill, Whole, Claussen, 1 oz.	4	<1	<1	na	na	0
Cucumber, fresh-pack slices, 2 slices (1½-in. diameter, ¼-in. thick)	10	tr	na	tr	na	0
Cucumber, sweet gherkin, small, 1 pickle (whole, about 2½-in. long, ¾-in. diameter)	20	tr	na	tr	na	0
POTATOES						
Baked (about 2 per lb. raw), flesh only, 1 potato	145	tr	na	tr	na	0
Baked (about 2 per lb. raw), with skin, 1 potato	220	tr	na	<1	<1	0
Boiled (about 3 per lb. raw), peeled after boiling, 1 potato	120	tr	na	tr	na	0
Boiled (about 3 per lb. raw), peeled before boiling, 1 potato	115	tr	na	tr	na	0
Canned, Whole New, Del Monte, ½ cup	45	0	0	0	0	0
French-Fried, Microwave Crinkle-Cut, Ore-Ida, 3 oz.	163	7	39	na	na	0
French fried, strip (2 to 3½ in. long), fried in vegetable oil, 10 strips	160	8	45	3	17	0
French fried, strip (2 to 3½ in. long), oven heated, 10 strips	110	4	33	2	16	0
Sweet, candied, 2½×2-in. piece, 1 piece	145	3	19	1	6	8
Sweet, canned, solid packed, mashed, 1 cup	260	1	3	<1	<1	0
Sweet, cooked (baked in skin), 1 potato	115	tr	na	tr	na	0
Sweet, cooked (boiled w/o skin), 1 potato	160	tr	na	<1	<1	0
Sweet, vacuum pack, 2¾×1-in. piece	35	tr	na	tr	na	0
Twice-Baked, Ore-Ida, 5 oz.	200	8	36	na	na	0

FOOD/PORTION SIZE	CAL.	FAT		SAT. FAT		CHOL. (mg)
		Total (g)	As % of Cal.	Total (g)	As % of Cal.	
Wedges, Frozen Homestyle, Ore-Ida, 3 oz.	110	3	35	tr	na	0
PUMPKIN						
Canned, 1 cup	85	1	11	<1	4	0
Cooked, from raw, mashed, 1 cup	50	tr	na	<1	2	0
Solid Pack, Libby's, 1 cup	80	1	11	0	0	0
RADISHES						
Raw, stem ends and rootlets cut off, 4 radishes	5	tr	na	tr	na	0
SPINACH						
Cooked, drained, from frozen (leaf), 1 cup	55	tr	na	<1	2	0
Cooked, drained, from raw, 1 cup	40	tr	na	<1	2	0
Raw, chopped, 1 cup	10	tr	na	tr	na	0
SQUASH						
Summer (all varieties), cooked, sliced, drained, 1 cup	35	1	26	<1	3	0
TOMATOES						
Chili Style Chunky Tomatoes, Del Monte, ½ cup	30	<1	<1	na	na	na
Italian Style Pear-Shaped, Contadina, ½ cup	25	<1	<1	na	na	na
Juice, canned, 1 cup	40	tr	na	tr	na	0
Pasta Ready, Contadina, ½ cup	50	2	36	tr	na	0
Paste, canned, 1 cup	220	2	8	<1	1	0
Paste, Contadina, 2 oz.	50	<1	<1	na	na	na
Puree, canned, 1 cup	105	tr	na	tr	na	0
Raw, 2⅗-in. diameter (3 per 12-oz. pkg.), 1 tomato	25	tr	na	tr	na	0
Sauce, Canned, Contadina, ½ cup	30	1	30	0	0	0
Stewed, Canned, Contadina, ½ cup	35	1	26	0	0	0
Stewed, Canned, Italian Style, Del Monte, ½ cup	30	0	0	0	0	0
Stewed, Canned, Original Style, Del Monte, ½ cup	35	0	0	0	0	0
Vegetable Juice, V-8, 6 fl. oz.	35	0	0	0	0	0
Whole Peeled, Contadina; ½ cup	25	<1	<1	na	na	na

FOOD/PORTION SIZE	CAL.	FAT		SAT. FAT		CHOL.
		Total (g)	As % of Cal.	Total (g)	As % of Cal.	(mg)
VEGETABLES WITH SAUCE						
Broccoli with Cheese Sauce, Birds Eye Cheese Sauce Combination Vegetables, 5 oz.	120	6	45	2	15	5
Broccoli with Creamy Italian Cheese Sauce, Birds Eye Cheese Sauce Combination Vegetables, 4½ oz.	90	6	60	3	30	15
Brussels Sprouts with Cheese Sauce, Birds Eye Cheese Sauce Combination Vegetables, 4½ oz.	120	6	45	2	15	5
Cauliflower with Cheese Sauce, Birds Eye Cheese Sauce Combination Vegetables, 5 oz.	110	6	49	2	16	5

Yogurt

FOOD/PORTION SIZE	CAL.	FAT		SAT. FAT		CHOL.
		Total (g)	As % of Cal.	Total (g)	As % of Cal.	(mg)
Blueberry, Dannon, 8 oz.	259	3	10	2	7	11
Blueberry, Dannon Fresh Flavors, 8 oz.	216	4	17	2	8	0
Blueberry, Dannon Light, 8 oz.	100	0	0	0	0	5
Blueberry, Lite n' Lively, 5 oz.	150	1	6	na	na	10
Blueberry, Yoplait, 6 oz.	190	3	14	2	9	11
Cherry, Yoplait 150, 6 oz.	150	0	0	0	0	5
Lemon, Dannon, 8 oz.	200	3	14	na	na	15
Plain, Dannon, 8 oz.	140	4	26	na	na	na
Raspberry, Yoplait Fat Free, 6 oz.	160	0	0	0	0	5
Strawberry, Dannon Fresh Flavors, 8 oz.	216	4	17	2	8	11
Strawberry, Light, Yoplait, 6 oz.	80	0	0	0	0	<5
Strawberry, Lite n' Lively, 5 oz.	150	2	12	na	na	10
Strawberry, Weight Watchers Ultimate 90, 8 oz.	90	0	0	0	0	5
Strawberry, Yoplait 150, 6 oz.	150	0	0	0	0	5
Vanilla, Dannon, 8 oz.	200	3	14	na	na	15

Index

INDEX

Dietary habits
  Finland, 18
  Japan, 18, 33
  Mediterranean, 13, 19, 33
  Netherlands, 18, 19
  United States, 18
Diet(s)
  Air Force Diet, 58
  allowances in, 72
  American Heart Association, 49–50
  analysis, 4–5
  Atkins Diet, 58
  Basic Four Food Groups, 51–52
  Calories Don't Count Diet, 58
  and cancer, 28, 30, 34–35
  cancer protecting, 34–35, 48, 52–53, 58
  changing, 68–78
  cholesterol-lowering, 19–20, 22
  choosing, 56
  fad, 61
  failure of, 54
  fasting, 61
  Food Guide Pyramid, 52
  Good Calorie Diet, The, 61
  Grapefruit Diet, 58
  guidelines, 48–49, 68–69
  high-fiber, 37
  high-protein, 59–61
  Last Chance Diet, The, 60
  low-calorie, 56–57
  low-carbohydrate, high-fat, 58–59
  low-fat, 4–5, 17, 34, 36, 49–50, 54, 57–58
  Mayo Diet, 58
  Mediterranean, 52, 53
  National Cancer Institute, 53
  need for fat in, 8
  recommendations, 48–49
  Scarsdale Diet, 59
  Ski Team Diet, 58
  Step One/Step Two, 50–51
  Stillman Diet, 59
  vegetarian, 17, 19, 21, 33, 35
  Zone Diet, The, 61
DNA, 29, 32, 34, 37, 53
Doll, Richard, 28
Drugs
  antidepressant, 47
  blood pressure, 14
  cancer, 30
  cardiac, 14
  cholesterol-lowering, 17, 19–20, 21, 27, 51
  pravastatin, 20
  statins, 20
  tranquilizers, 47
Dysgammaglobulinemia, 25, 27

E
Eggs, 13, 77
Energy, 6
  providing, 8
  storage, 6
Enzymes, 9, 12
Estradiol, 30–31, 32
Estrogen, 35, 64
  and cancer, 30
  replacement therapy, 16, 18, 26
  and weight, 42
Exercise, 5, 46, 55, 57, 62–67
  aerobic, 21, 24, 54, 62–64, 65
  and back pain, 64
  and cholesterol, 11, 20, 24, 25

Exercise (continued)
  effects of, 64
  and high blood pressure, 62, 64
  high-intensity, 65–66
  importance for children, 47
  low-intensity, 65–66
  precautions, 66–67
  programs, 65
  regular, 4
  strength building, 65–66
  strength training, 62, 64–65
  stretching, 66
  warm up, 66
  weight-bearing, 64

F
Fast food, 12
Fasting, 61
  and cholesterol, 25
Fat, body. See Body fat.
Fats, 4–5
  animal, 6
  and blood cholesterol, 9–13
  calories from, 13, 72, 74
  and cancer, 30, 32–34, 35, 36–37
  craving for, 69–70
  energy in, 6
  health risks of, 6
  and heart disease, 14–22
  "hidden," 7
  importance of, 8
  as insulation, 8
  nature of, 6
  need for, 8, 70
  provision of energy from, 8
  sources of, 70
  substitutes, 71
Fats, monounsaturated, 6, 7, 13, 19, 50, 52, 53, 58, 68, 69, 72, 73
Fats, polyunsaturated, 6, 7, 8, 13, 50, 53, 58, 68, 69, 72, 73
Fats, saturated, 4, 6–7, 11, 12–13, 18, 25, 32, 50, 58, 68, 72, 73
Fatty acids, 6–7, 12
  energy in, 8
  omega-3 group, 6, 7, 32, 69, 73
  omega-6 group, 6, 32
  omega-9 group, 6, 7
  trans, 6–7, 9, 11, 12, 33, 73, 76
Fiber, 11, 12, 37, 49, 52, 53, 56, 57, 58, 59, 68, 73, 74
Finland, 18
Fish, 7, 13, 19, 32, 51, 58, 72, 76–77
Food and Drug Administration, 60, 75
Food Guide Pyramid, 52
Food labeling, 73–75
Food processing, 12, 13, 73
Framingham Heart Study, 15–16, 17, 19, 24
Free radicals, 29, 30, 32, 35, 37, 53

G
Gallbladder, 9, 58
Gallstones, 42, 60
Gender
  and cancer, 30
  and cholesterol, 25
  and overweight, 42–43
  risk factors, 17
  as treatment factor, 20, 21
Glucose, 63–64
Goldstein, Joseph, 10–11
Good Calorie Diet, The, 61

Gout, 42
Grains, 51, 53, 58, 73, 77–78
Grapefruit Diet, 58
Greenland, 33

H
Harvard School of Public Health, 51–52
HDL. See Lipoproteins, high-density.
Heart attacks, 14, 15, 16, 17, 19, 20, 25, 26, 27
Height and weight tables, 40, 41
Helsinki Heart Study, 20
HMG-CoA reductase inhibitors, 20
Hormones
  aldosterone, 9
  and cancer, 30, 32
  and cholesterol, 9
  cortisol, 9
  estrogen, 16, 18, 26, 30, 32, 35, 42, 64
  imbalance, 46–47
  insulin, 30, 42, 52, 61, 63–64
  progesterone, 64
  prolactin, 35
  prostaglandins, 8, 32, 58
  sex, 9
  side effects of, 64
  steroid, 9, 10, 30
  testosterone, 42
  thyroid, 25
Hydrogenation, 7, 11, 13, 73, 76
Hypercholesterolemia, 11, 17
Hypertension. See Blood pressure, high.
Hyperthyroidism, 46–47
Hypoglycemia, 59, 61
Hypothyroidism, 25, 27

I
Immune system, 29, 32, 53
Insulin, 30, 42, 52, 61, 63–64, 69
International Atherosclerosis Project, 18
Iron, 51

J
Japan
  breast cancer in, 33
  colon cancer in, 36
  dietary habits, 18, 33
  prostate cancer in, 35

K
Ketoacidosis, 59, 61
Ketones, 59

L
Last Chance Diet, The, 60
LDL. See Lipoproteins, low-density.
Legumes, 52, 58
Leiden Study, 19
Linoleic acid, 32, 33, 58
Lipid peroxide, 32, 53
Lipid Research Clinics Coronary Primary Prevention Trial, 20
Lipids, 9, 10
  fasting, 17
Lipoproteins, high-density, 10, 13, 17, 19, 24, 26, 27, 53, 68–69
  alcohol in, 25
  and exercise, 63, 66
  measurement, 23–24, 25–26
  and overweight, 42
  raising, 20, 21
  role in coronary heart disease, 24